張建君
Zhang Jian-Jun

Published on the occasion of Zhang Jian-Jun: Vestiges of a Process, organised by iPRECIATION

Published, designed and edited by
iPRECIATION
T : (65) 6339 0678
F : (65) 6438 2080
1 FULLERTON SQUARE, #01-10
SINGAPORE 049178
www.ipreciation.com

ISBN: 981-05-6474-0

張建君

Zhang Jian-Jun

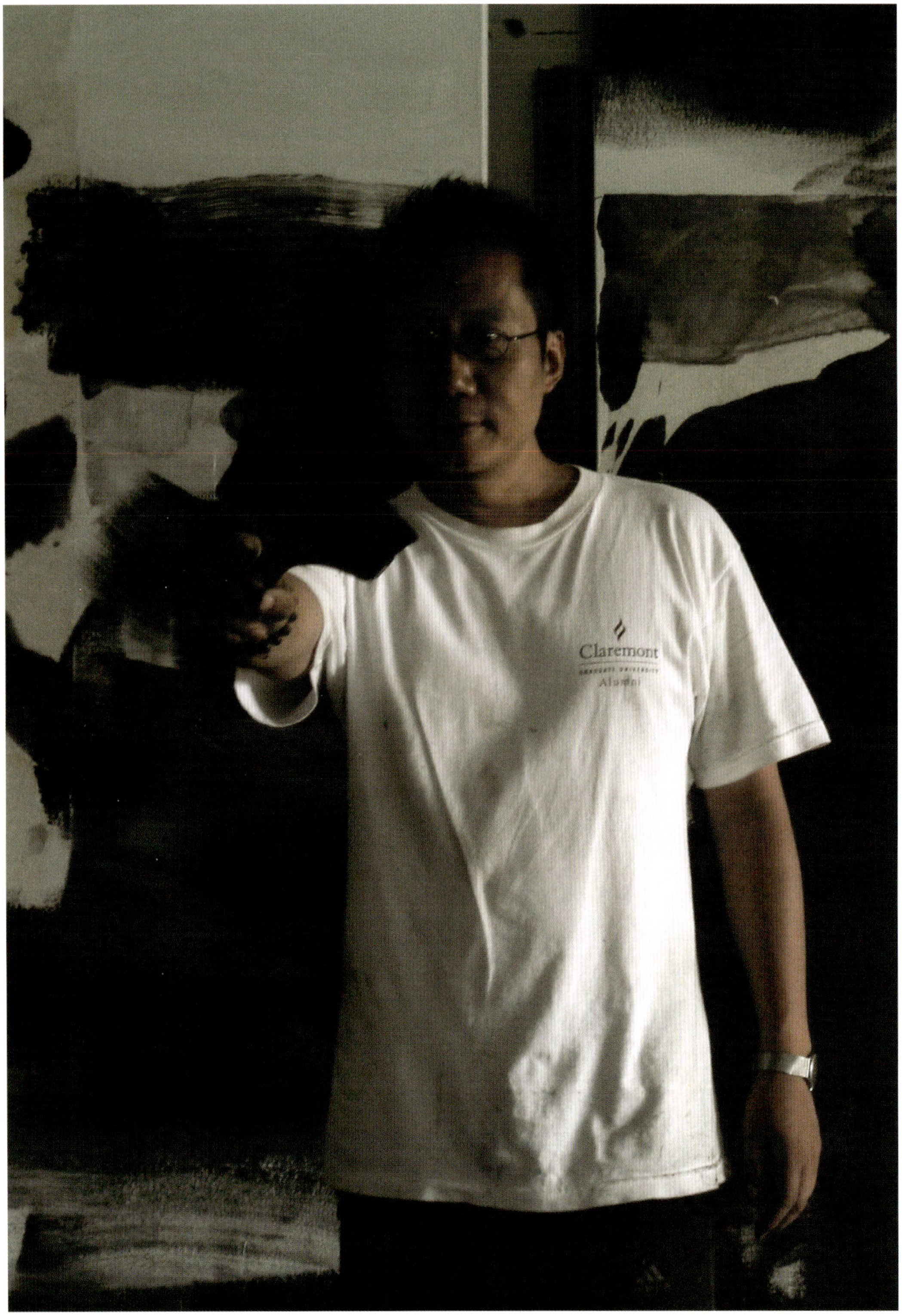

Photograph 攝影: MaoMao 毛毛

CONTENT

目錄

Message

Helina Chan

One of the most talented and disciplined Chinese contemporary artists of our time, Zhang Jian-Jun (b. 1955) was part of the graduating cohort of the 1978 Shanghai Drama Institute Department of Fine Arts. For years, Zhang shared a professional kinship with the Shanghai Art Museum where he was the first Director of the Curatorial and Art Research Department, afterwards the Assistant Director of the Museum. In 1987, Zhang was invited by the Asian Cultural Council to the United States for a fellowship. He decided to permanently settle down in New York in 1989; this personal experience in his East-West migration most probably has influenced his art today.

Over the years, Zhang has had more than 15 solo exhibitions and over 100 group exhibitions in China, the United States and other parts of Asia and Europe. Some of the world's most prestigious museums at which his works have been showcased include the Shanghai Art Museum, the Posnan Art Museum in Poland, and many other art museums and international Biennales. Today, Zhang is an Adjunct Professor at the New York University's Fine Arts Department.

Zhang's works come in various forms including oil paintings, watercolour paintings, photography, drawings and outdoor sculpture installations. Through his art, one sees the intertwining of the old and the modern as well as the East and West, articulating his novel visions of these elements.

Playing with modernist shapes and antique Chinese vessels in "2000 Years in Motion," featured in this catalogue, Zhang blends modern Western influences with ancient Eastern touches. Adding shapes and colours to photographs like in the "Vestiges of a Process" series that includes watercolour and oil paintings, he redesigns historical and modern architecture – transforming the archaic to modern and thrusting the new into the past. Yet another inclusion in this catalogue is the "Garden" series comprised of works such as *Mirage Garden Part 1* and *Blue Mountain*. Displaying his artistic ability to redefine time, these contemporary works were skillfully re-created with modern materials, such as silicone

前言

陳淑娟

放眼我們這個時代的華人當代藝術家，張建君可稱得上是最為才華橫溢且律己最嚴的一位。他生於1955年，1978年自上海戲劇學院美術系畢業，多年來一直與上海美術館保持著密切的專業聯系。他曾經是該美術館的首任策展及學術研究部主任，隨后更擔任館長助理。1987年，張建君應亞洲文化協會的邀請，前往美國從事學術研究，后來在1989年決定移居紐約。這種從東方移居西方國家的個人經歷，極可能影響了他今日所從事的藝術創作。

張建君這些年來已舉行過十五次個展，並參加了超過一百次的群展，參展地點遍及中國、美國、其他亞洲國家以及歐洲。他的作品曾在世界頂尖知名美術館中展出，包括上海美術館、波蘭波茲南美術館以及其他多處。國際雙年展中亦屢見其蹤。張建君現任紐約大學藝術系客座教授。

張建君的創作形式多樣，有油畫、水彩畫、攝影、素描以及戶外雕塑裝置藝術等。觀其作品，傳統與現代、東方與西方的深切交織昭然可見，清楚傳達了藝術家對這些元素的新穎之見。

在本畫冊所介紹的作品《行進中的2000年》當中，張建君對一些現代主義式形體和中國古器皿予以創意處理，將古代東方情致融合了現代西方產物。在包含水彩畫及油畫的《過程的瞬間》系列作品中，我們又看到他如何為照片添加圖形與色彩，重新設計歷史及現代建筑，化古為今，以舊納新。包含《幻園 #1》和《藍山》等作品、在本畫冊中亦有所介紹的《園林》系列，則體現了張建君善於重新界定時間的高超藝術功力。這組當代藝術作品，靈感得自超過千年以前為中國文人所喜愛的天然觀賞石“太湖石”，以硅膠等現代材質進行巧妙的再創造。羅伯特•C•摩根博士在關於張建君作品的精辟論述中，認為：“他（張建君）…的作品，透過‘感知’這一行為明確表達了時間之流逝、歷史以及記憶。”[1] 我也覺得張建君的藝術似乎對人類文化的長久延綿不斷，有精要的體悟，傳達了記憶

rubber, with inspiration drawn from Chinese scholar's rocks which are naturally occurring objects appreciated by Chinese scholars. An insightful examination into Zhang's work by Dr. Robert C. Morgan suggests "His (Zhang's) work articulates a process of time, history and memory through the act of perception."[1] It appears to me as well that Zhang's art seems to encompass an essence of the continuity of human culture through the ages, conveying the importance of remembering.

This publication contains a retrospective collection of Zhang's amazing creations dating from the 1980s to 2007. Here we will all be able to admire Zhang's art that is *distinctive* and *contemporary*!

I also wish to thank Mr. Fang Zengxian, Director of the Shanghai Art Museum, for penning the Afterword; and Dr. Robert C. Morgan, renowned art historian and author, for his article contribution.

I am pleased to present to you the art collection of Zhang Jian-Jun. I hope you will be as delighted by it as I have been!

[1] Robert C. Morgan, *Zhang Jian-Jun: Memory and the Process of Historical Time*, 2006

的重要性。

本刊物屬回顧性質，網羅了張建君從1980年代至2007年的多件瑰奇杰作。通過畫冊，我們都將得以欣賞張建君氣派獨得而又富有當代精神的藝術！

我謹在此感謝上海美術館館長方增先先生為畫冊撰寫后跋，也感謝著名藝術史學家兼作家羅伯特•C•摩根博士撰文相助。

我很榮幸能把張建君的藝術作品集呈獻給大家。希望您能與我一樣，為之歡欣、喜悅！

[1] 羅伯特·C·摩根：〈張建君：記憶以及歷史時間的進程〉（2006年）。

MEMORY AND THE PROCESS OF HISTORICAL TIME

by Robert C. Morgan

Robert C. Morgan is a writer, artist, critic, curator and art historian. He is the author of several books, monographs, and catalogs on contemporary art. He teaches graduate level seminars at Pratt Institute and Hunter College in New York City. In 2005, Dr. Morgan was the recipient of a Fulbright Fellowship as a senior scholar in the Republic of Korea.

張建君：記憶以及歷史時間的進程

羅伯特·C·摩根

羅伯特·C·摩根是作家、藝術家、藝術評論家、策展人兼藝術史學家。他曾撰寫過幾部關於當代藝術的書籍、專論和畫冊。他目前在紐約市普瑞特設計學院及亨特學院教授研究生課程。摩根博士曾於2005年以資深學者的身份，獲得富布萊特研究基金到韓國從事研究。

To speak of time and history as qualities that great artists from the past have instilled within their works may sound too hermetic for today's media-driven art world. Yet artists have always worked in relation to history, often appropriating temporal concepts to which they attribute major significance. They come to terms with the raw material of history not only through the pursuit of form, but also through the linguistic structure of their concepts that function in terms of what we might call historical memory. This approach to art is basically a conceptual one in which the idea supercedes the object in the pure sense. Such an approach to art requires a lucid awareness of the historical moment, the turning point whereby the persistence of change appears inevitable. For example, there are artists who know how to capture these rarefied moments – not so much as trends – but as historical realities. For them, history is less an archive of the past than an essential living part of the omnipresent human condition. Were it not for the insights of Picasso, Duchamp, Malevich, Pollock, Beuys, or Andy Warhol to find the pulse within the course of Western Modernism, it is questionable whether their careers would have had any meaning. Most recently, Warhol raised the question as to how an artist wishing to identify with today's "cutting edge" might discover something original that has never been calculated or intuited in quite the same way before? Given this precedent, is it not possible that focusing on the process of historical time might prove beneficial as artists attempt to reinterpret their understanding of our current transcultural environment? If so, how does this happen?

In contrast to earlier postmodern assumptions, it may still be possible for an artist to work in relation to history. This being the case, it may still be possible for artists to offer an original point of view about the present. Artists may seek to discover a new syntax in terms of how objects, events, architecture, and natural forms from all cultures affect the way we understand the conflicts of the present. This is to suggest that the artist's work is more or less limited to the time that he or she is alive, and that his or her experience within the present becomes the raw material by which significant art is made. Some postmodernists may argue that experience in art is less important than academic readership, but I think not. For an artist to work within history is to become part

將時間和歷史說成是歷代藝術大師灌注於本身作品之中的兩種特質，對今日為媒體所推動的藝術界而言，或許有點太玄。然而，一直以來，藝術家確實是參照著歷史來創作的。他們往往借用各種有關時間的概念，並賦予它們重大的意義。他們不僅通過對藝術形式的追求，也通過按所謂“歷史記憶”運作的、概念的語言結構，來看待原始歷史材料。這基本上是一種概念化的處理方式，是以理念取代純粹意義上的客體。依此而行的藝術家，必須對歷史性時刻（也就是事物的持續變化已顯得不可違逆的那個轉捩點）有清楚的意識。舉例而言，有些藝術家懂得如何捕捉這種凝練的時刻，不將之視為趨勢的體現，而更多的是作為歷史實況。在他們看來，歷史與其說是對往事的存檔，其實更像是普世人生境況不可或缺的、活生生的一部分。畢加索、杜尚、馬列維奇、波洛克、波依斯或安迪•沃霍若不是能以精妙之見求取西方現代主義進程的脈動，他們的藝術事業會否有任何意義也是值得懷疑的。時代離我們最近的沃霍曾經質疑：一個藝術家如果想在當今“時代尖端”那裡自得其所，應該如何發現過去未曾以同樣方式構想出來或（通過直覺）感知到的原創事物呢？既然前人有此一問，當藝術家在嘗試重新詮釋他們對當今跨文化環境的理解時，如果能將注意力放在歷史時間的進程上，有沒有可能會有所助益呢？倘若答案是肯定的，這個過程又是如何開展的呢？

雖然前人的后現代式假設不以為然，藝術家其實還是有可能聯系歷史進行創作的。在這種情況下，藝術家或許還可以就現今提出創見。他們可能會尋求一種新序列，探索來自多種文化的物體、事件、建筑和自然形態到底如何影響我們對當前各種沖突的理解。這意味著，一個藝術家的創作多少受其生活年代所限制，而他在當前時日之中的體驗，即成為造就藝術大作的原始素材。有些后現代主義者或許會辯駁說：藝術當中的體驗，並不比學術性的評析還來得重要。然而，我

of one's time. This happens through the process of intuiting new ways of thinking, seeing, and feeling, and also by discovering new mediumistic processes whereby one may project the past into the present. By grappling with images of the relative past, the artist may project a concept of time in relation to the future.

This is precisely what the Shanghai-born artist Zhang Jian-Jun has shown in a provocative series of works over the past decade and a half, from the late twentieth into the early twenty-first century. His work articulates a process of time, history and memory through the act of perception. For Zhang, time is essential to how the human beings perceive and acculturate themselves to the existing transitional environment. In one sense, he is dealing with a structuralist argument, but not entirely. While all the signs of existence may ultimately add up to survival, the multifarious approaches within the enormous spread of culture today may suggest a matrix that is far more profound. Zhang wants to trace a pattern of ideas through the observation of worldly phenomena, often laminating signs of the historical process against the other. Village architecture inside China may suddenly appear in suspension between two worlds, vessels from the Shang Dynasty (or earlier) may challenge certain assumptions as to how we perceive our reality today, and portraits of human beings that we identify according to race, gender, or class may reveal traits about themselves that were previously unknown or unconsidered in terms of the sociological classifications employed in two previous centuries. All of these subjects are within the purview of Zhang Jian-Jun's investigations.

Even so, we have to consider that his inquiry into these topics may exceed the limits of investigation normally reserved for the social sciences. There is more than a hint that the intuition of the artist may have the capacity to move history forward. For example,

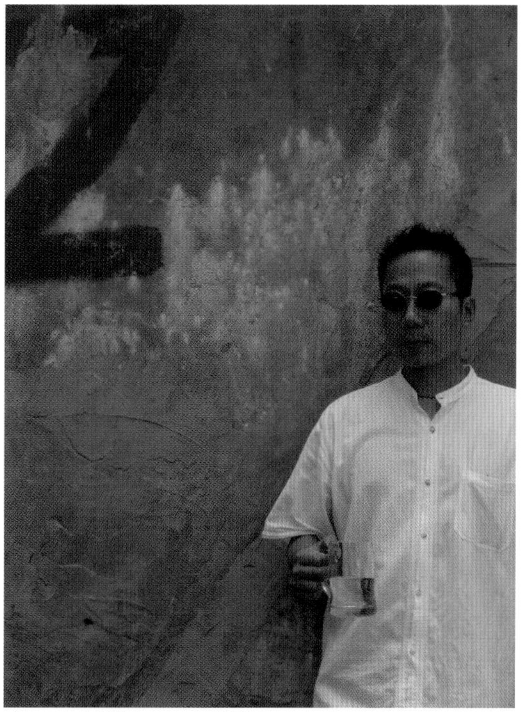

Photograph 攝影: MaoMao 毛毛

Zhang Jian-Jun 張建君

對此並不苟同。一個在歷史當中創作的藝術家，憑著直覺來把握思考、觀看及感受事物的新方式，並且又發現嶄新的借尸還魂之法，得以將過去投射於當下，便等於是成為本身所處時代的一部分。藝術家在與相對屬於過去的影像周旋時，或許能投射出一種時間觀念，與未來互為觀照。

出生於上海的畫家張建君正好就表現了這一點。從二十世紀后期到本世紀初的十五年間，他一系列發人深省的作品，透過“感知”這一行為明確表達了時間之流逝、歷史以及記憶。對於現有的、處於轉變當中的環境，人類是如何加以認識及與其同化的呢？對張建君而言，時間於此當中是極為關鍵的。從某種意義上來看，他所面對的是一種結構主義式的論述，但又並不完全如此。盡管生命“存在”的所有符號或許最終都指向“生存”，覆蓋面極為巨大的當今文化之中卻又存在著五花八門的切入角度，仿佛意味著人文底下另有更為深遠的母體。通過對世俗現象的觀察，張建君志在找出一種理念的規律，並經常在此過程中，將歷史進程中的各種不同符號相互疊合。他會突然將原屬中國鄉村的建筑懸置於兩個世界之間，或者利用商朝（或更早以前）的器皿震撼我們就如何看待眼前現實而秉持的某些假設。我們依據種族、性別或階級來辨識的人物肖像，可能會展現出某些特征，而且是過去兩個世紀的社會學分類法所不曾知道或不曾正視過的特征。這些都屬於張建君所要探討的課題范圍。

盡管如此，我們還必須考慮到：張建君對這些課題的探究，已經超出了一般專屬社會科學的研究范疇。他顯然認為藝術

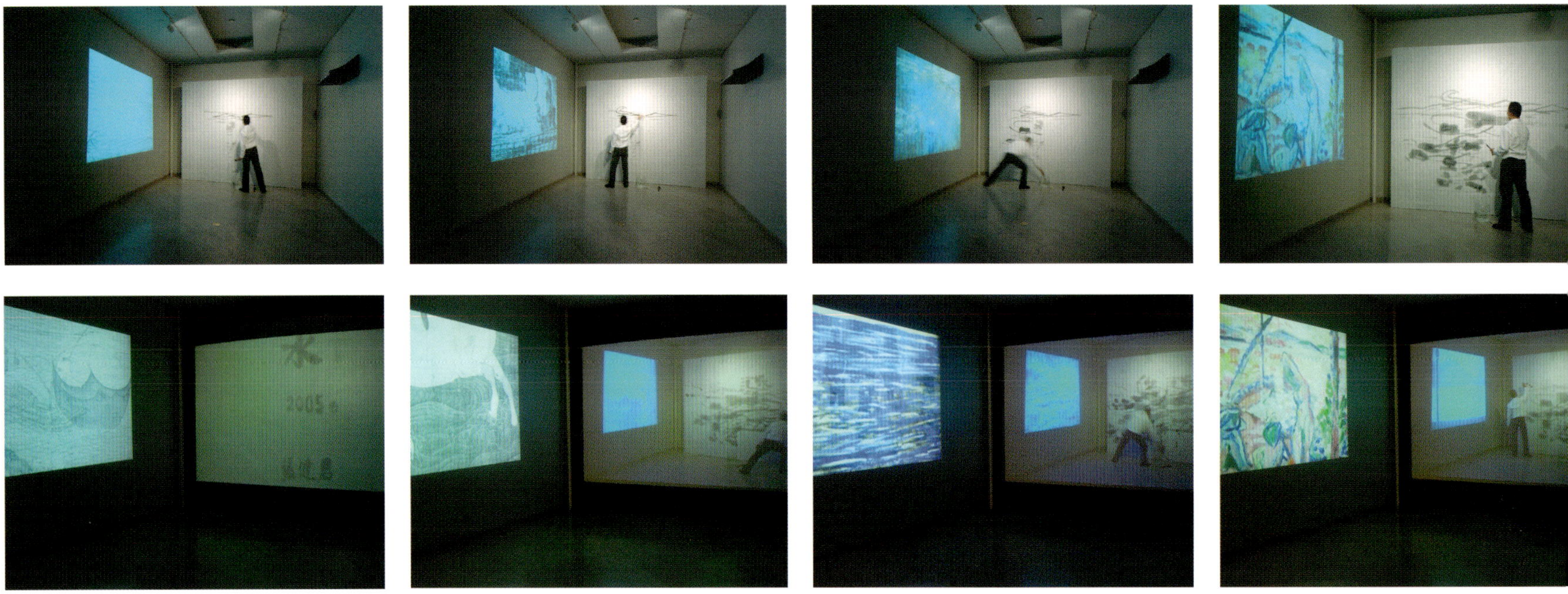

Vestiges of a Process: Water (Part 1) 過程的瞬間：水（第一部分）, *Time, water, black board, rice paper, performance, video, 2005*

At the Shanghai Art Museum, China.
上海美術館，中國。

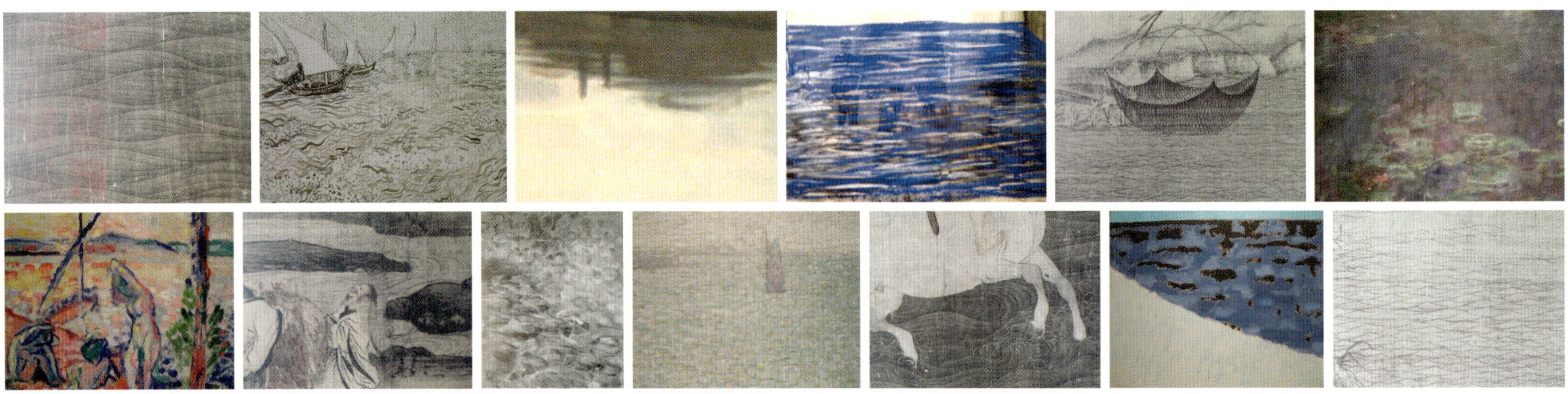

Vestiges of a Process: Water *(water images)* 過程的瞬間：水 *（輔助圖片資料）, 2005*

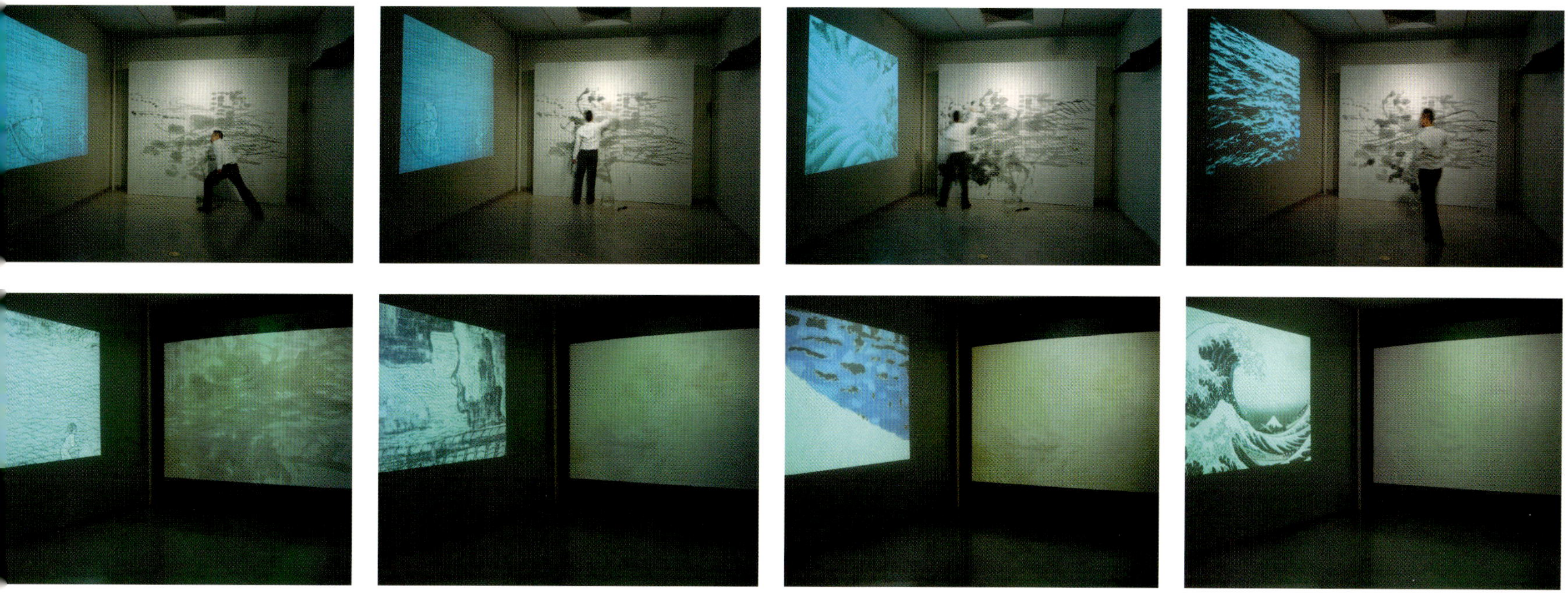

in Vestiges of a Process: Water (Part I) from 2005, Zhang projects an image from a painting of water on one wall, while on an adjacent wall, he copies the images by painting with traditional ink brushes and plain water. The painting is done on rice paper mounted on a black board, so that the observers can see the appearance of the forms that he is painting in reference to the projected image of Monet's Water Lilies or Hokusai's Great Wave. Upon completing the painting – using only water on the rice paper – Zhang's copy of the original works will eventually disappear. As the water dries under the halogen lights, Zhang's work becomes invisible. What replaces the evaporated images on the sheets of rice paper is a projected DVD documentation of the artist painting the various copies in relation to each of the projections of works by art historical masters.

家的直覺或許具有推動歷史前進的能力。比如：張建君在2005年的《過程的瞬間：水》（第一部分）當中，將以水為題材的畫作投影在一面牆上，再用毛筆蘸清水，在連接的另一面牆上加以臨摹。他在宣紙上作畫，宣紙又附於黑板上，故此觀畫者能清楚看到，他以莫內《睡蓮》或葛飾北齋《巨浪》等畫作的投影為本的形體如何漸漸顯現。這些僅用清水在宣紙上完成的臨摹畫作，最終都消失無蹤。隨著水分在鹵素燈下蒸發，張建君的畫化為無形。宣紙上蒸發掉的畫像，接著被一段投射的DVD錄像所取代。錄像所顯示的，正是畫家臨摹所投射的歷代藝術大師之作的過程。

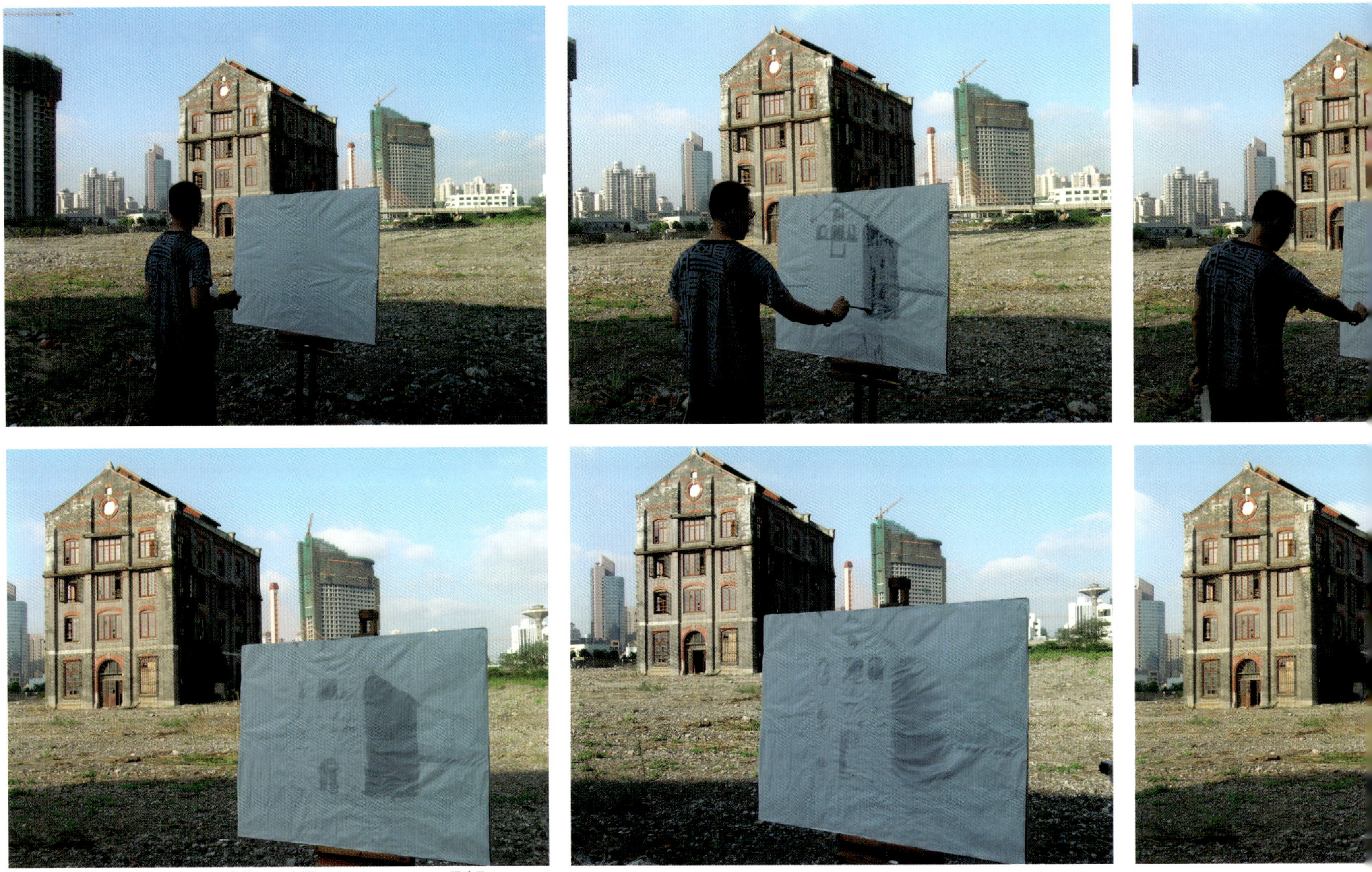

Photographs 攝影：Barbara Edelstein 芭芭拉・艾德斯坦 and Zhang Jian-Jun 張建君

Vestiges of a Process: Shanghai Project 過程的瞬間：上海計劃, *Time, water, rice paper, black board, old building, 2004*

The structure of this work is related to his on-going Vestiges of a Process series of the past few years, including his Shanghai Project from 2004. In contrast to his indoor projection/performance work, Zhang also paints out-of-doors using a Western-style easel that he places in front of an isolated five-storey building built in the early twentieth century. The old building was situated by itself in an enormous vacant lot where (one would imagine) other similar

這件藝術作品的結構，與張建君過去幾年持續創作的《過程的瞬間》系列（其中作品包括2004年的《上海計劃》）有所關聯。除了室內投影/行為藝術作品以外，張建君也有一些戶外創作。他將西式畫架放置在一棟建於二十世紀初期的五層獨立建筑物的前方。這棟老建筑單獨矗立在一大片空地上，使人自然聯想到：

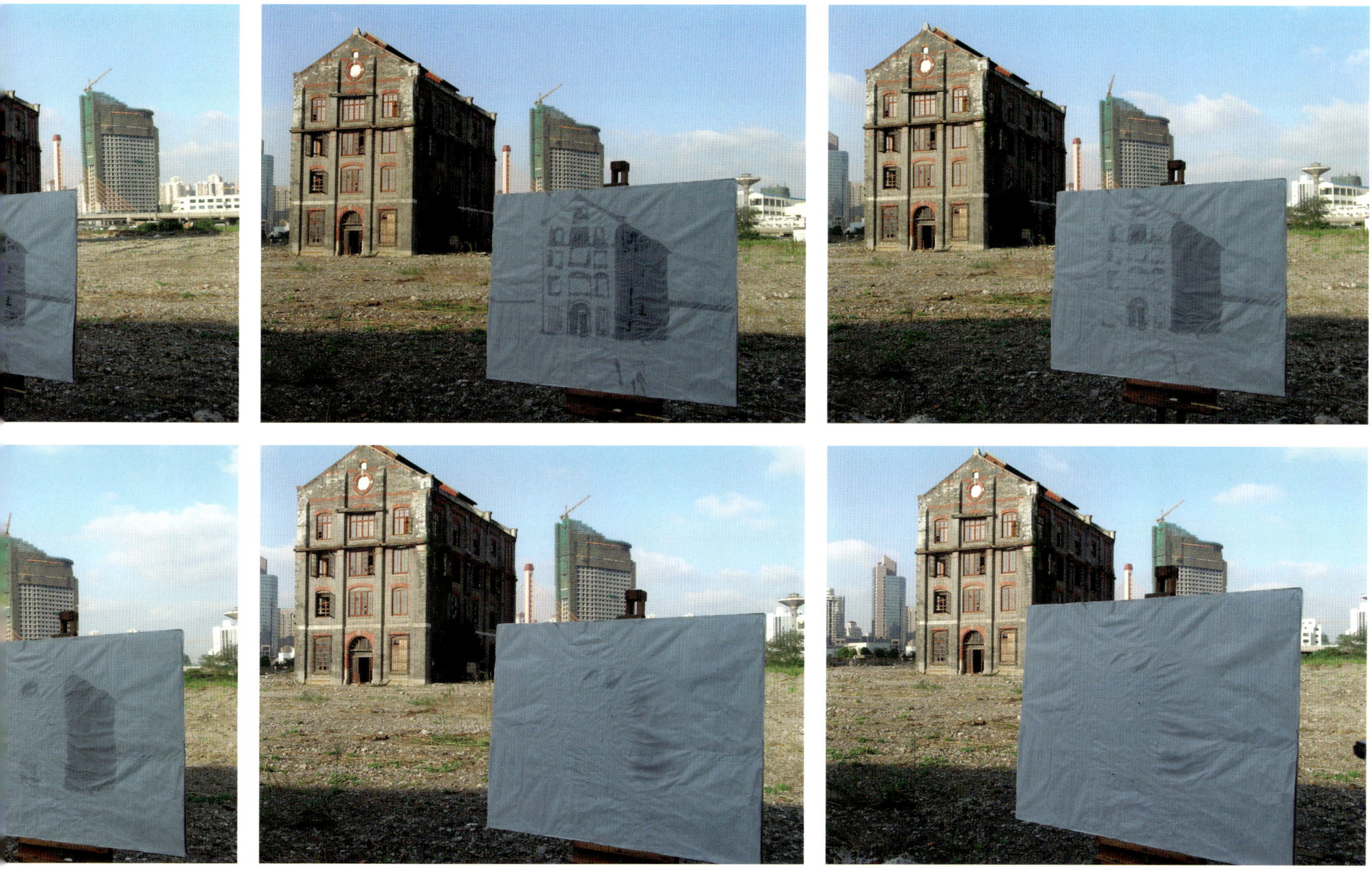

buildings once stood. Here the artist paints in water on rice paper covering a sumi-ink board in the Western plein air manner. Once completed, the water painting was left on the easel outside to dry until the image, previously defined by the sumi-ink board, was no longer there. Zhang's method of painting absence instead of presence relates directly to the process of historical time. The inevitable disappearance of this lone building corresponds to the disappearance

該處曾有其他類似的舊樓。藝術家於此用宣紙覆蓋著墨板，在老建筑前用清水以外光畫法在紙上作畫。完成后的水畫被擱在畫架上晒干，直到先前被墨板框起來的畫像已了無痕跡為止。張建君這種畫“無”不畫“有”的方法，與歷史時間的推移有直接關聯。這孤立的老建筑最終必然無可避免地消失。這與張建君宣紙

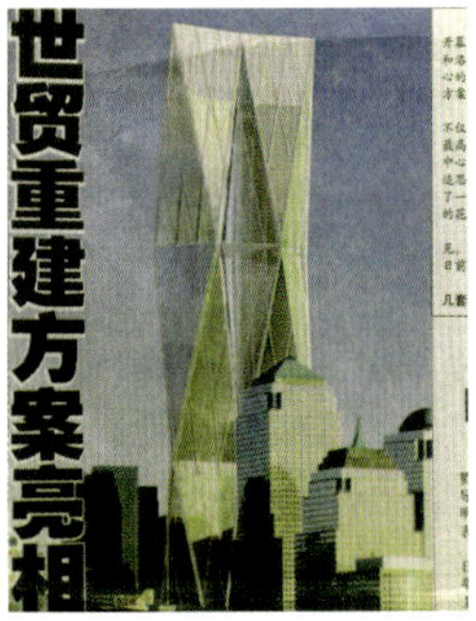

New York, USA

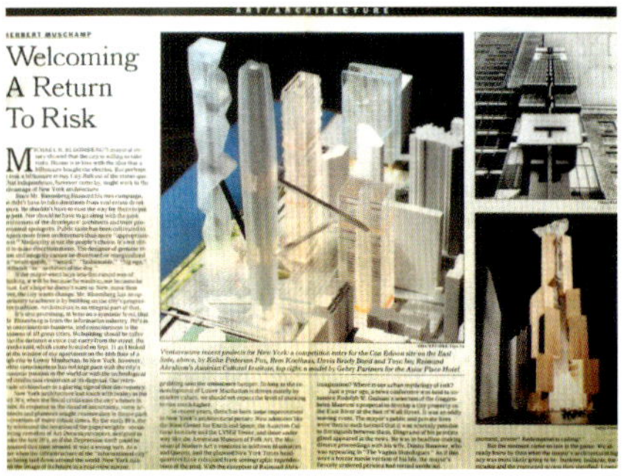
Welcoming A Return To Risk

New York, USA

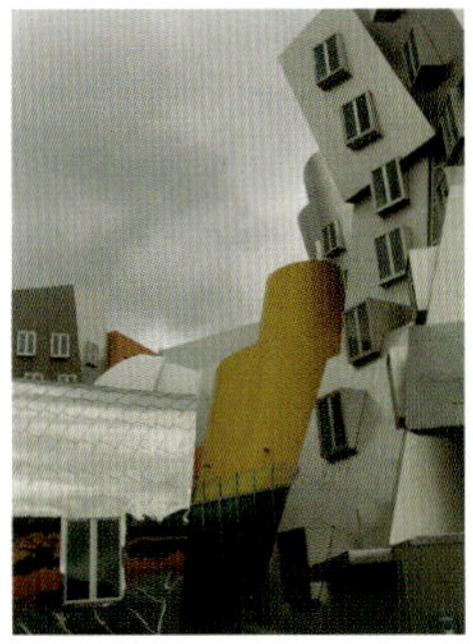
Boston, Massachusetts, USA

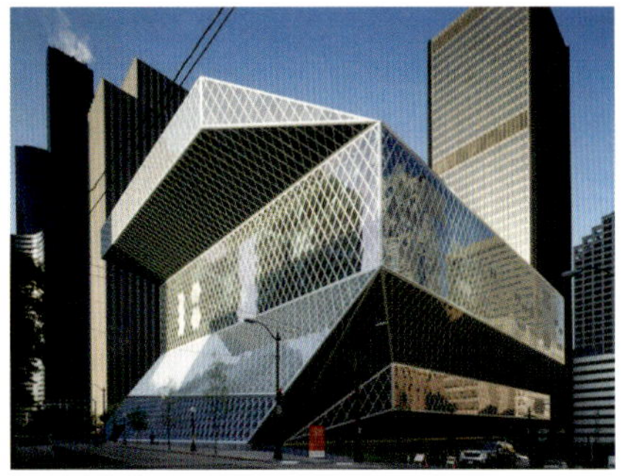
Seattle, Washington, USA

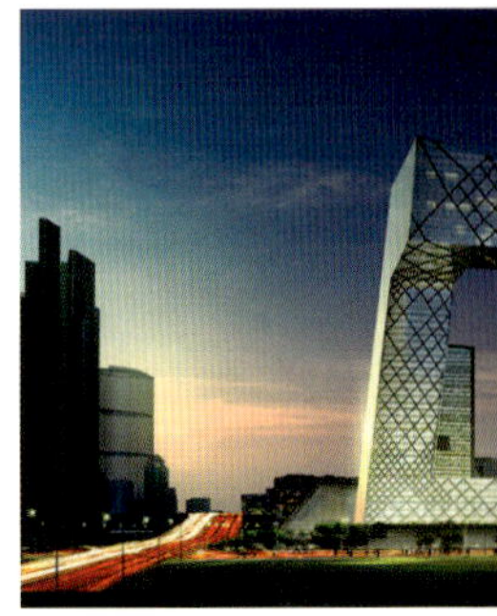
Beijing, China

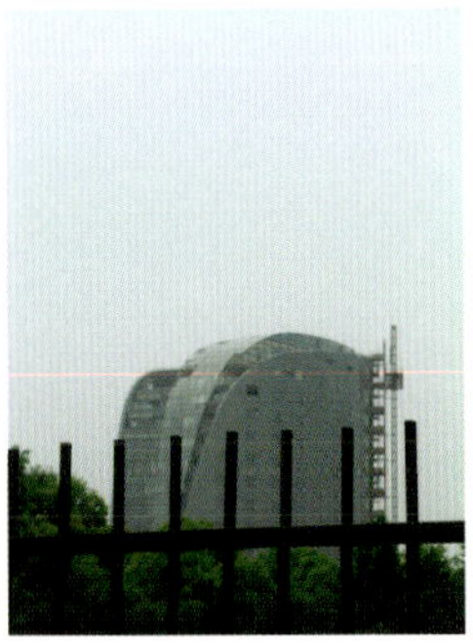
Shanghai, China

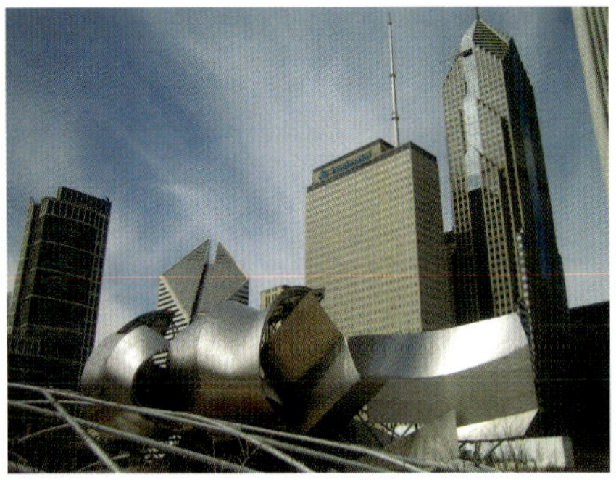
Chicago, Illinois, USA

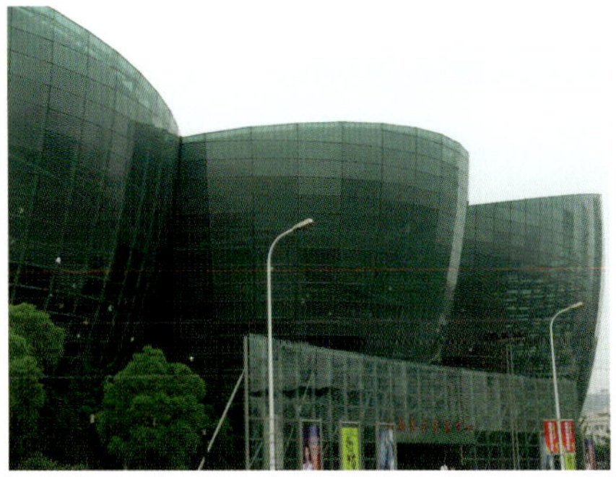
Shanghai, China

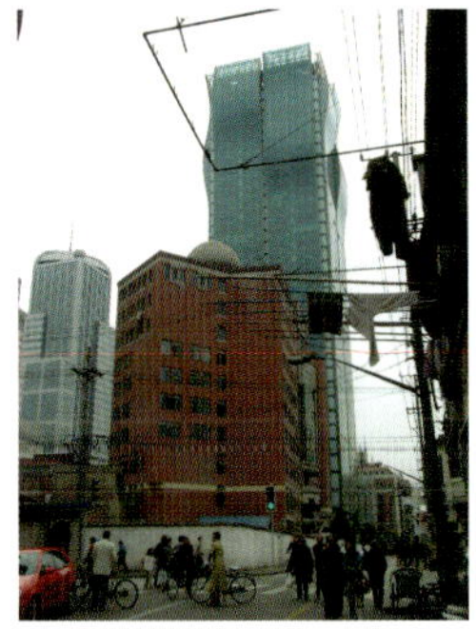
Shanghai, China

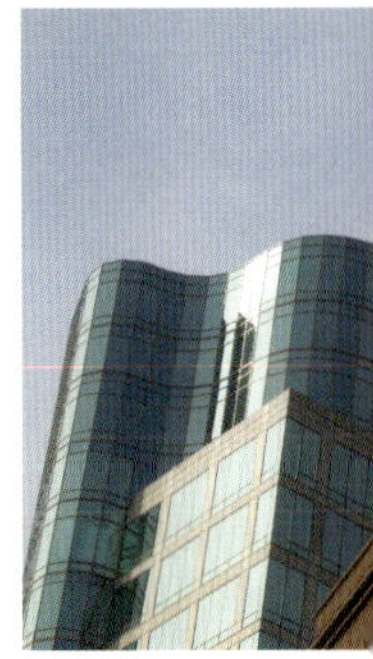
New York, USA

Document of images of Contemporary Architecture 時尚建筑圖像 *（輔助圖片集料）*

of Zhang's invisible painting of the building on the rice paper.

The Shanghai Project from 2004 is about a reciprocal disappearance. The building is painted and then the image disappears. This action on the part of the artist equals the act of a building being built and later destroyed, thereby suggesting the presence of historical time and to recognize its ability to transform presence into absence and thereby to destroy the object and its representation. To take this concept further would suggest that historical time in China is generally perceived over a longer duration than in the Western world. The act of representation and disappearance in Zhang's recent artistic practice is not only in reference to the duration of historical time -- as far back as the Neolithic era -- but also in reference to a culturally specific action and (for a better word) a psycho-sociological trace that signifies a perennial culture embedded within the structure of Chinese thought and language.

Zhang Jian-Jun was born, raised, and educated in Shanghai. He graduated from the Fine Arts Department of the Shanghai Drama

上無形舊樓畫的消失，正好互相呼應。

2004年的《上海計劃》實以互作消逝為主旨。藝術家畫了建筑物，接著畫像又消失了。他這樣的行為等同於人們對房子先建后毀的行為。這於是就暗示了歷史時間的存在，承認時間確實能化“有”為“無”、將客體以及對客體的描繪一並消滅。倘若就此再進一步思索，可以說就被感知的時間長短而言，中國的歷史時間大體上比西方世界的還要漫長。張建君近期創作中“先畫后逝”之舉，不僅是指涉歷史時間之長短（最早可追溯到新石器時代），同時也指涉了某種屬於特定文化的行為，以及某種心理社會意義上的殘跡（這麼說應該更為恰當）。這一殘跡，無非體現了埋藏在中國思維與語言的結構之中的一種文化常態。

上海是張建君出生、成長和受教育的地方。他在1978年畢業

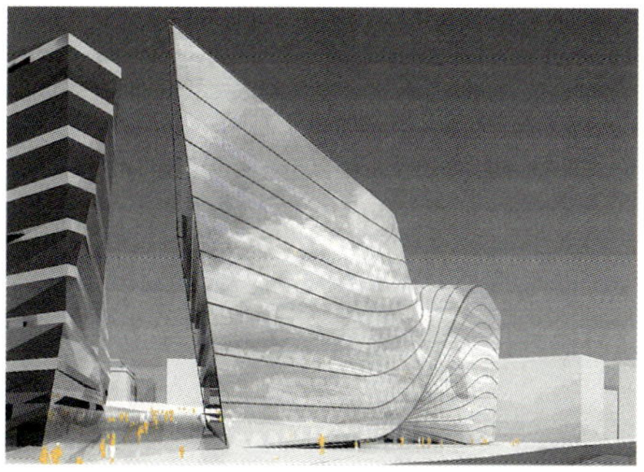

London, England

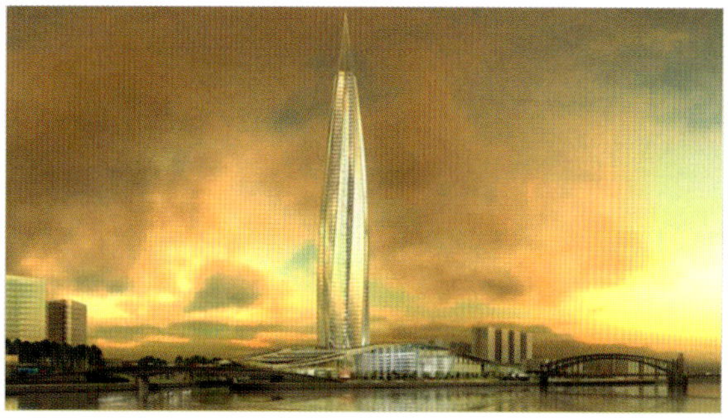

St. Petersburg, Russia

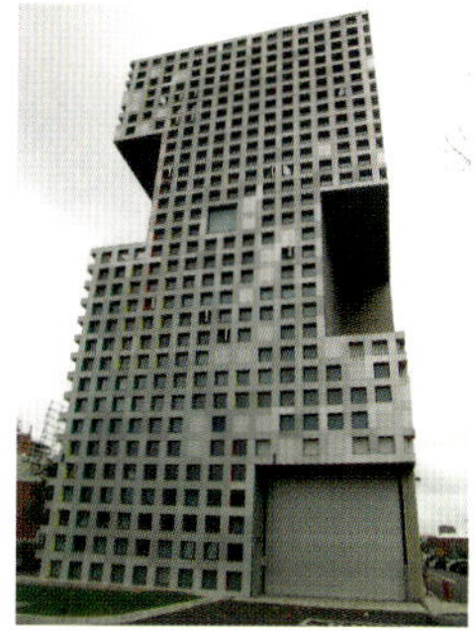

Boston, Massachusetts, USA

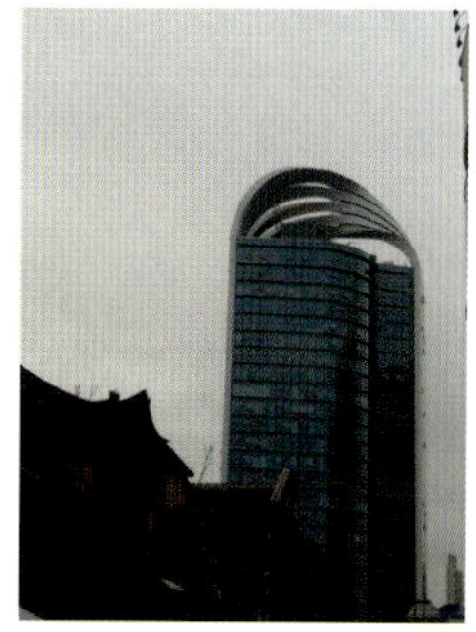

Shanghai, China

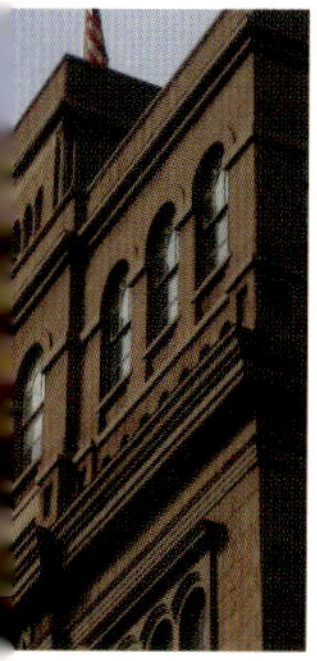

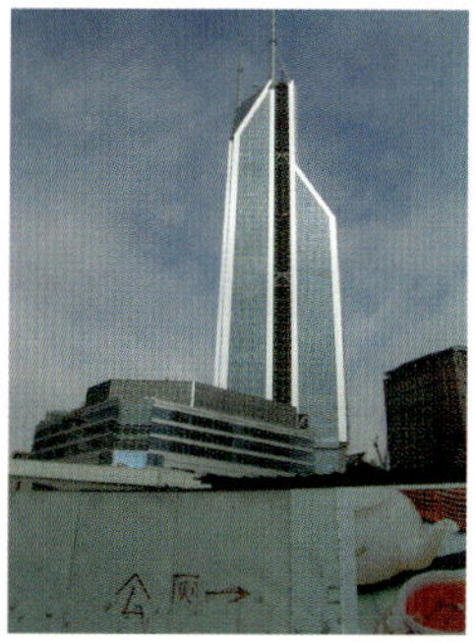

Shanghai, China

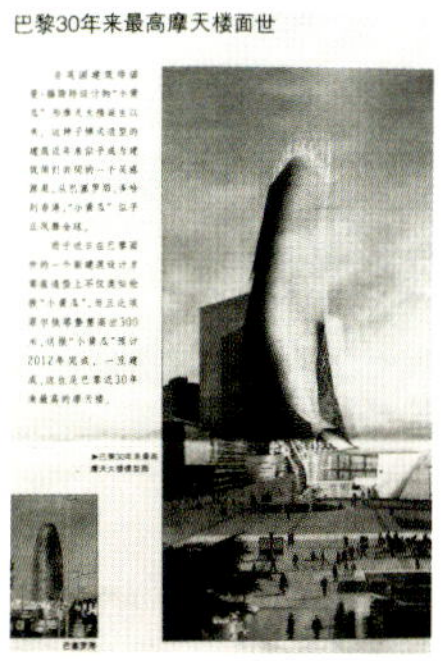

Paris, France

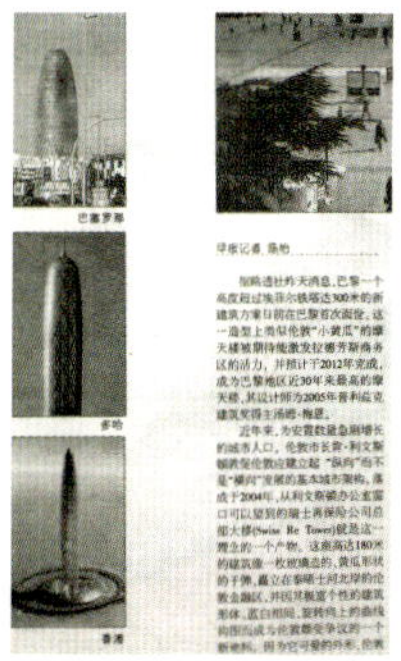

Barcelona, Spain

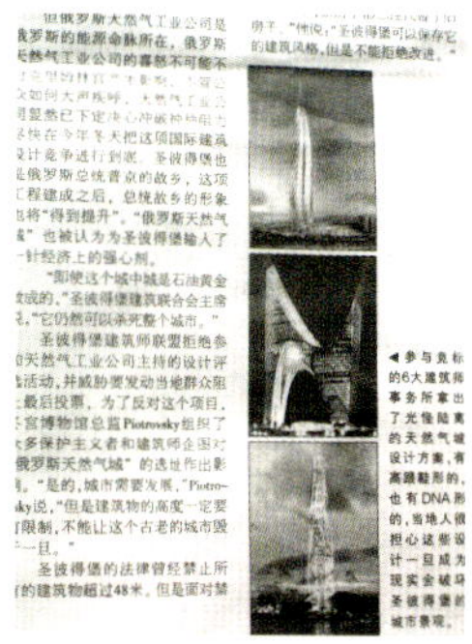

St. Petersburg, Russia

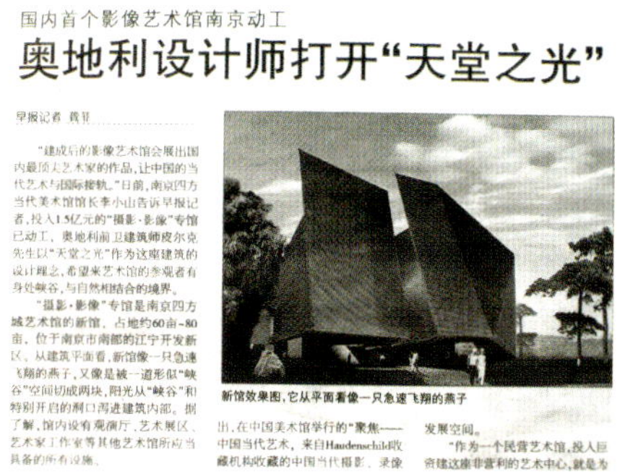

Nanjing, China

Institute in 1978. He became involved as an abstract painter and exhibited his work in the early eighties (for which he paid a certain price). By the mid-eighties, things began to change. Over the past two decades, Zhang has been held various curatorial, directorial, and advisory positions in association with the Shanghai Art Museum. In 1989 he moved to New York where his met his wife, the artist Barbara Edelstein (with whom he has collaborated on many projects), and was in many important exhibitions. Since 1997, Zhang has been an Adjunct Professor at New York University and has continued to travel frequently between his native China and New York. This suggests that Zhang has been acculturated into American life-styles while maintaining a clear focus in terms of his Chinese heritage. Rather than seeing current history in terms of the negative, Zhang reflects but does not hesitate. He forges ahead exploring new terrains that embed his sense of historical time within the conflicts of the present-day.

As his projects move forward, Zhang employs subject matter from the West while at the same time adhering to a structure of time, history, and memory that is essentially Eastern. He works

於上海戲劇學院美術系，於1980年代早期從事抽象繪畫，展出作品（並為此付出一些代價）。到了1980年代中期，情況才開始出現變化。張建君過去二十年多次與上海美術館合作，負責過策展、領導及咨詢方面的各項職務。他1989年移居紐約，在那裡認識了畫家芭芭拉・愛德斯坦。兩人就多個項目進行合作，最終結為夫妻。張建君此時還參加了不少重要的展覽。他自1997年起擔任紐約大學客座教授，並繼續頻密往返中國和紐約兩地。這其實表示，張建君已經融入美國的生活，但同時又明確著眼於自己的中國根底。他並不褒古貶今；他對於當前的歷史有所思考，卻又毫不遲疑。他以向前邁進的精神，穩健地探索新疆域；在那裡，他的歷史時間感是深植於屬於今日的各種沖突當中的。

張建君在推展他的藝術項目的同時，既採用西方題材，又依循基本屬於東方的時間、歷史與記憶三重結構。他以耐心和

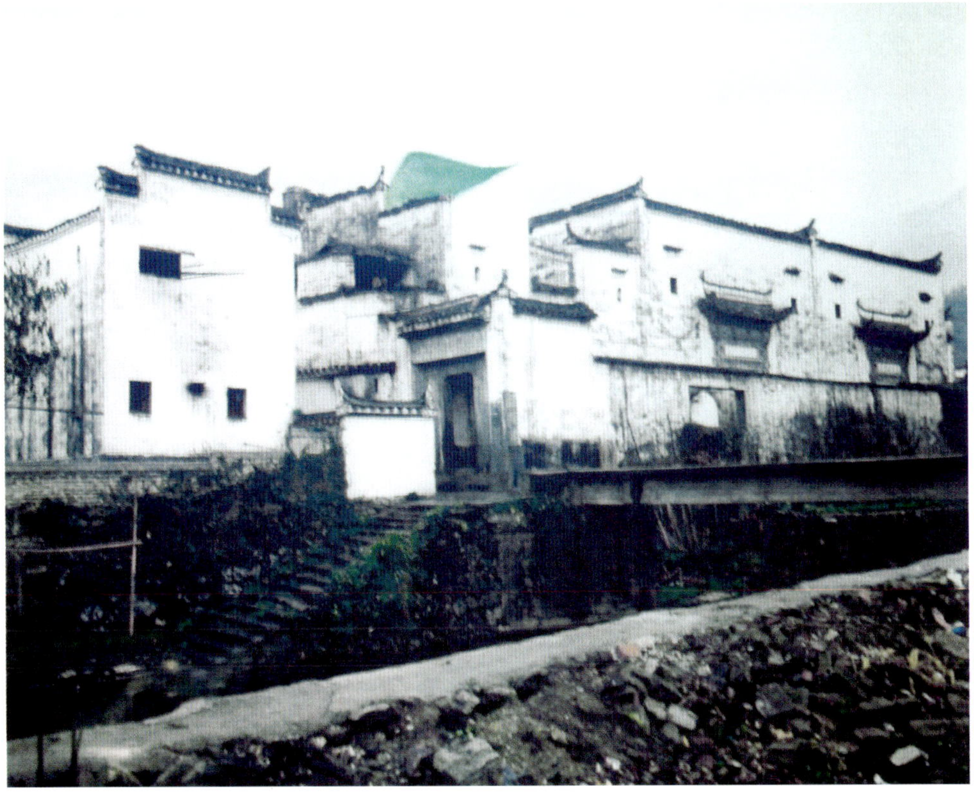

China Chapter: Xiao Qi Village #1
中國篇：曉起 #1
Oil paint on photo
100 x 120 cm
2004

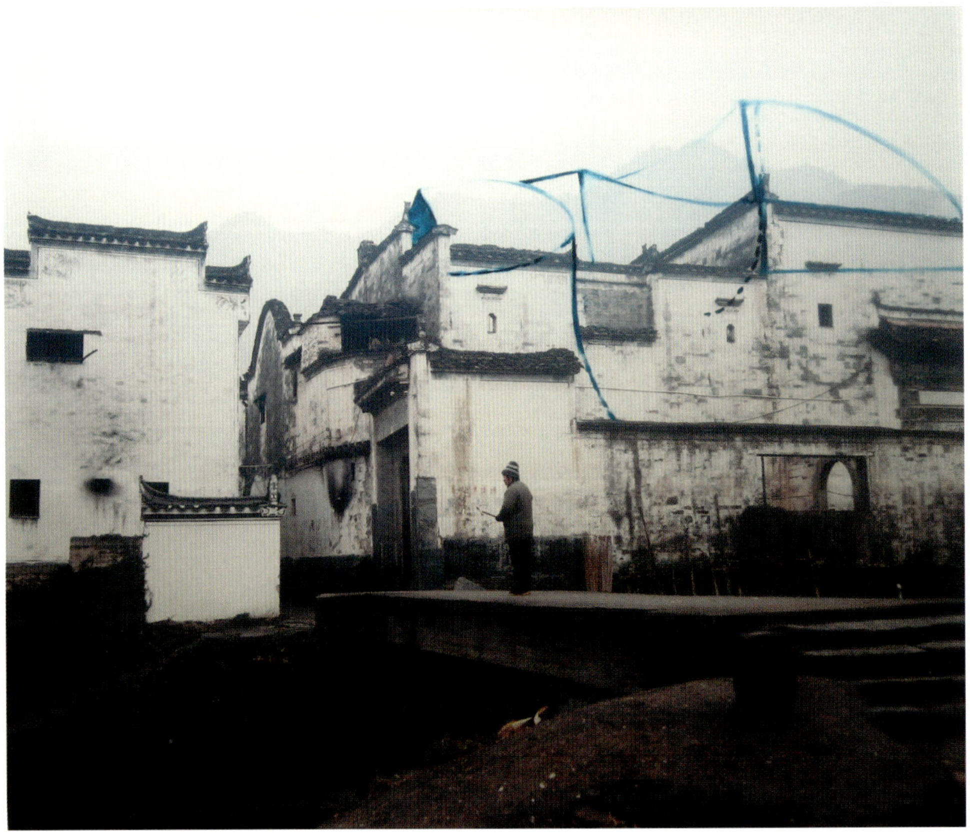

China Chapter: Xiao Qi Village #2
中國篇：曉起 #2
Oil paint on photo
100 x 120 cm
2004

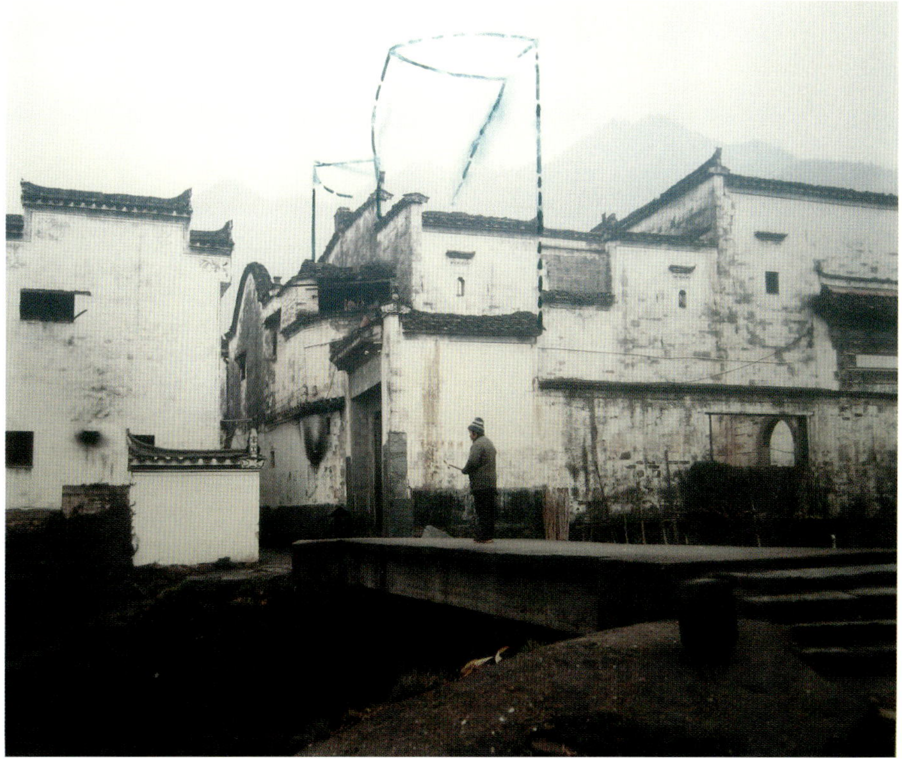

China Chapter: Xiao Qi Village #3 中國篇：曉起 #3

Oil paint on photo
100 x 120 cm
2004

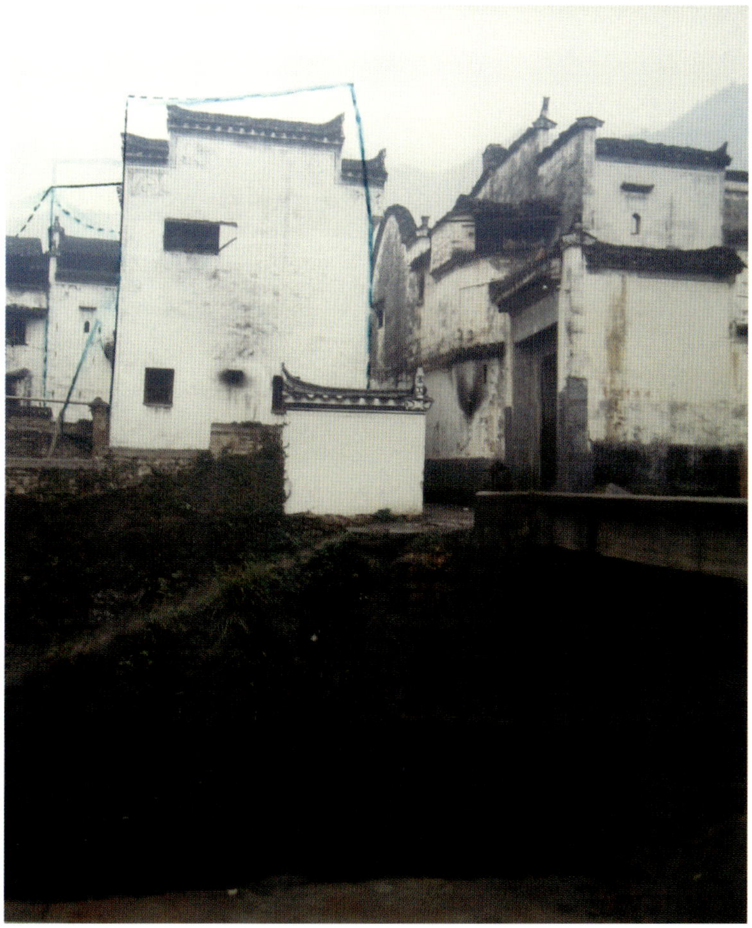

China Chapter: Xiao Qi Village #5 中國篇：曉起 #5

Oil paint on photo
120 x 100 cm
2004

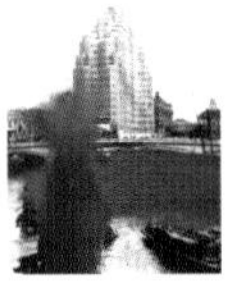

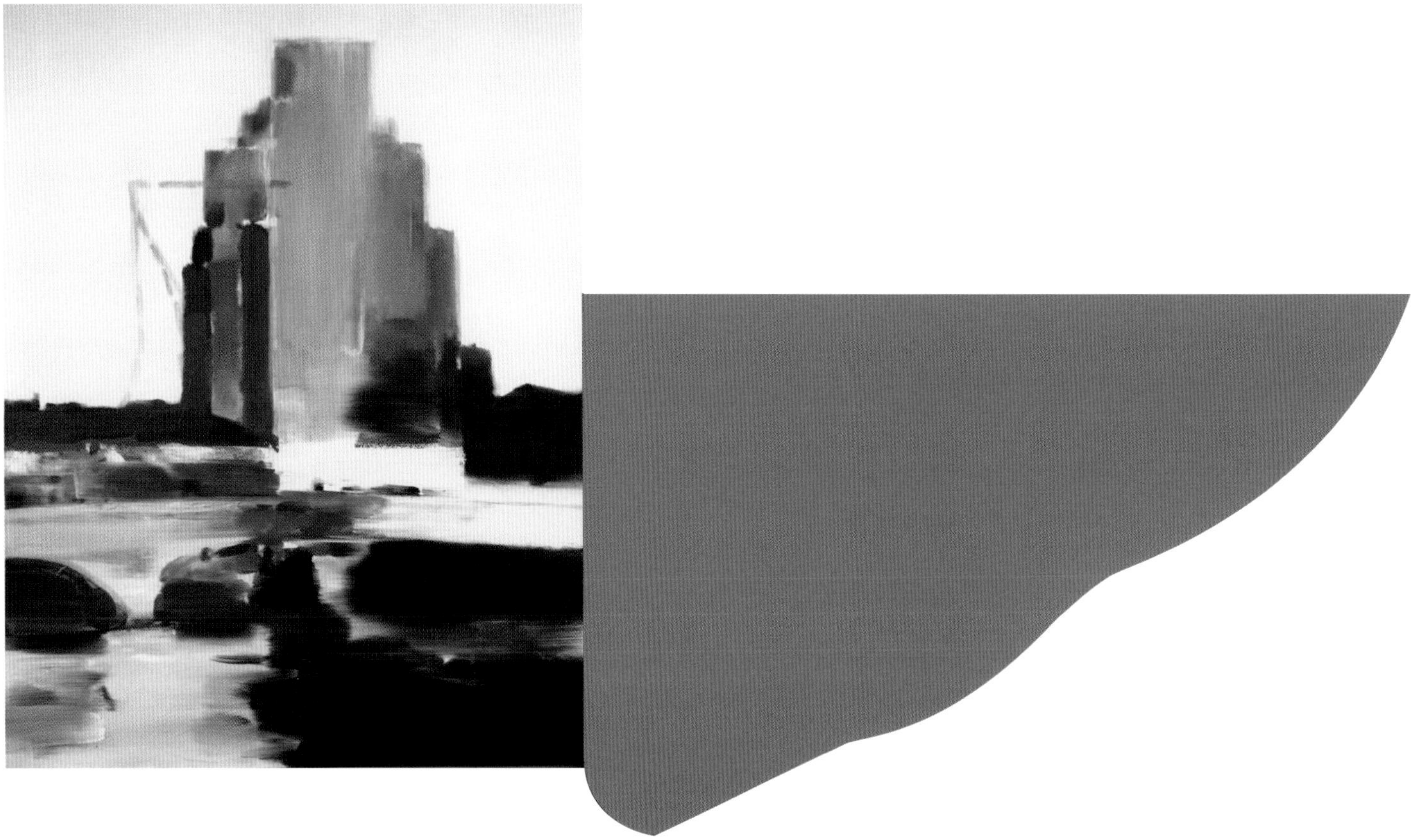

Vestiges of a Process: Shanghai Project 2006 #1 過程的瞬間：上海計劃
Oil on linen, photo
176 x 335 cm
2006

with patience and humility in his attempt to represent an extended duration of time. For example, the linear oil paint markings that appear above the rooftops of the sepia-toned photograph entitled China Chapter: Xiao Qi Village #2 do little more than suggest the immanence of change, that is, the inevitability of architectural renovation over time. The same is true with Xiao Qi Village #3 in which different hand-painted markings occur on a reproduction of the same photograph. In comparing the two works, one may decipher than the later configuration more closely resembles the looming presence of Frank Gehry's Guggenheim Museum in Bilbao, but not intentionally.

These architectural photographs with accompanying oil paintings tend to encapsulate most clearly Zhang's interest in memory and in the process of historical time. "Culture largely influences architectural style," says Zhang. This could be no more apparent than in another work entitled Vestiges of a Process: Shanghai Project.

謙遜的態度進行創作，試圖表現更為漫長的時間。比如作品《中國篇：曉起 #2》，褐色調照片中屋頂上方的油彩線條標記，即隱隱暗示了變遷的內在性－也就是建筑隨著時間流逝，無可避免將必須進行整修的事實。《曉起 #3》亦是如此，唯獨它是上述照片的復制品，上面畫有另一些不同的手繪標記。我們若是對這兩件作品進行比較，或許會覺得后者的構圖無意間更接近法蘭克・蓋瑞所設計的畢爾巴鄂古根漢美術館兀然聳立之狀。

這些各附油畫的建筑照片，往往就張建君對記憶及歷史時間進程的興趣有最清楚的集中反映。他曾表示：“文化的影響所及，以建筑風格為主。” 把這一點展現得最淋漓盡致的，莫過於《過程的瞬間：上海計劃》。在其中一個副題為

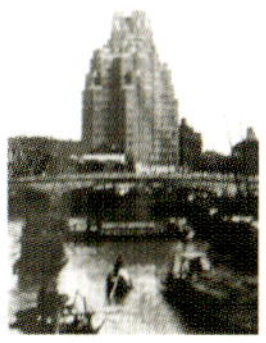

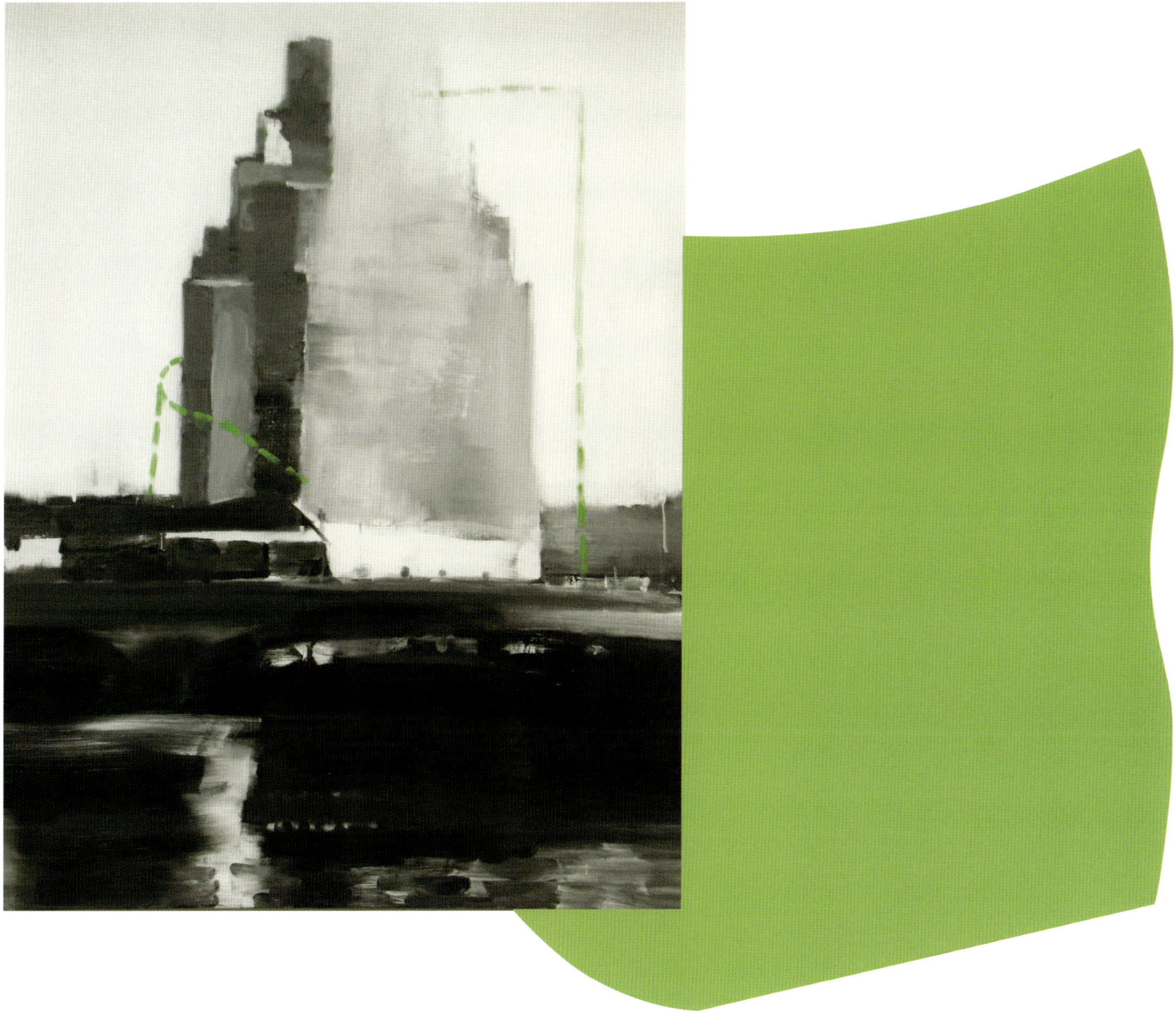

Vestiges of a Process: Shanghai Project 2006 #2 過程的瞬間：上海計劃

Oil on linen, photo
180 x 288 cm
2006

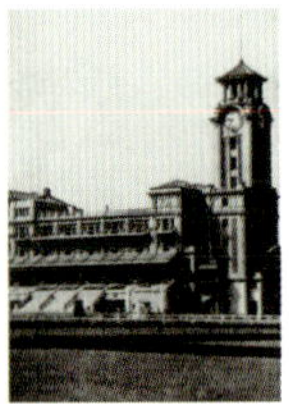

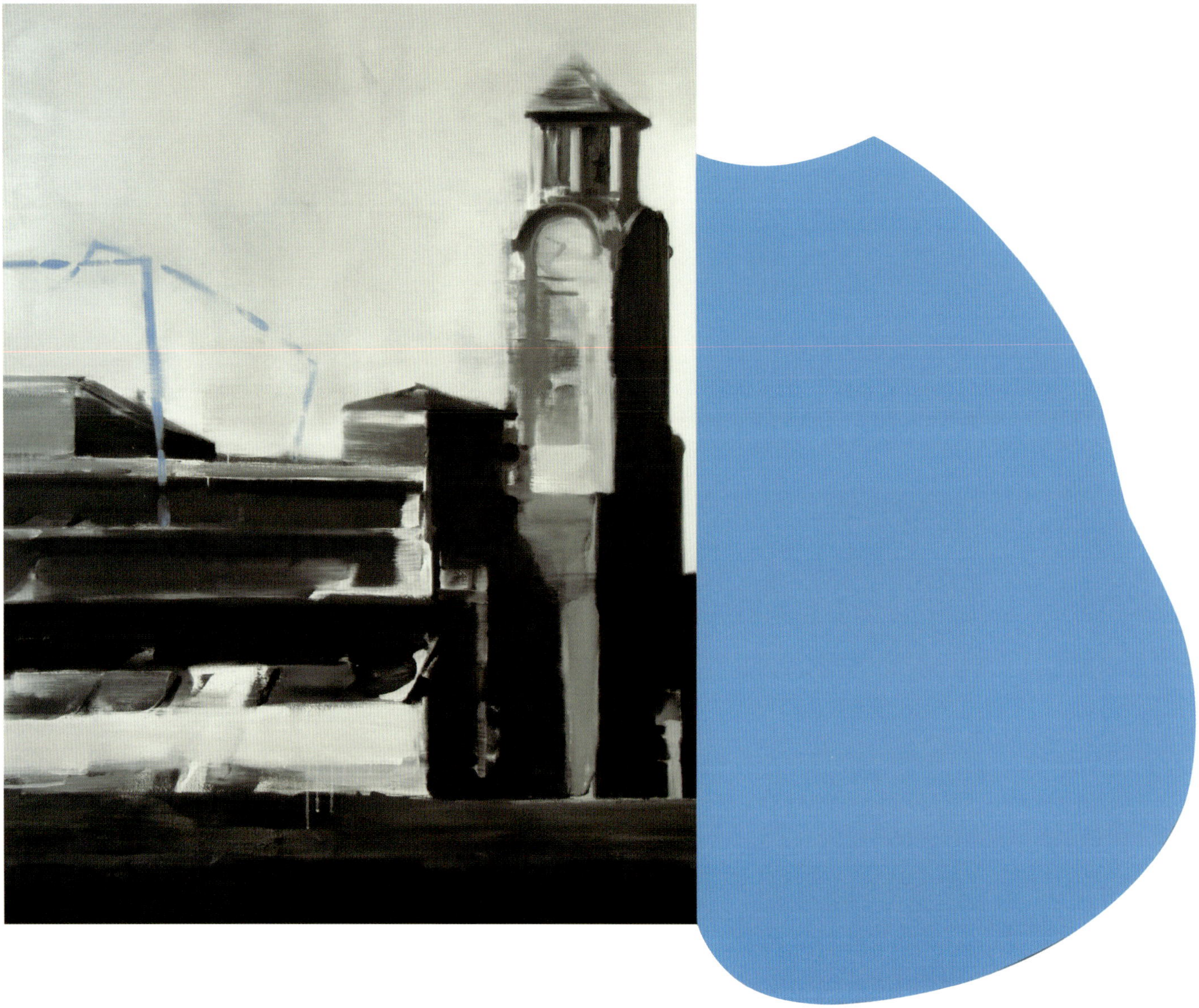

Vestiges of a Process: Shanghai Project 2006 #3 過程的瞬間：上海計劃
Oil on linen, photo
182 x 262 cm
2006

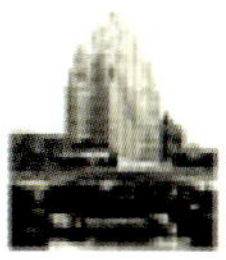

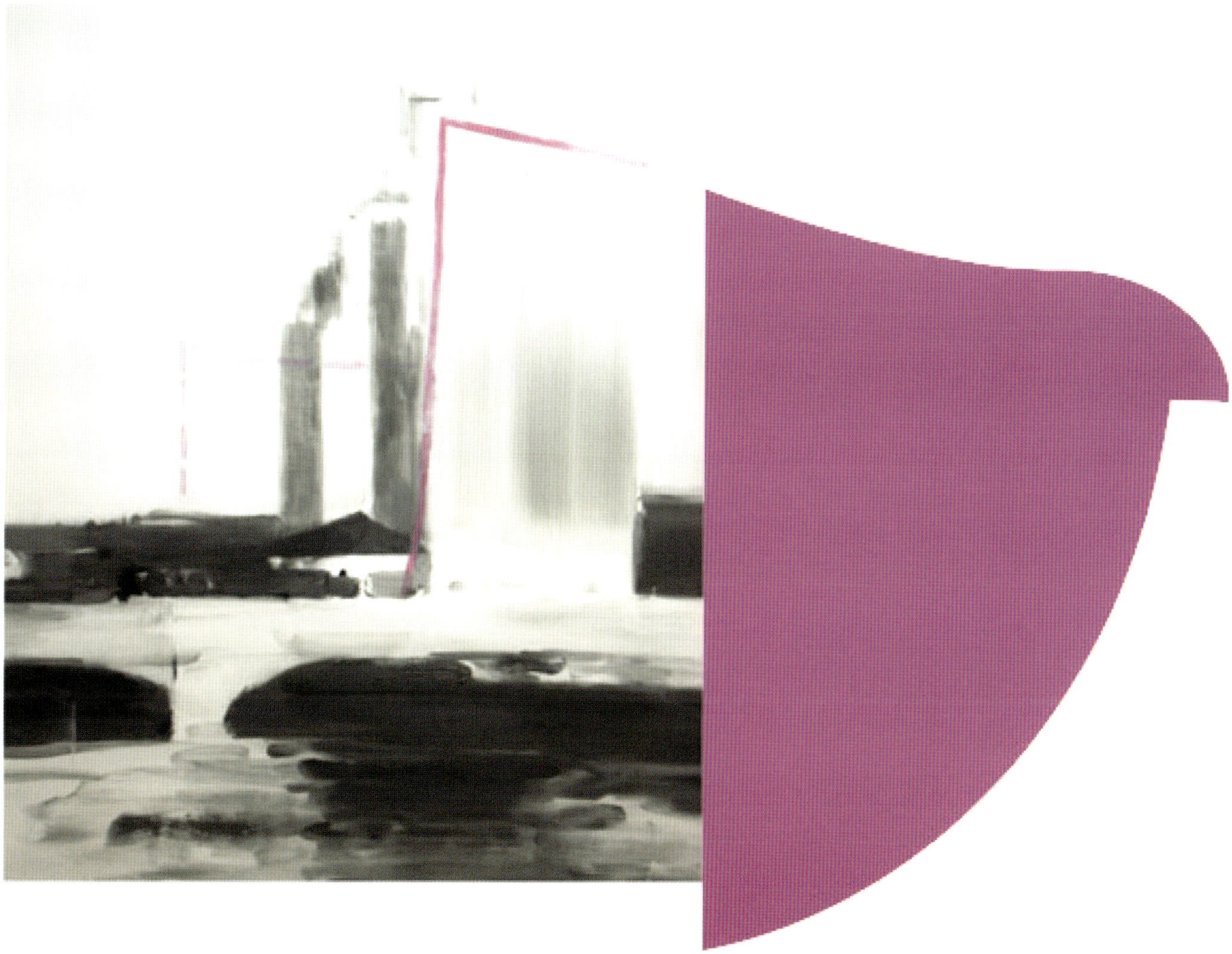

Vestiges of a Process: 2007 Shanghai Project #2 過程的瞬間：2007 上海計劃 #2

Oil on linen, photo
151 x 279 cm
2007

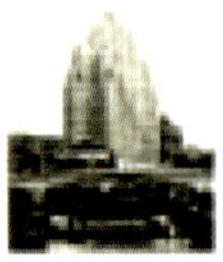

Vestiges of a Process: 2007 Shanghai Project #3 過程的瞬間：2007 上海計劃 #3
Oil on linen, photo
152 x 245 cm
2007

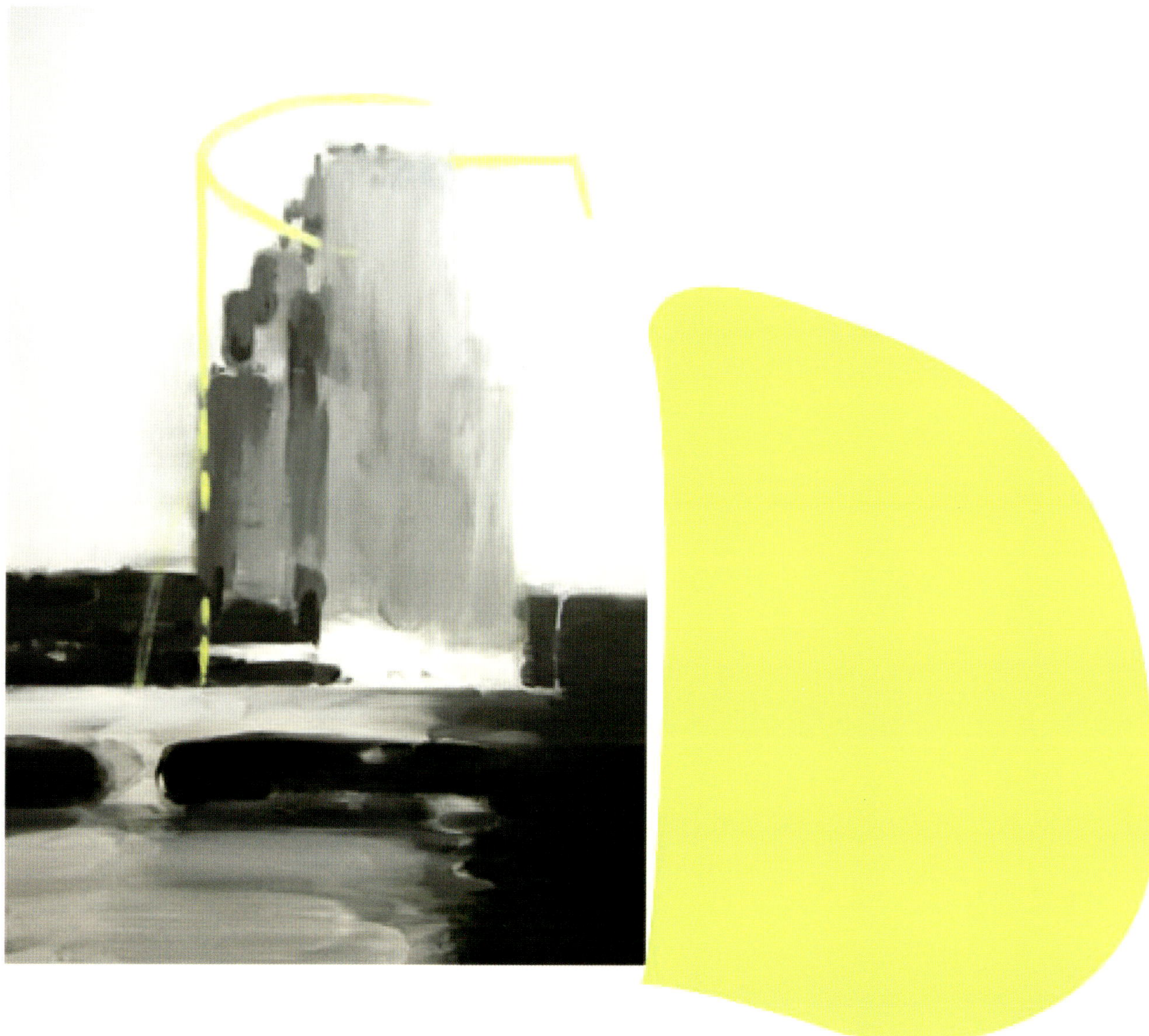

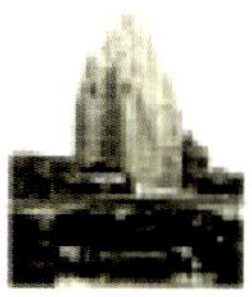

Vestiges of a Process: 2007 Shanghai Project #5 過程的瞬間：2007 上海計劃 #5

Oil on linen, photo
125 x 185 cm
2007

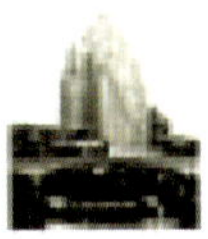

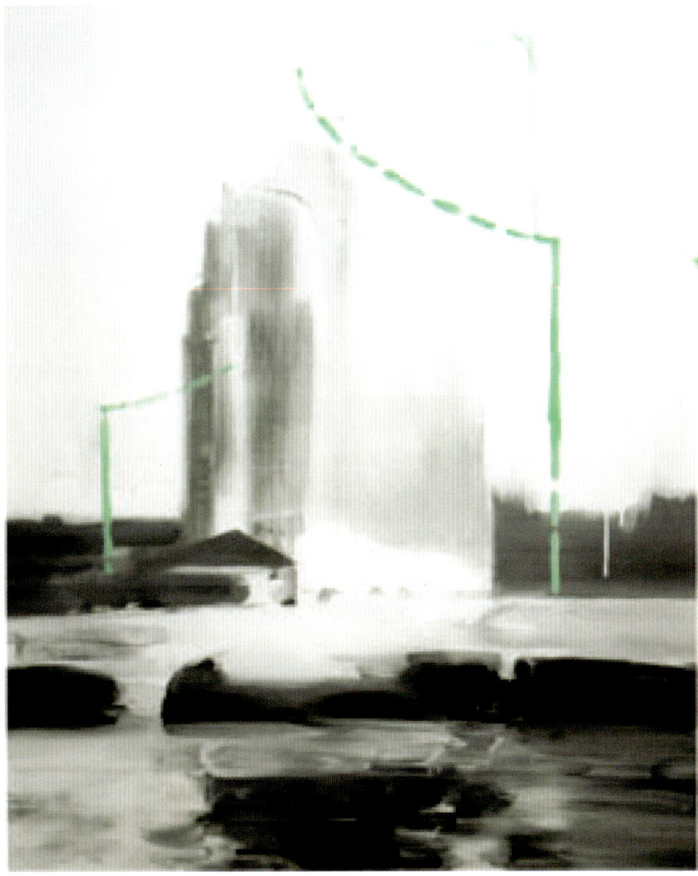

Vestiges of a Process: 2007 Shanghai Project #6 過程的瞬間：2007 上海計劃 #6

Oil on linen, photo
161 x 260 cm
2007

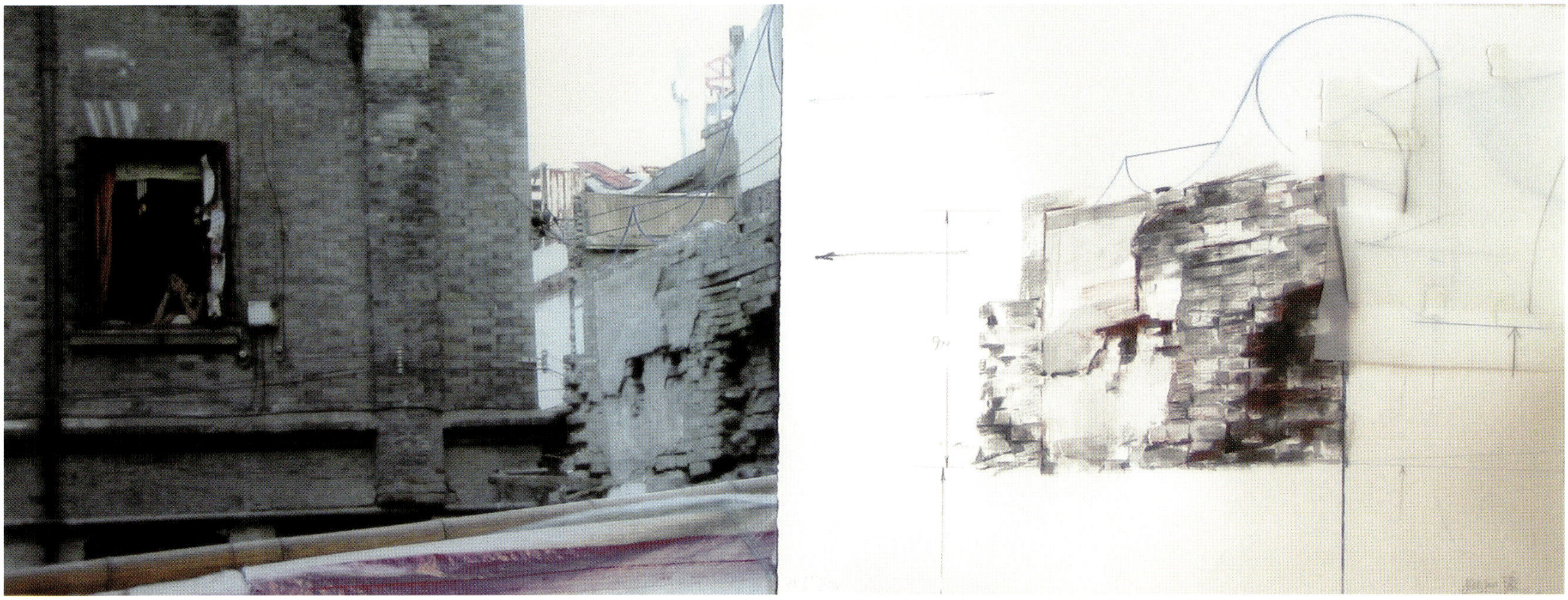

Vestiges of a Process: Shanghai Project 過程的瞬間：上海計劃 2003 - 2005

Watercolor and graphite on paper, photo
51 x 122 cm
2003-2005

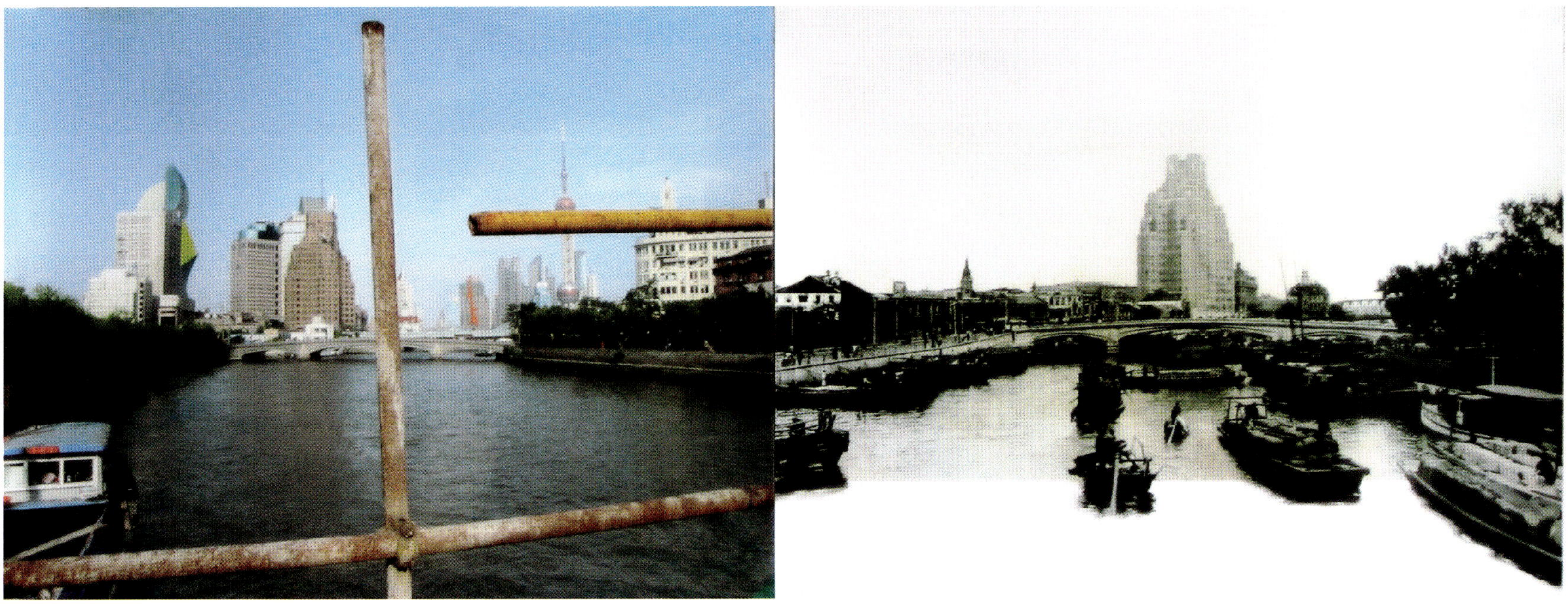

Vestiges of a Process: Shanghai Project 過程的瞬間：上海計劃 2003 - 2005

Oil on photo
51 x 122 cm
2003-2005

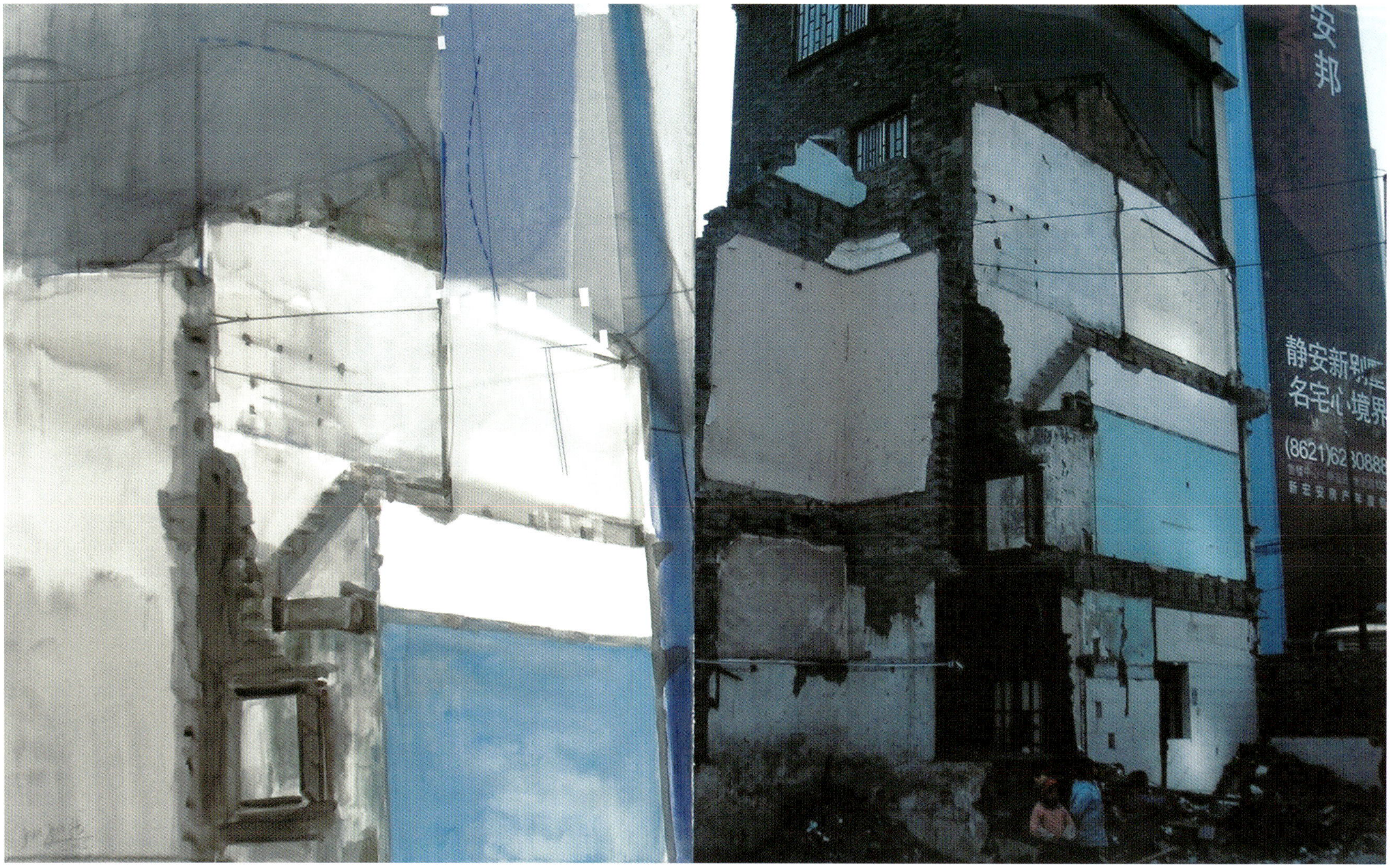

Vestiges of a Process: Shanghai Project 過程的瞬間：上海計劃2005
Watercolor on paper, photo
122 x 200 cm
2005

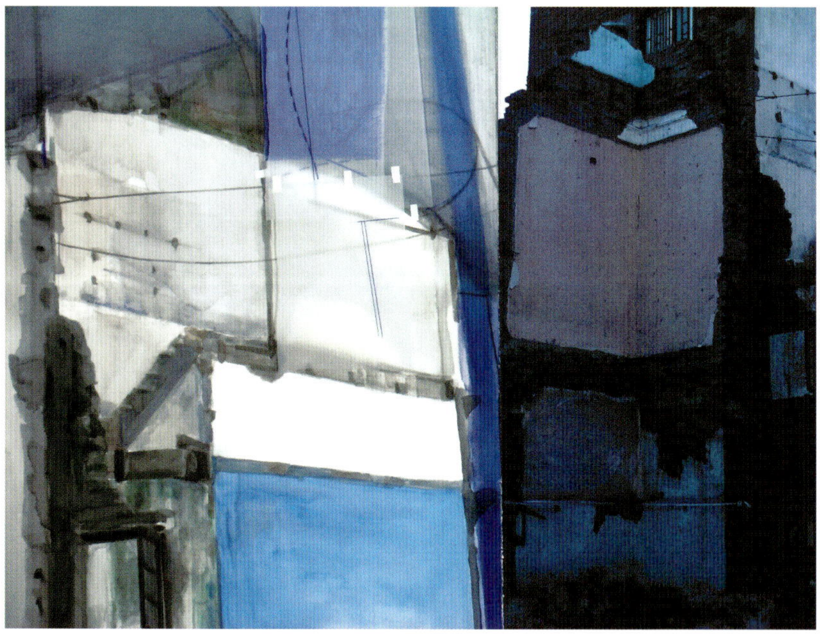

Vestiges of a Process: Shanghai Project (detail)
過程的瞬間：上海計劃 2005（局部）
Watercolor on paper, photo
122 x 200 cm
2005

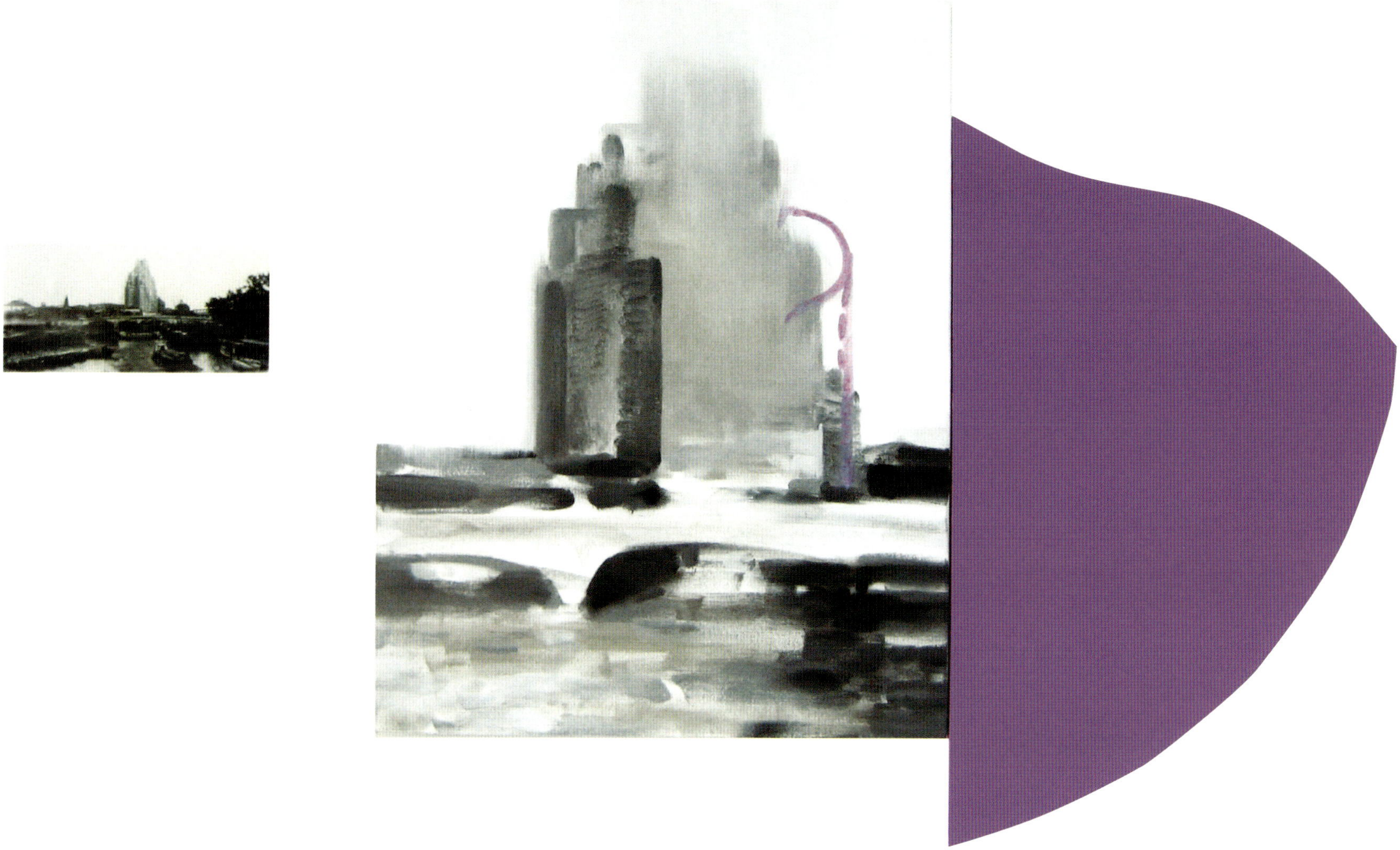

Vestiges of a Process: Shanghai Project (Broadway Building/Suzhou Creek) #1 過程的瞬間：百老匯大廈/蘇洲河 #1 ,
Oil on canvas, photo, 88 x 146 cm, 1935 - 2006

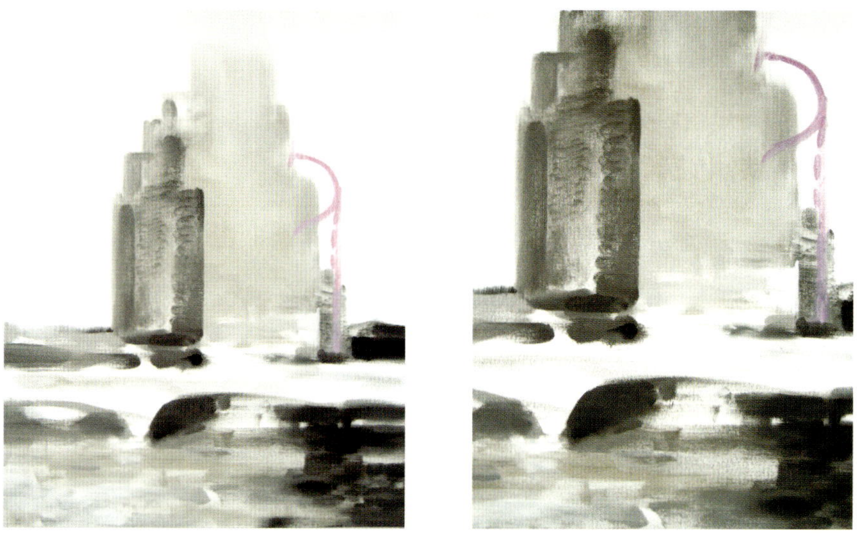

Vestiges of a Process: Shanghai Project (Broadway Building/ Suzhou Creek) #1 (detail)（局部）, *Oil on canvas, photo, 88 x 146 cm, 1935 - 2006*

In one version, sub-titled Broadway Building/Suzhou Creek #1, 1935 - 2005, the artist shows a tripartite arrangement consisting of a small black and white photograph of the area explained in the sub-title, a larger painting that focuses on the Broadway Building, and a pink-colored shaped canvas off to the right side, which is an enlargement of the pink lines in the painting that indicate what the future of this building is going to resemble.

《百老匯大廈 / 蘇州河 #1》的版本中，張建君呈現了一種三分布局，構成部分為：一小張副題所指地區的黑白照片，一幅較大的、以百老匯大廈為主的繪畫，以及右側一片修剪過的粉紅色帆布。帆布其實是在模仿畫中的粉紅線，隻是尺寸增大了。這粉紅線的用意，原是標明有關建筑物未來的模樣。

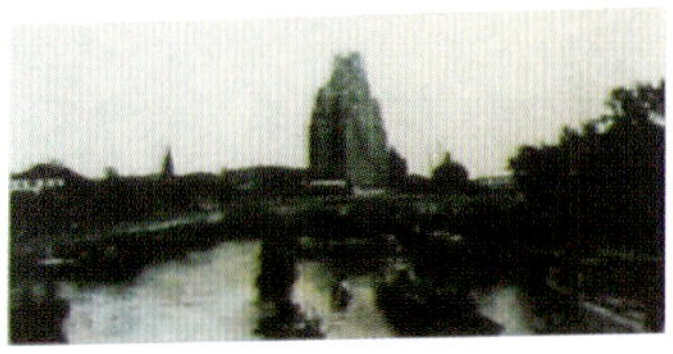

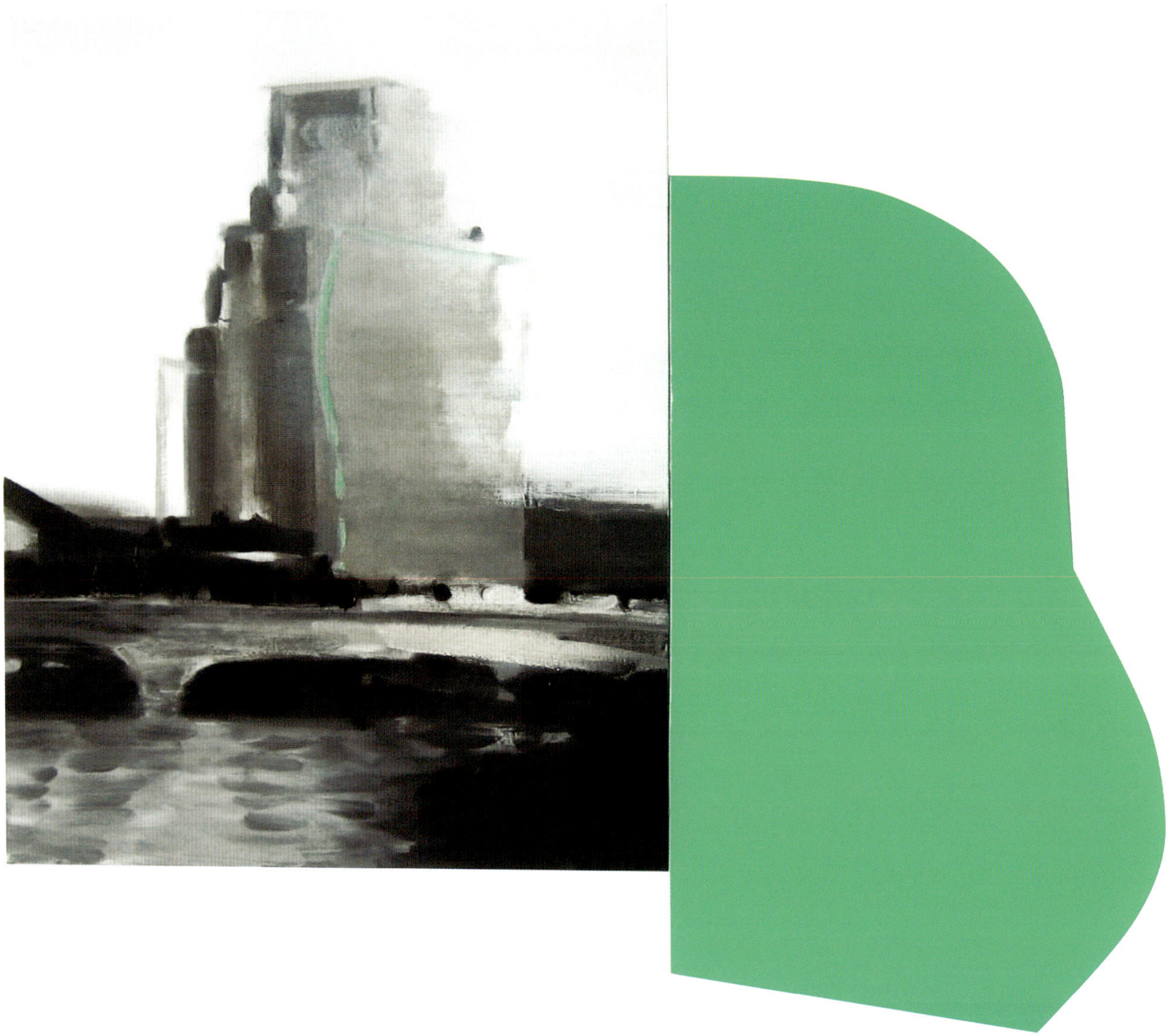

Vestiges of a Process: Shanghai Project (Broadway Building/Suzhou Creek) #2 過程的瞬間：百老匯大廈/蘇洲河 #2,
Oil on canvas, photo, 90 x 147 cm, 1935 - 2006

In version #2 of this subject matter, Zhang shows a different configuration of green lines sketched on the painting of the Broadway Building with a slightly altered free-form shape clinging to the right side of the painting. In both version, he has made clear his intentions that architecture – like mass media – comes from a cultural consensus. In this insistence, the cultural consensus does not refer to high art so much as to the

同樣題材的第二個版本，布局則有所不同。張建君於此在百老匯大廈的繪畫上加上了構成另一種形態的綠色線條。畫的右緣則緊貼著一個稍微修改過的不規則形狀。上述兩個版本都清楚表明了張建君的寓意：建筑跟大眾媒體一樣，都是文化共識的產物。在他看來，這文化共識，並非指高雅的藝術，而是因為有合成材料和

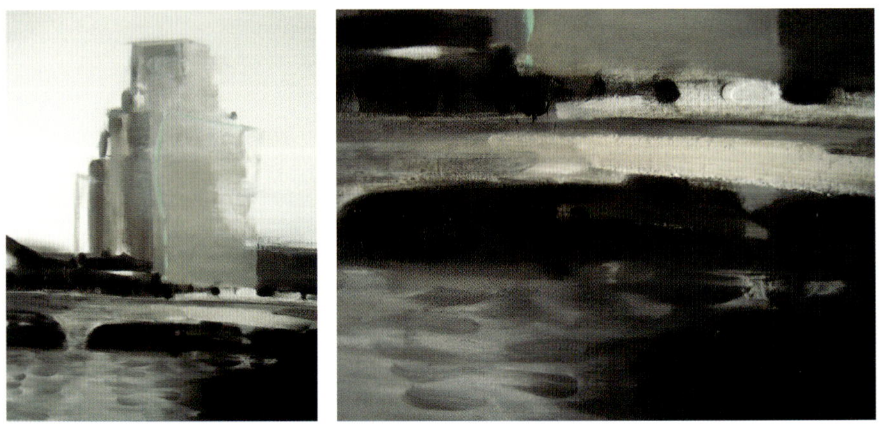

Vestiges of a Process: Shanghai Project (Broadway Building/Suzhou Creek) #2 (detail)（局部）, *Oil on canvas, photo, 90 x 147 cm, 1935 - 2006*

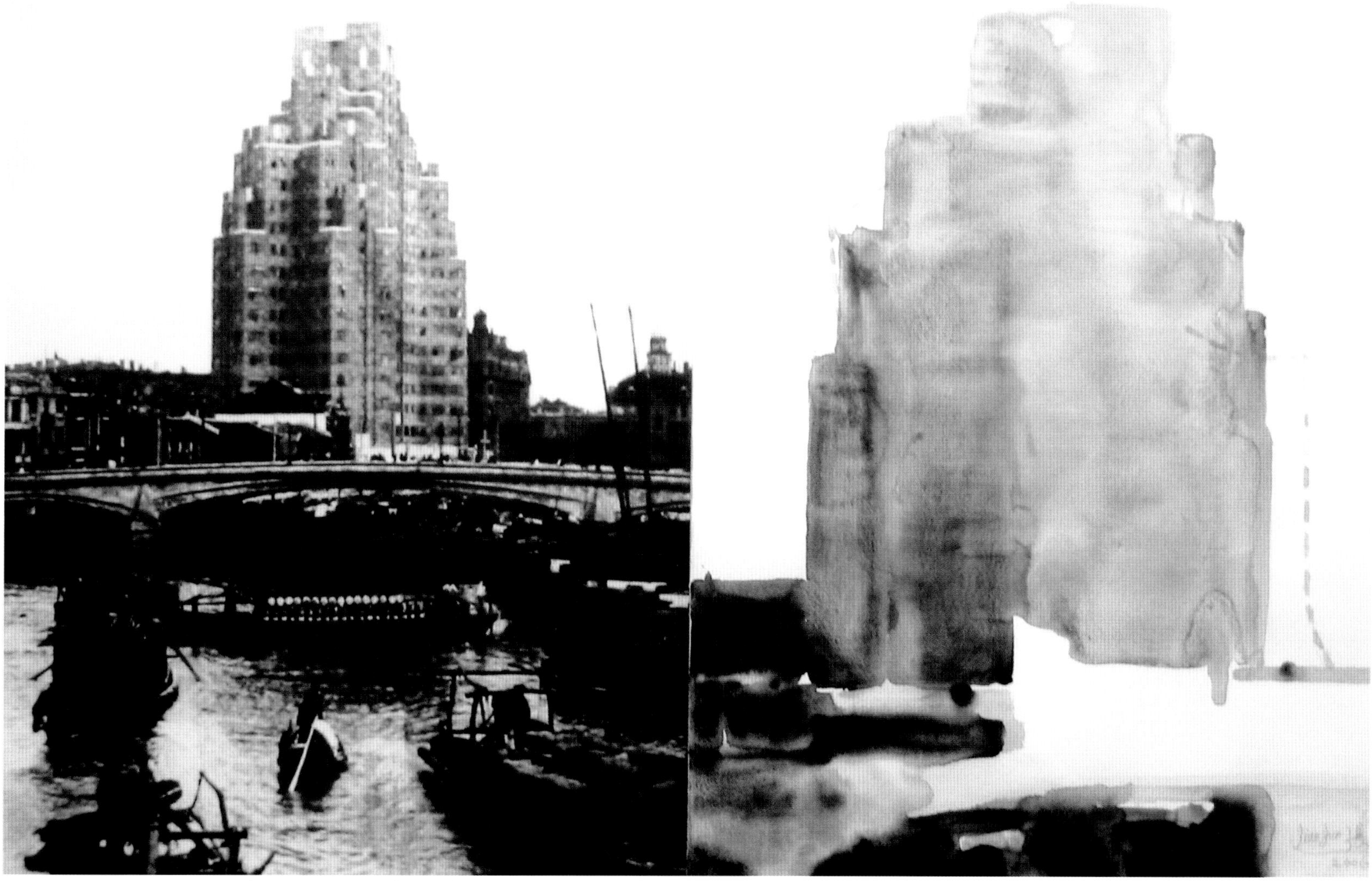

Vestiges of a Process: Shanghai Project (Broadway Building/Suzhou Creek) #9 過程的瞬間：百老匯大廈/蘇洲河 #9,
Watercolour on paper, photo, 76 x 112 cm, 1935 - 2006

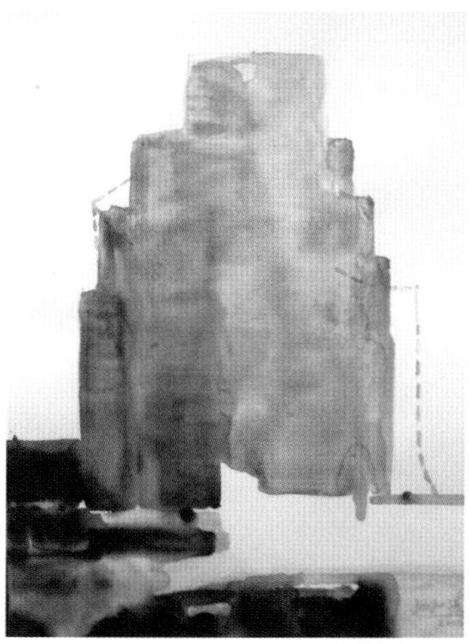

Vestiges of a Process: Shanghai Project (Broadway Building/ Suzhou Creek) #9 (detail)

public (commercial) expectations based on available synthetic materials and technologies. This is to suggest that these futuristic proposals may be culturally determined through a kind of subliminal programming in order to satisfy the imagined cravings of the ordinary populace. For better or for worse – and here Zhang remains relatively neutral – these challenges are not necessarily consistent with the desires of those who see high art in terms of enhancing the quality of life. Rather than taking a position at either end of the spectrum, Zhang is simply interested in the visual phenomena of how the demand for change in a rapidly progressing capitalist society – such as Shanghai and New York – offers a readymade solution based on

相應技術可用而形成的公眾（商業）期望。也就是說，這些頗具未來氣息的提案，也許是通過某種潛意識的設定，為了滿足一般群眾所自以為有的渴求而獲得文化上的定形。這樣的變化，不管是好是壞（對此，張建君保持相對的中立），其實都未必符合一些人的願望－這裡指認為高雅藝術應當提升生活質量的那些人。在這個問題上，張建君不堅守任何一個極端，隻是對某一個視覺現象感興趣。這個現象就是：諸如上海和紐約等迅速發展的資本主義社會對變革的需求，促使人們以半願景式的建筑模型為基礎，提出現

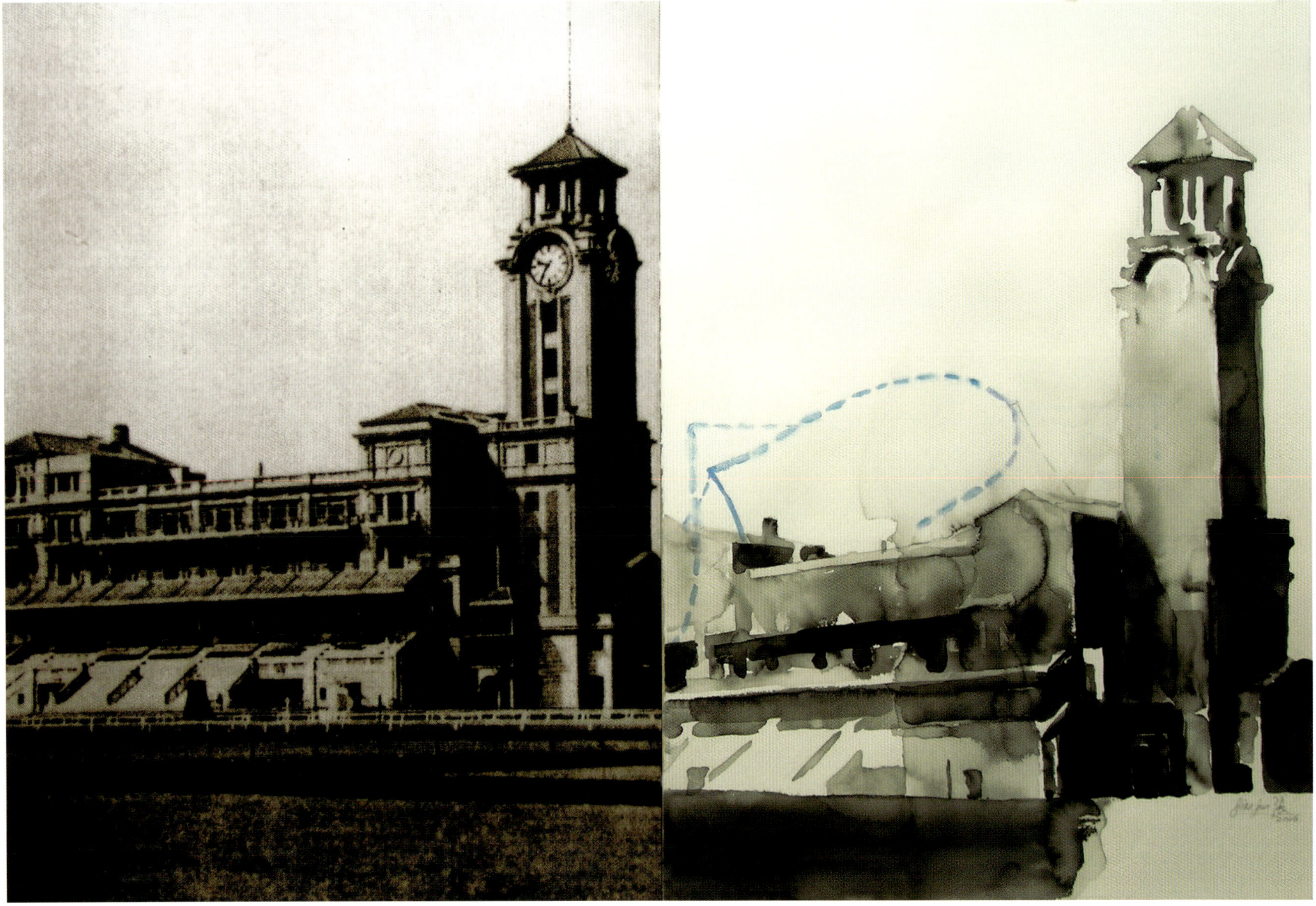

Vestiges of a Process: Clocktower Project #1 過程的瞬間：鐘樓計劃 #1
Watercolor on paper, photo
76 x 112 cm
1936 - 2006

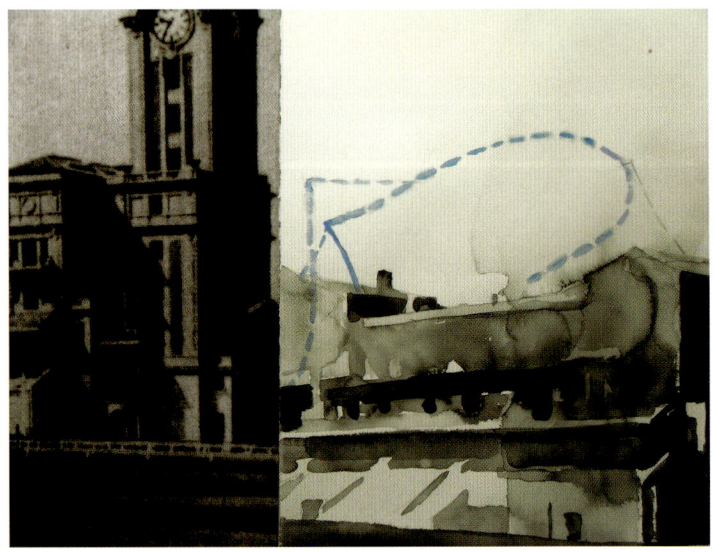

Vestiges of a Process: Clocktower Project #1 (detail)
過程的瞬間：鐘樓計劃 #1（局部）
Watercolor on paper, photo
76 x 112 cm
1936 - 2006

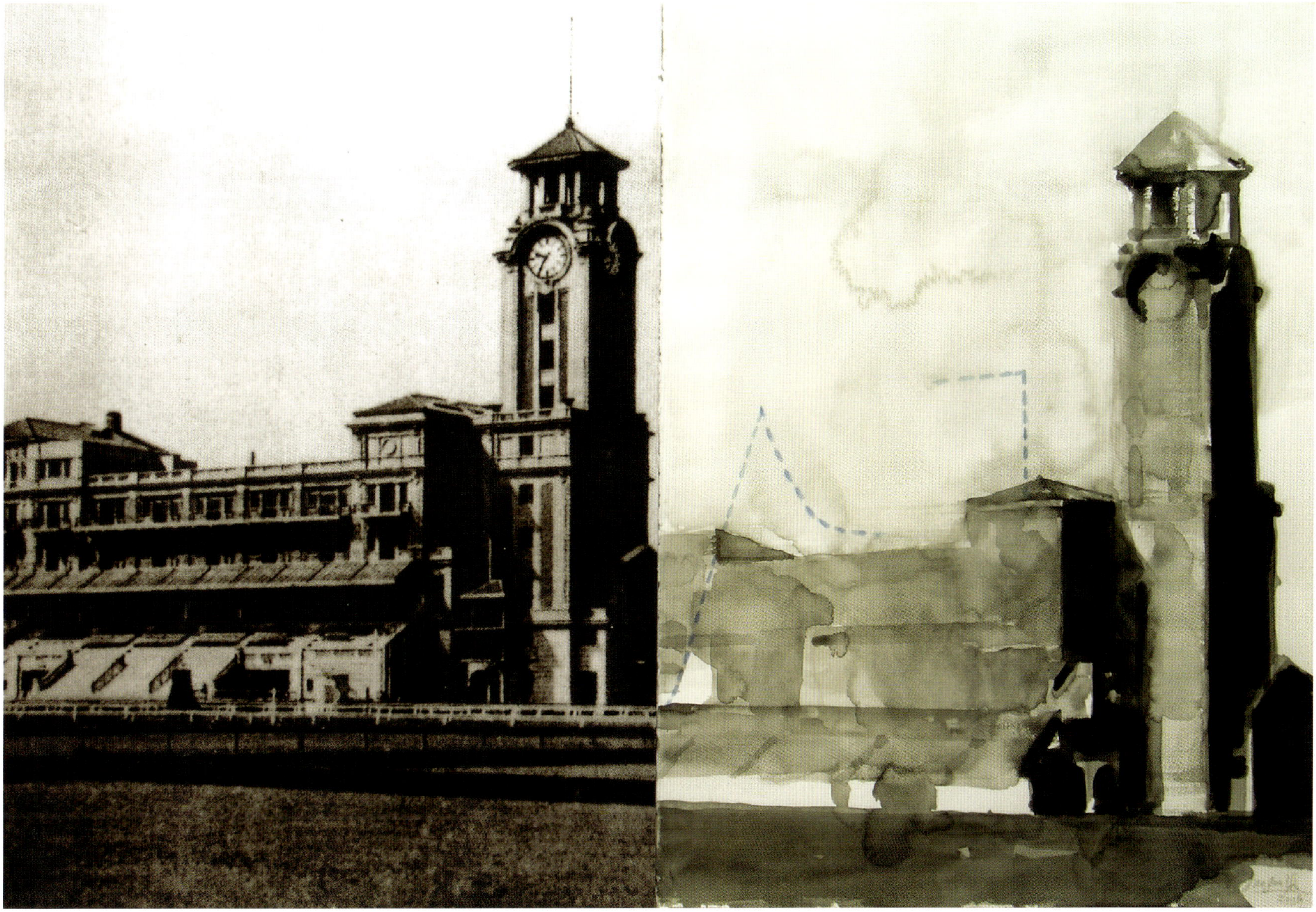

Vestiges of a Process: Clocktower Project #2 過程的瞬間：鐘樓計劃 #2

Watercolor on paper, photo
76 x 112 cm
1936 - 2006

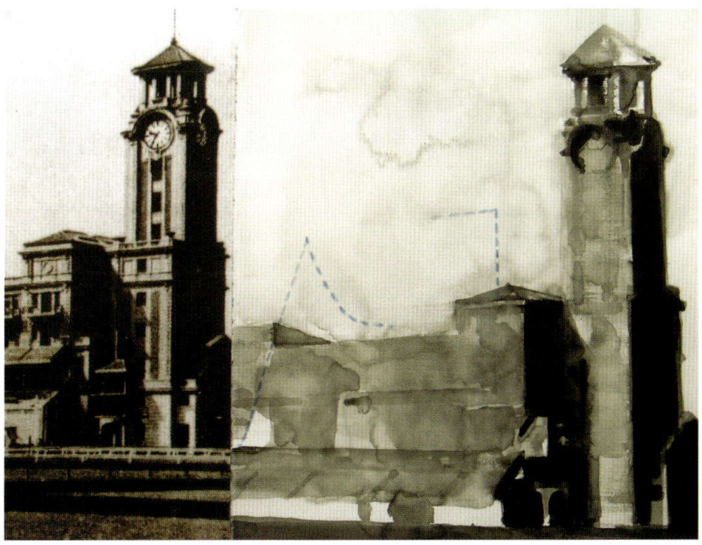

Vestiges of a Process: Clocktower Project #2 (detail)
過程的瞬間：鐘樓計劃 #2（局部）

Watercolor on paper, photo
76 x 112 cm
1936 - 2006

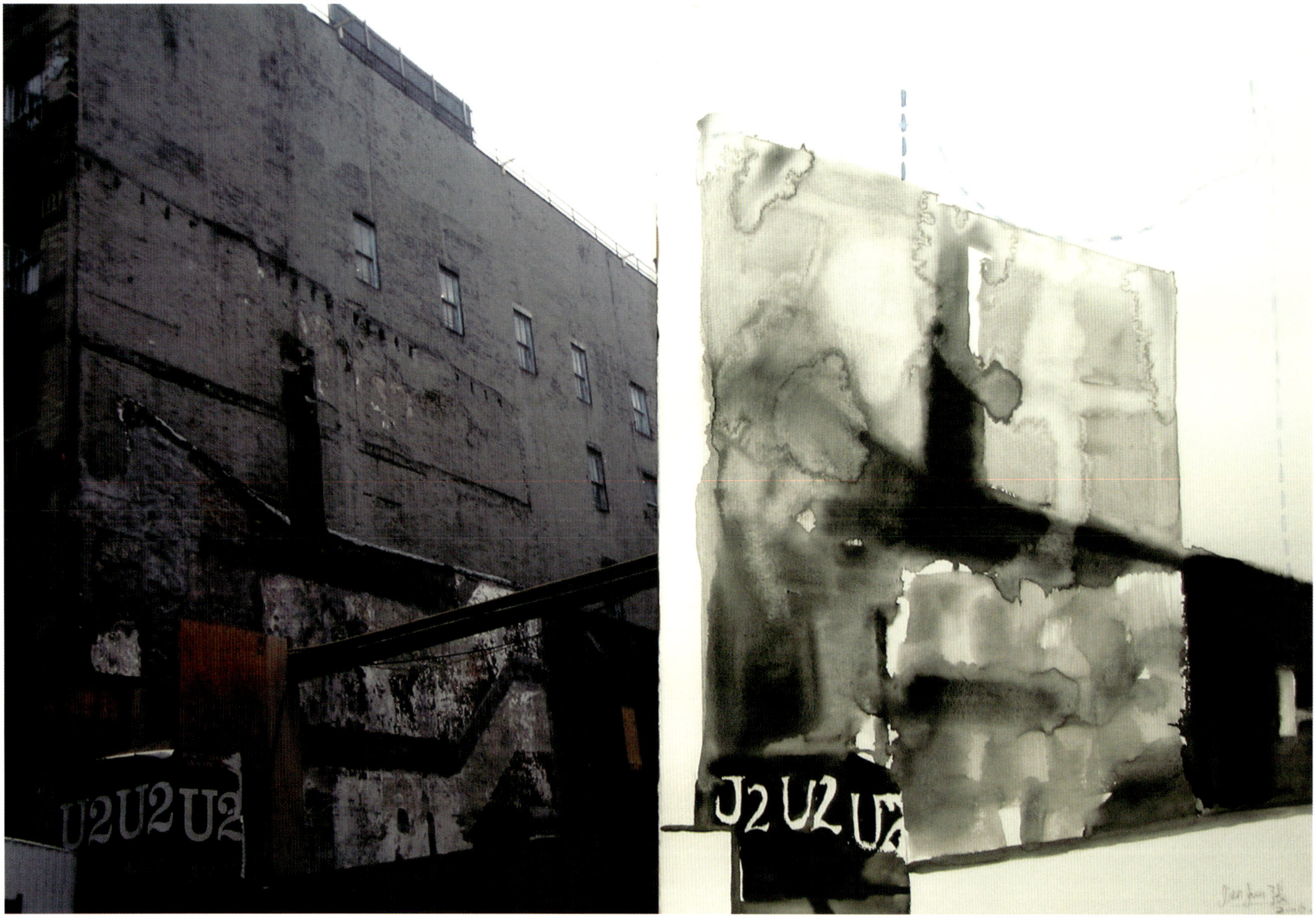

Vestiges of a Process: Bowery Project 2006 #1 過程的瞬間：包厘街 #1
Watercolor on paper, photo
76 x 112 cm
2004 - 2006

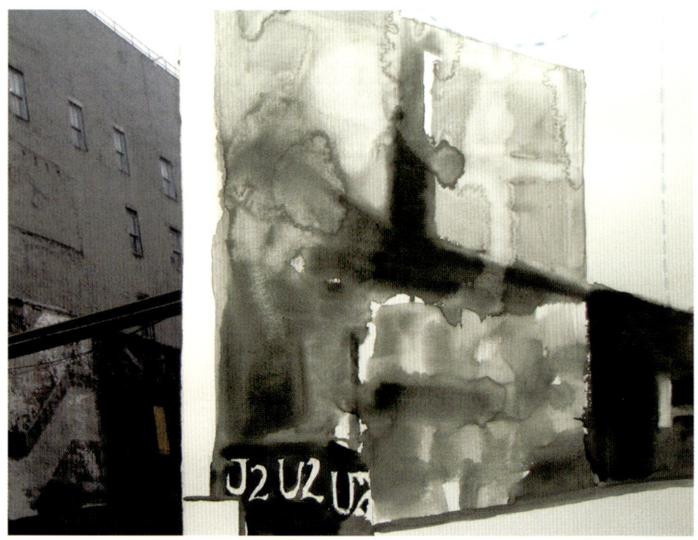

Vestiges of a Process: Bowery Project #1 (detail)
過程的瞬間：包厘街 #1（局部）
Watercolor on paper, photo
76 x 112 cm
2004 - 2006

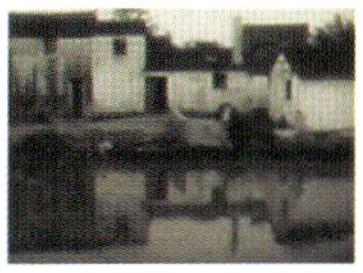

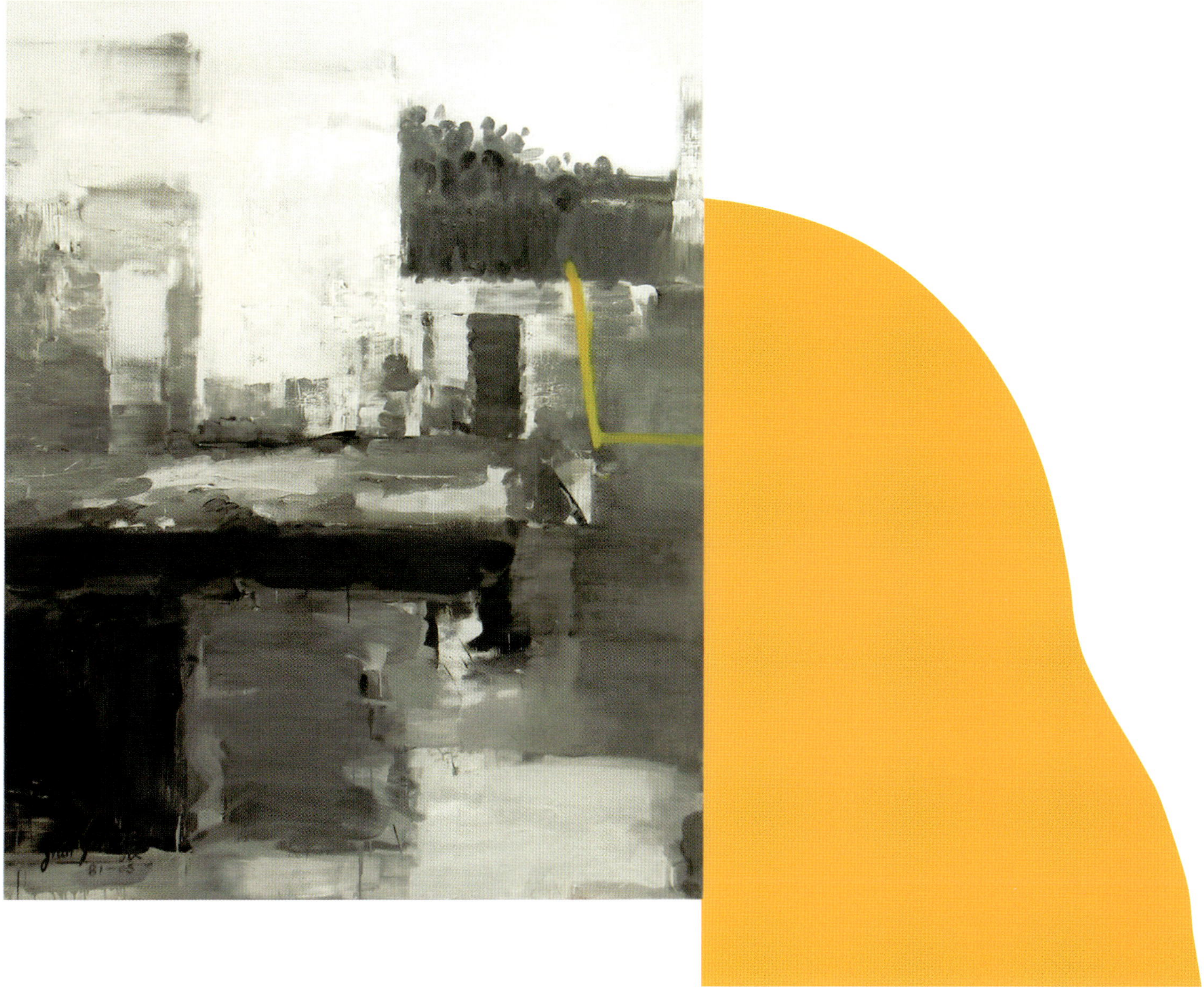

Vestiges of a Process: Zhou Zhuang Project #1 過程的瞬間：周庄 #1

Oil on linen, photo
277 x 419 cm
1981 - 2005

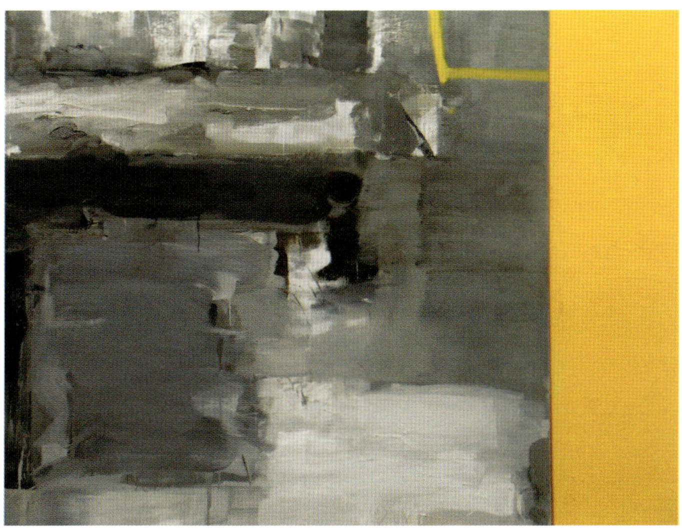

Vestiges of a Process: Zhou Zhuang Project #1 (detail)
過程的瞬間：周庄 #1（局部）

Oil on linen, photo
277 x 419 cm
1981 - 2005

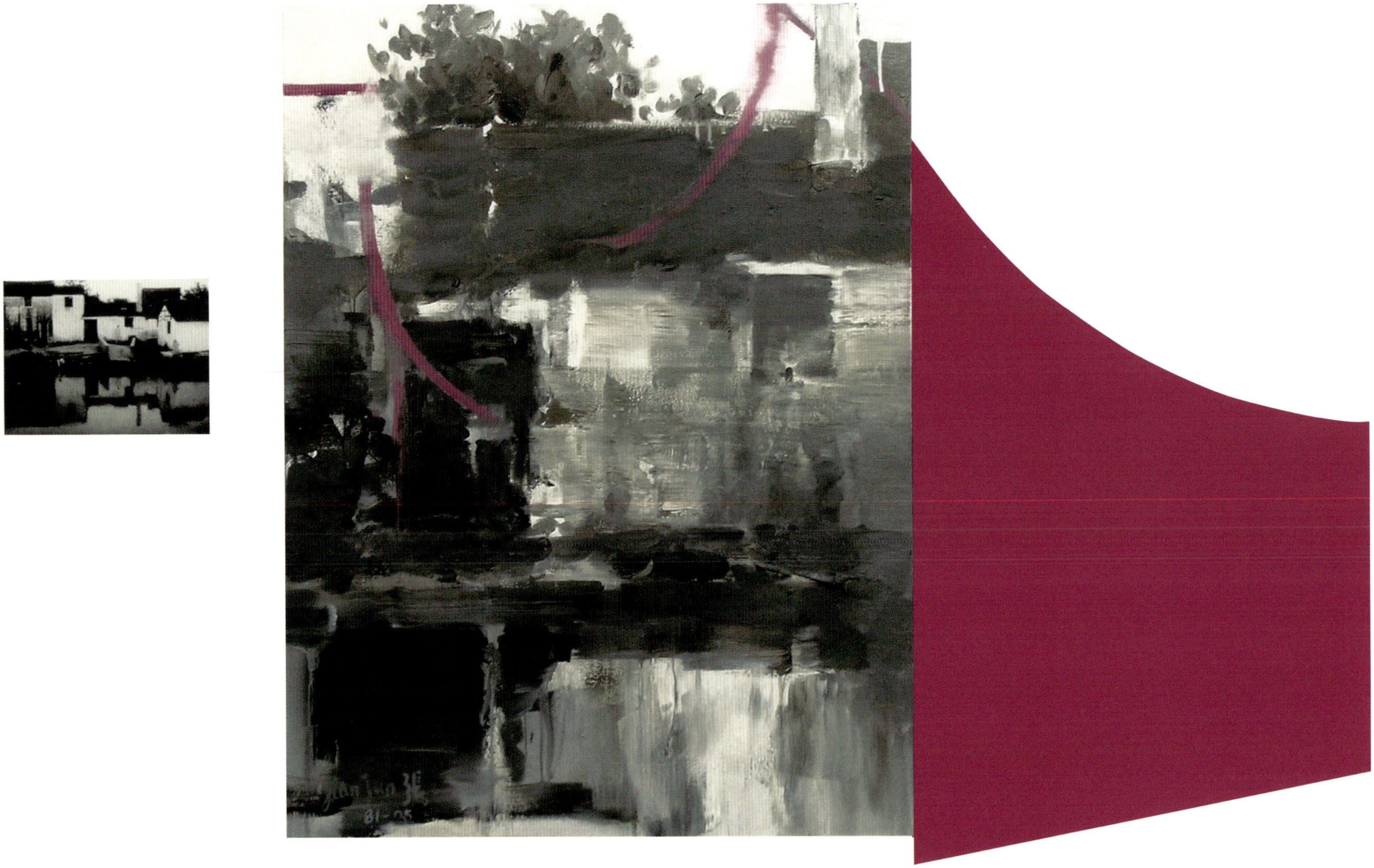

Vestiges of a Process: Zhou Zhuang Project #2 過程的瞬間：周庄 #2
Oil on linen, photo, 165 x 267 cm, 1981 - 2005

quasi-visionary architectural models. As further evidence of this phenomenon, there is little doubt that the current menu of proposals for new buildings by global all-star architects appears to show remarkable little variance in their attempts to envision or realize a new world order based on interesting conflicting ideas.

This process is not only found in major urban centers, but in the smaller villages as well. China's village landscape is also erupting with signs of capital as shown in Vestiges of a Process: Zhou Zhuang #3 (dated 1981-2005) in which a small photograph of the village scene is partially concealed by a greenish swatch of paint while the larger painting beside it is nearly impossible to decipher. The Ellsworth Kelly-style green shape to the right defines what will be built in its place.

成解決方案。目前環球明星建筑師所提呈的各項新建筑方案，雖然試圖在各種有趣的、互相沖突的理念基礎上展望或實現某種新世界秩序，在此方面卻都令人驚訝地大同小異。這無非是進一步証實了張建君所關注的上述現象確實存在。

上述過程不僅發生在主要的大城市裡，在較小的鄉鎮亦不乏其蹤。正如《過程的瞬間：周庄 #3》（1981至2005年）所顯示的，中國的鄉鎮景觀也處處爆發著資本橫流之象。在此作品中，一小張鄉景的照片被一抹綠彩部分掩蓋，旁邊較大的一幅畫則幾乎無法解讀。右側的綠色圖形有埃爾斯沃思•凱利（Ellsworth Kelly）的風格，指涉了即將於此處建立、對其取而代之的新事物。

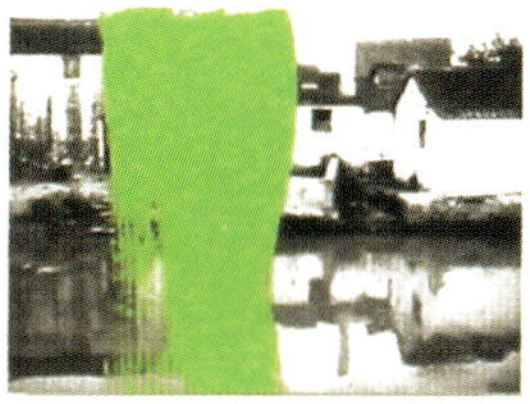

Vestiges of a Process: Zhou Zhuang Project #3 過程的瞬間：周庄 #3

Oil on linen, photo
175 x 275 cm
1981 - 2005

Vestiges of a Process: Zhou Zhuang Project #3 (detail)
過程的瞬間：周庄 #3（局部）

Oil paint on photo
175 x 275 cm
1981 - 2005

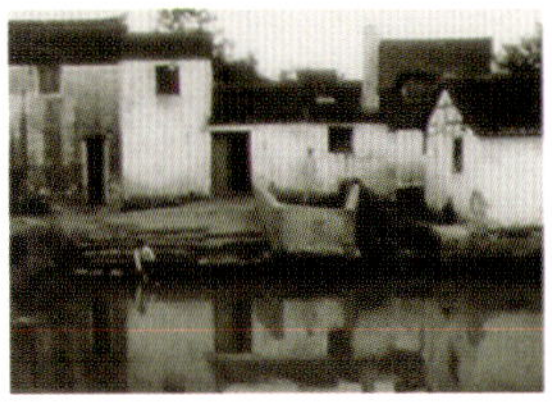

Vestiges of a Process: Zhou Zhuang Project #5 過程的瞬間：周庄 #5

Oil on linen, photo
102 x 149 cm
1981 - 2005

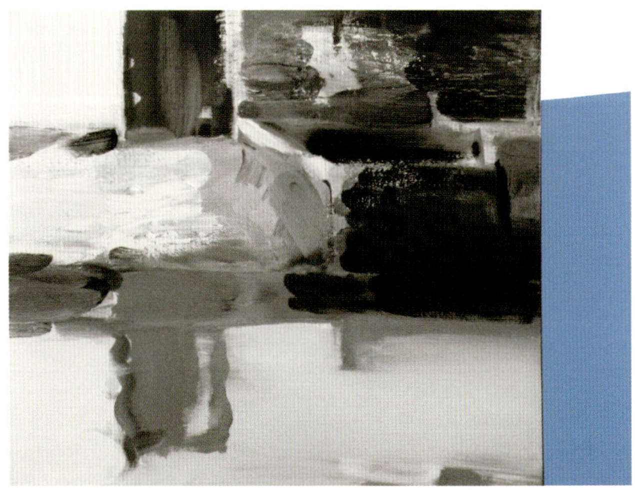

Vestiges of a Process: Zhou Zhuang Project #5 (detail)
過程的瞬間：周庄 #5（局部）

Oil on linen, photo
102 x 149 cm
1981 - 2005

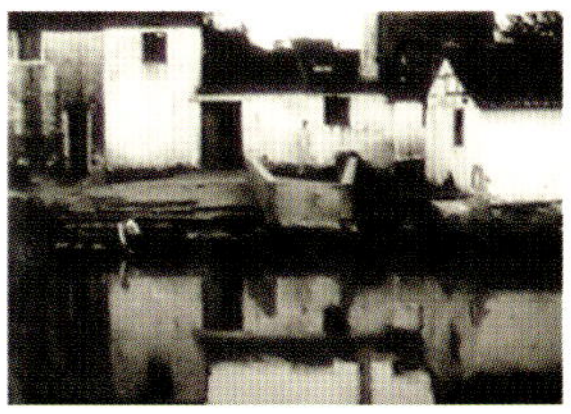

Vestiges of a Process: Zhou Zhuang Project #7 過程的瞬間：周庄 #7

Oil on linen, photo
98 x 142 cm
1981 - 2005

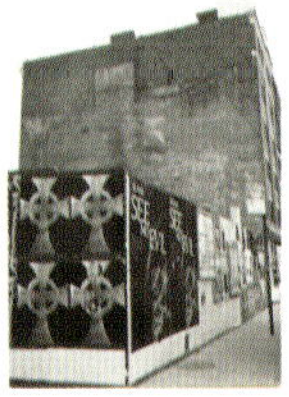

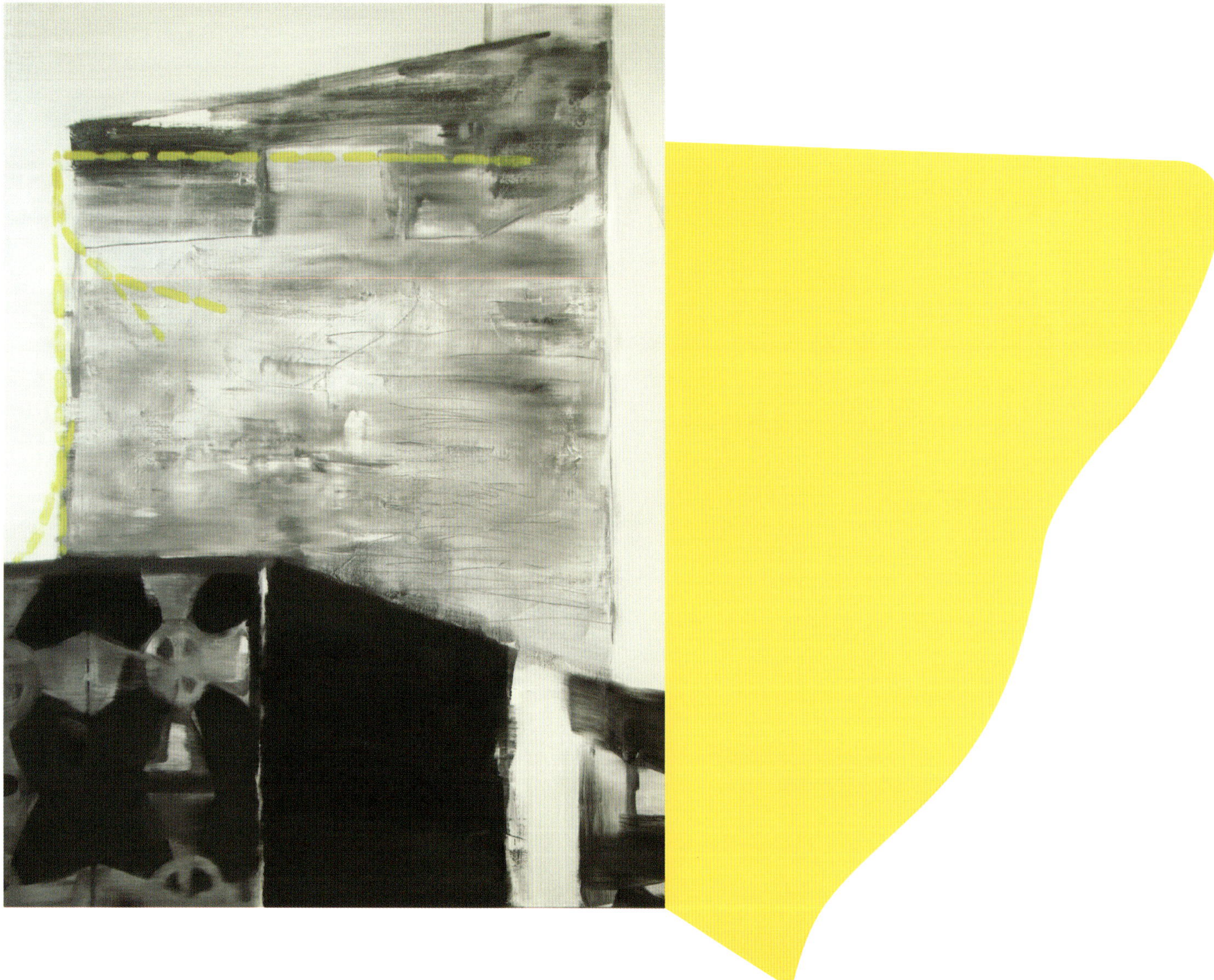

Vestiges of a Process: New York Project 2006 #1 過程的瞬間：紐約計劃

Oil on linen, photo
180 x 268 cm
2006

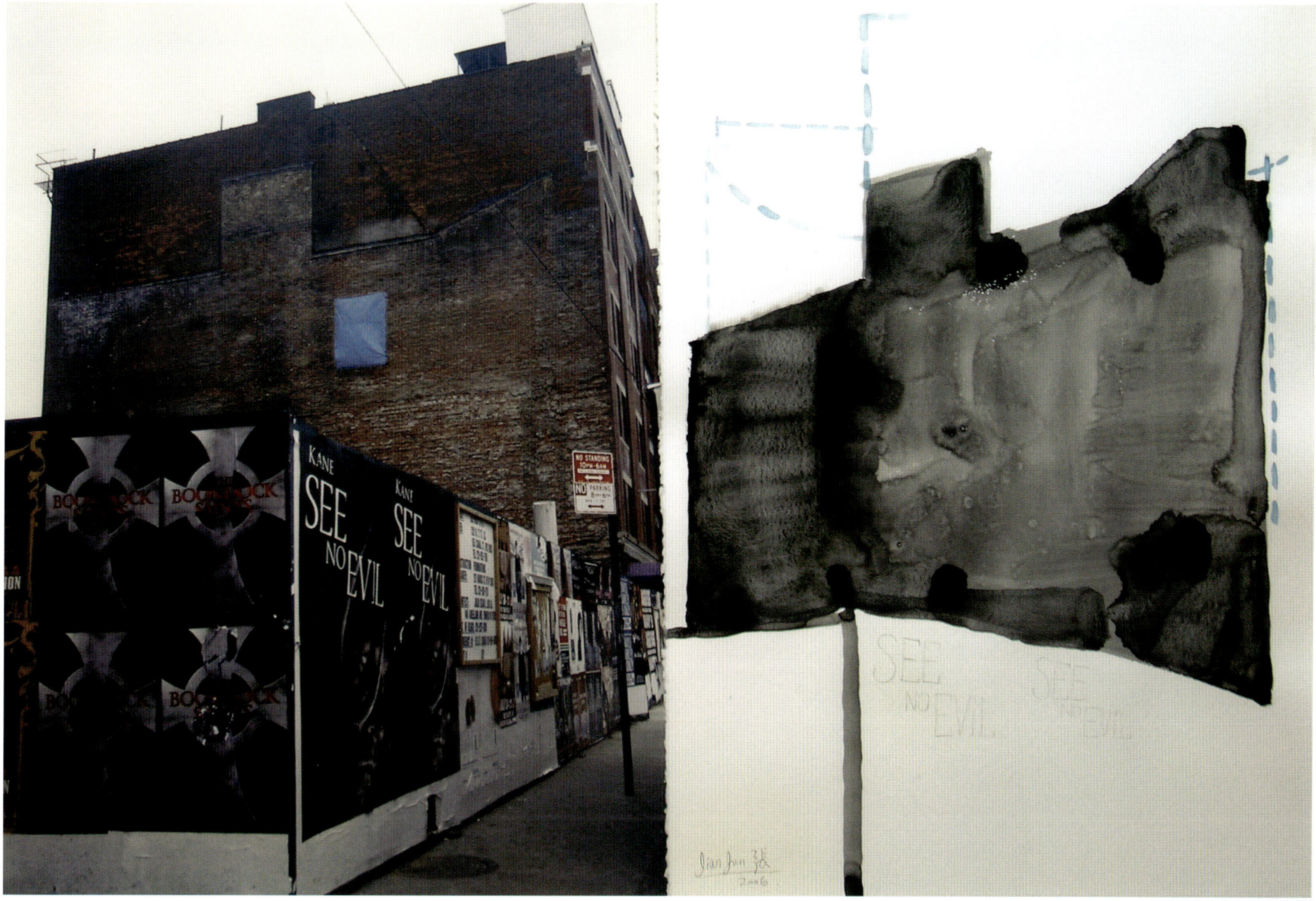

Vestiges of a Process: New York Project #3 過程的瞬間：紐約計劃 #3

Watercolor on paper, photo
76 x 112 cm
2005 - 2006

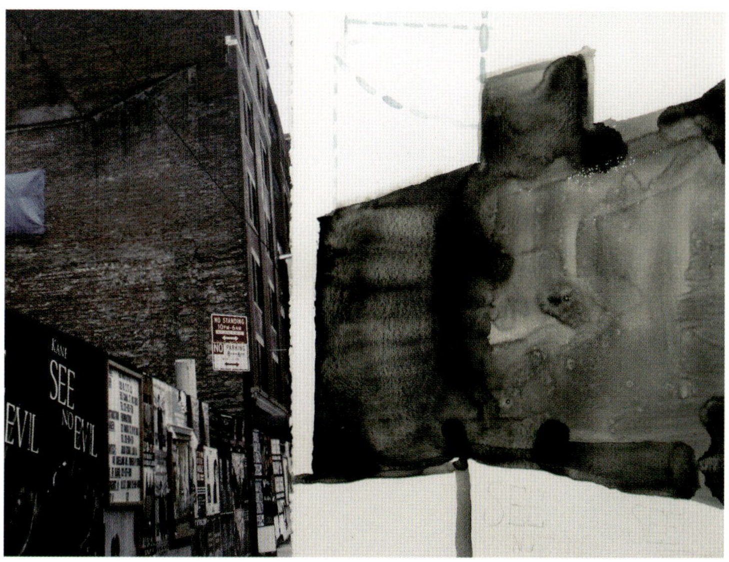

Vestiges of a Process: New York Project #3 (detail)
過程的瞬間：紐約計劃 #3（局部）

Watercolor on paper, photo
76 x 112 cm
2005 - 2006

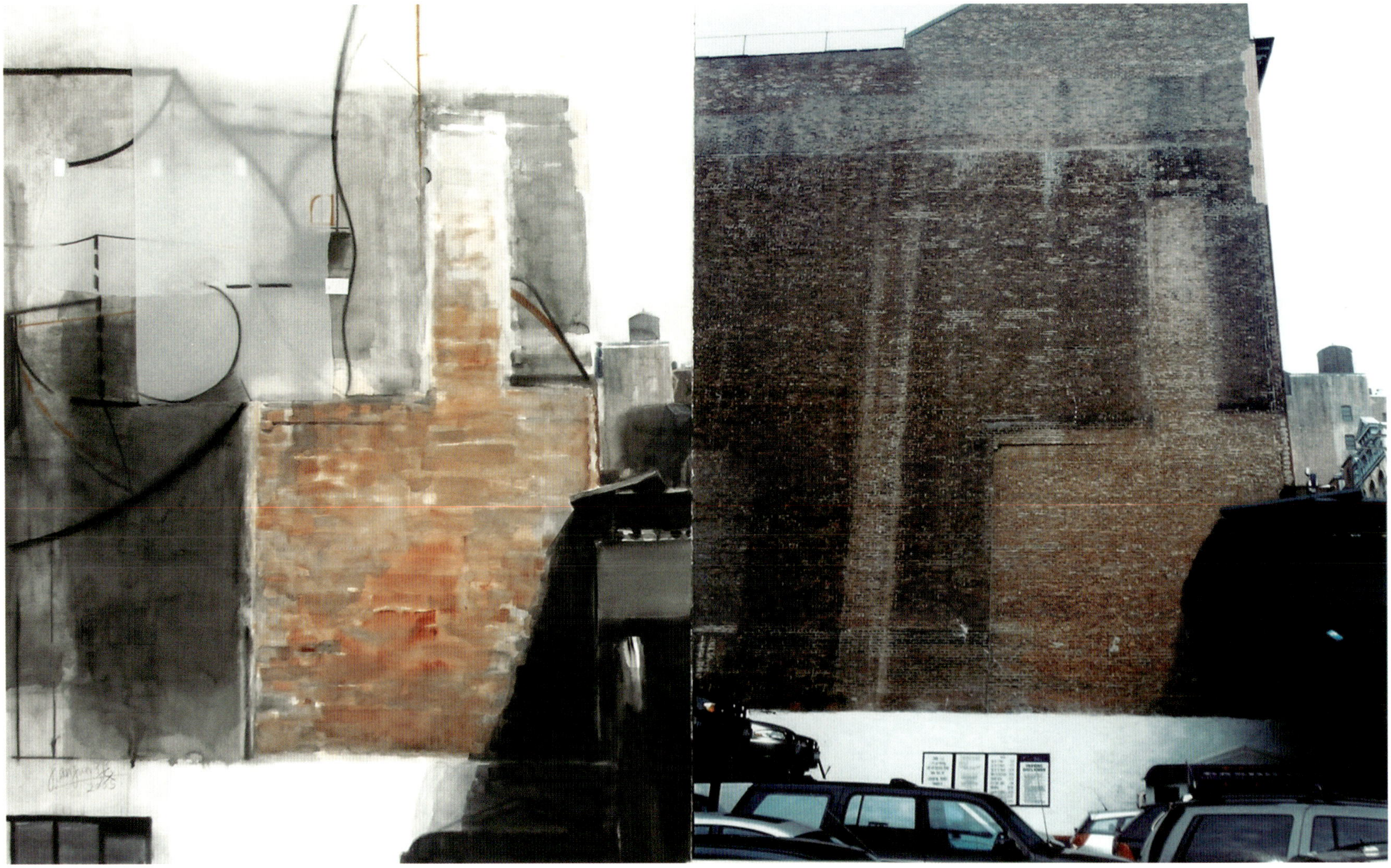

Vestiges of a Process: Soho Project
過程的瞬間：蘇荷計劃 2004 - 2005

Watercolor and graphite on paper, photo
122 x 200 cm
2004 - 2005

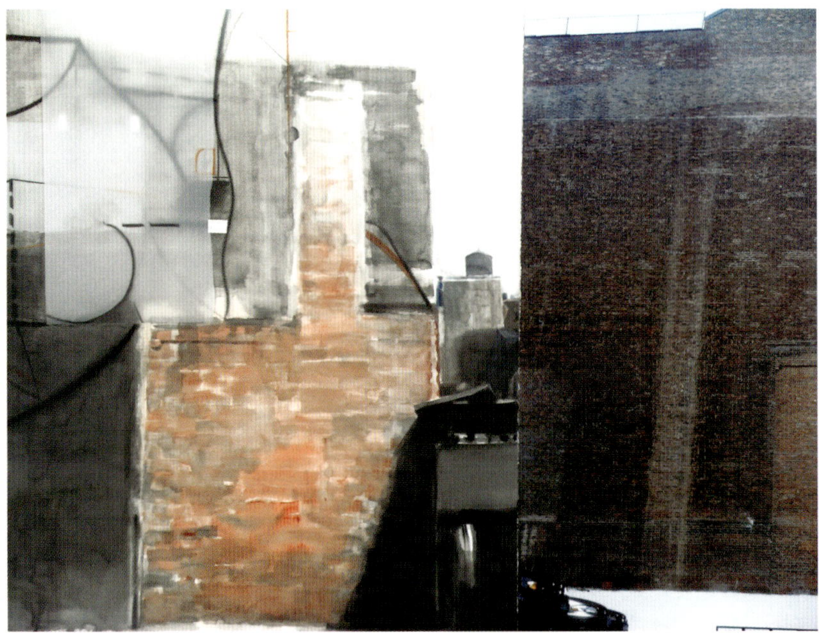

Vestiges of a Process: Soho Project (detail)
過程的瞬間：蘇荷計劃 2004 - 2005（局部）

Watercolor and graphite on paper, photo
122 x 200 cm
2004 - 2005

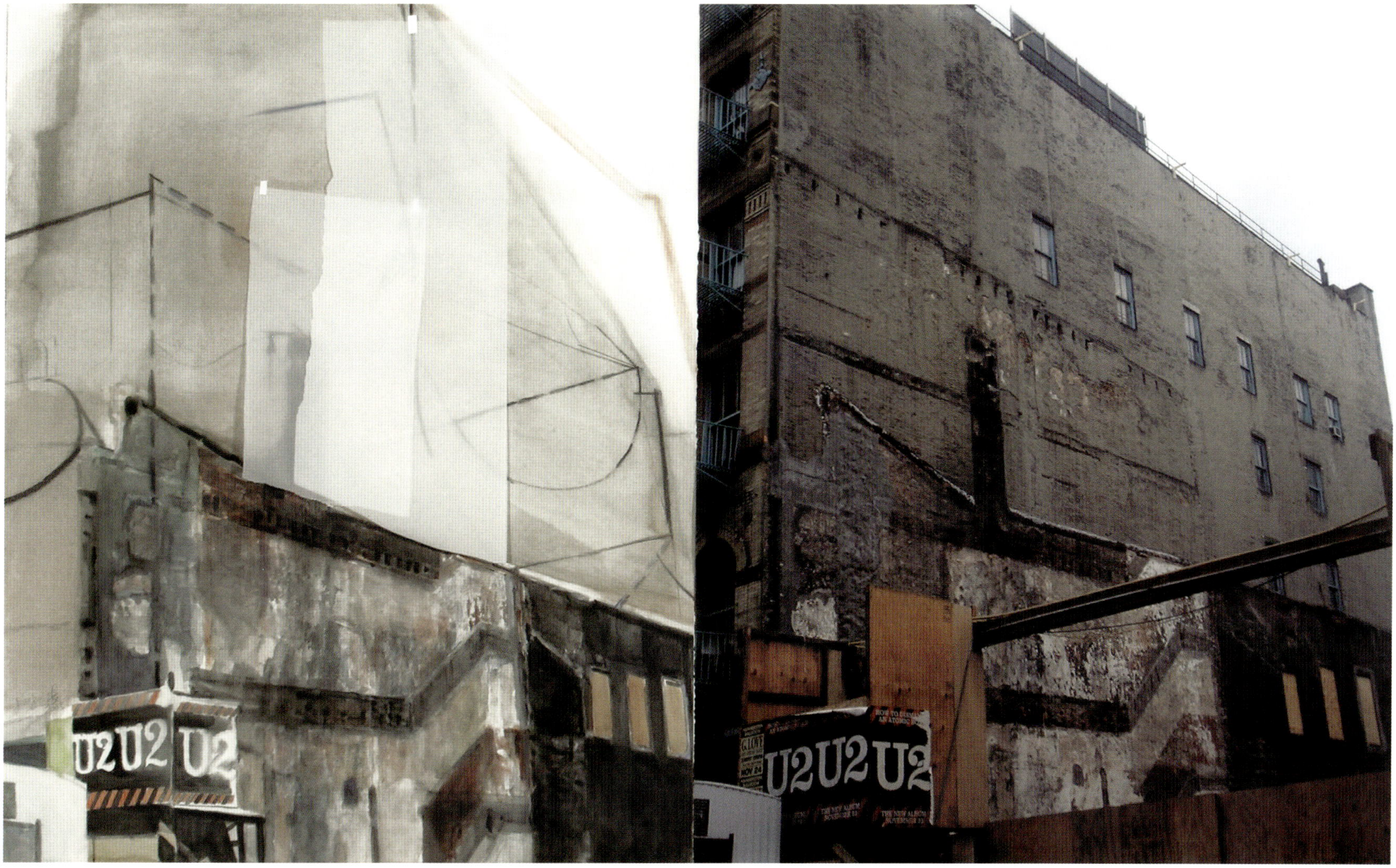

Vestiges of a Process: Bowery Project
過程的瞬間：包厘街計劃 2004 - 2005

Watercolor and graphite on paper, photo
122 x 200 cm
2004 - 2005

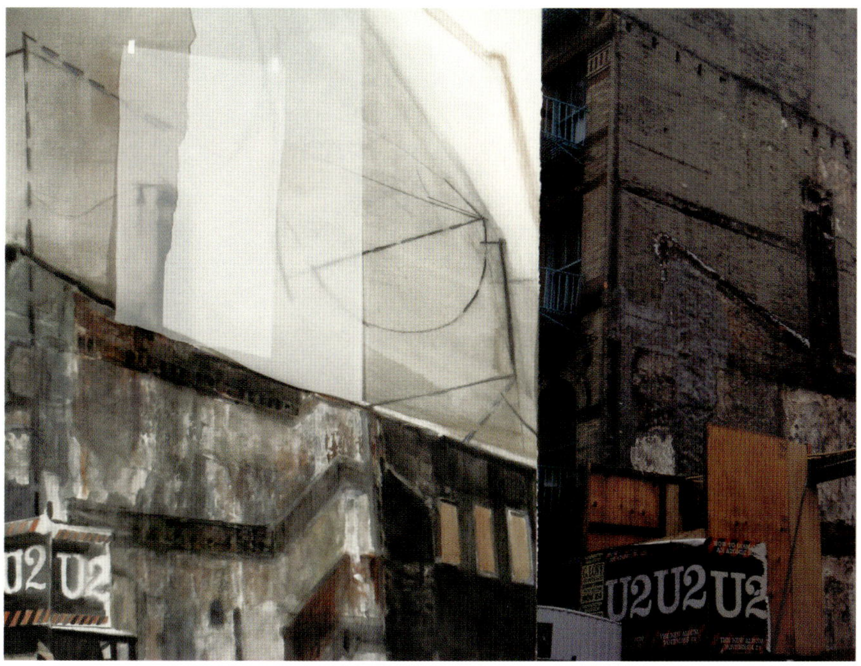

Vestiges of a Process: Bowery Project (detail)
過程的瞬間：包厘街計劃 2004 - 2005（局部）

Watercolor and graphite on paper, photo
122 x 200 cm
2004 - 2005

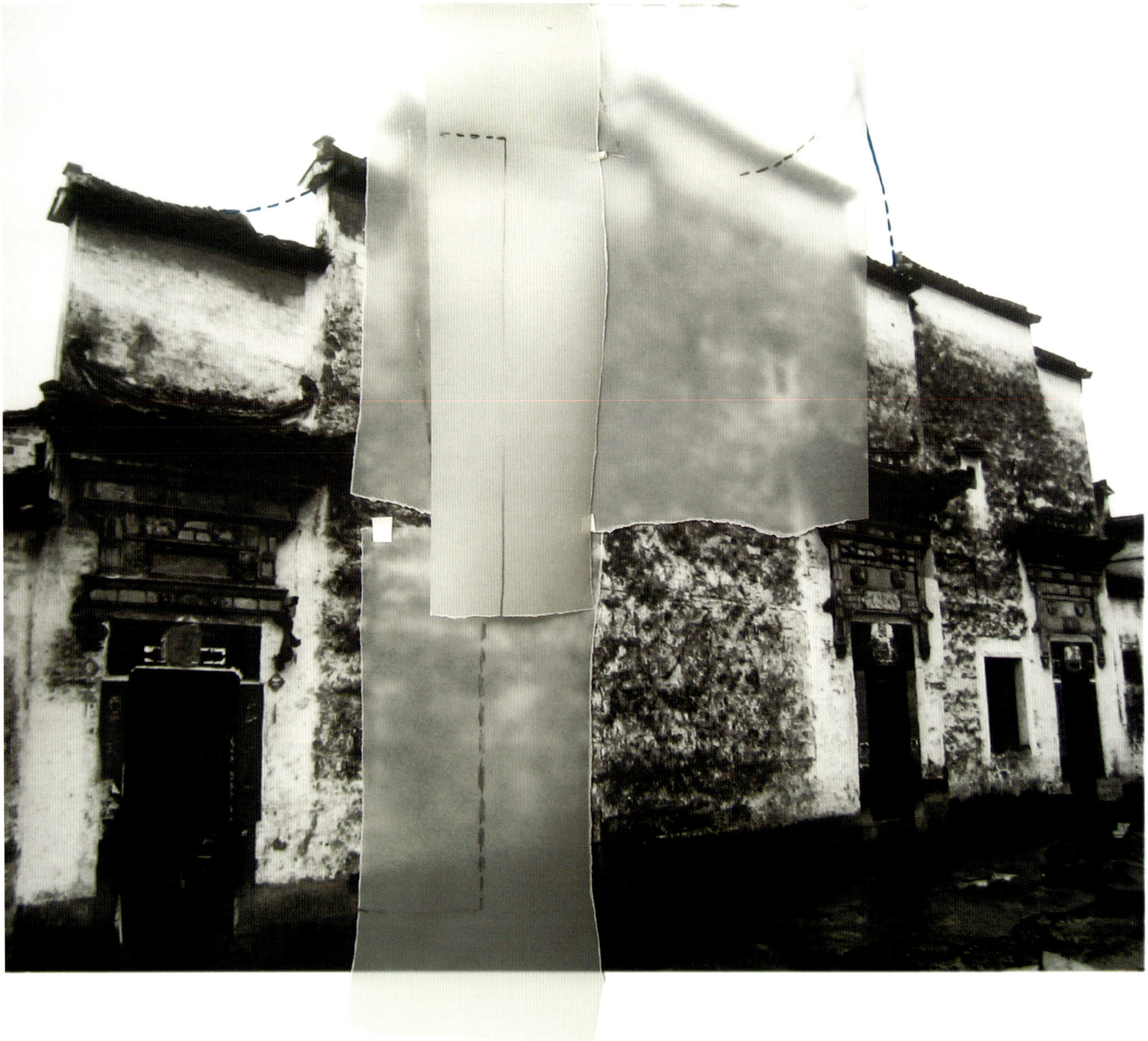

China Chapter: Xi Di Village 2006 #6 中國篇：西遞 #6
Oil paint, graphite, photo, vellum
53 x 61 cm
2006

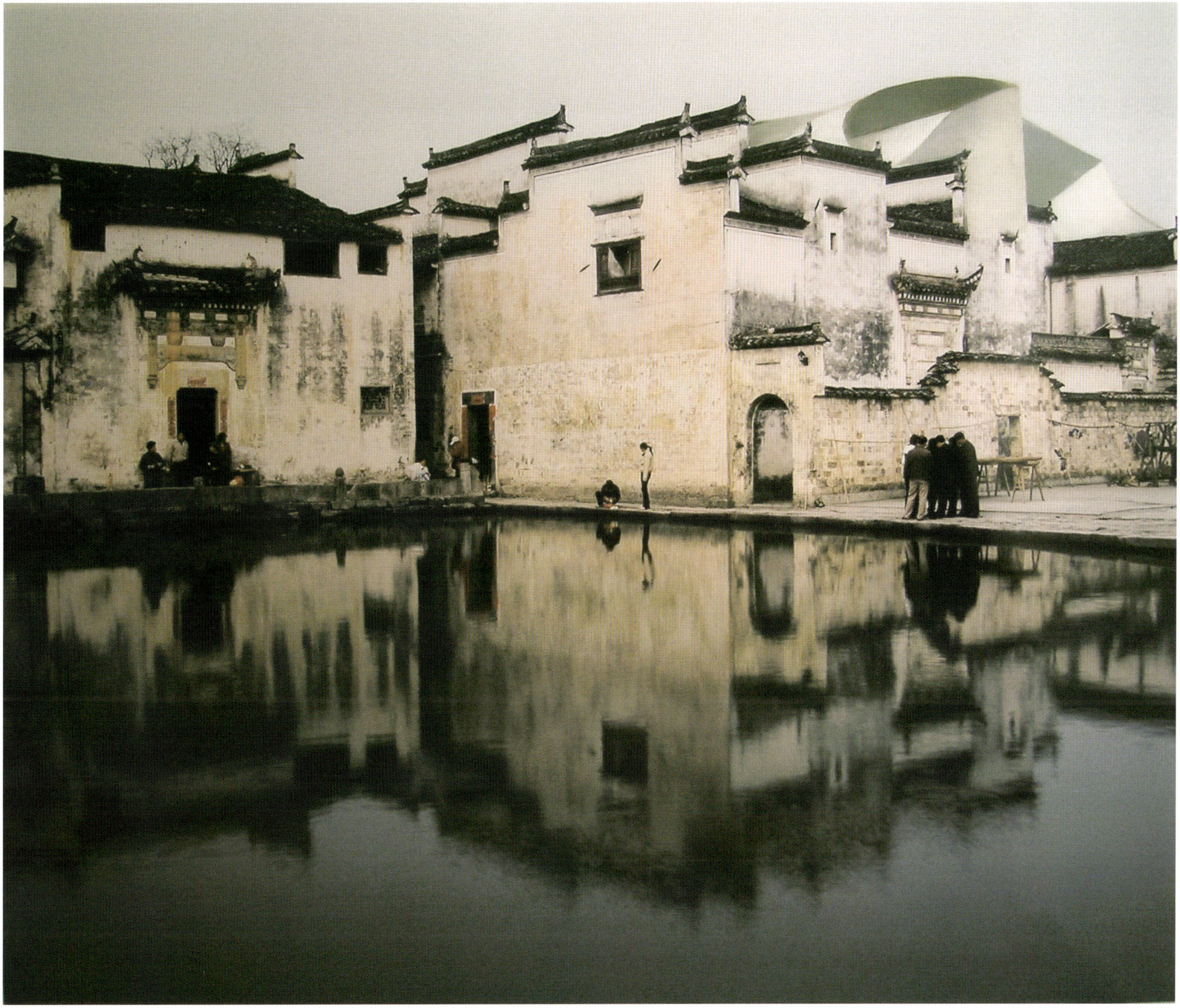

China Chapter: Hong Cun Village 中國篇：宏村 #1
Oil paint on photo
100 x 120 cm
2004

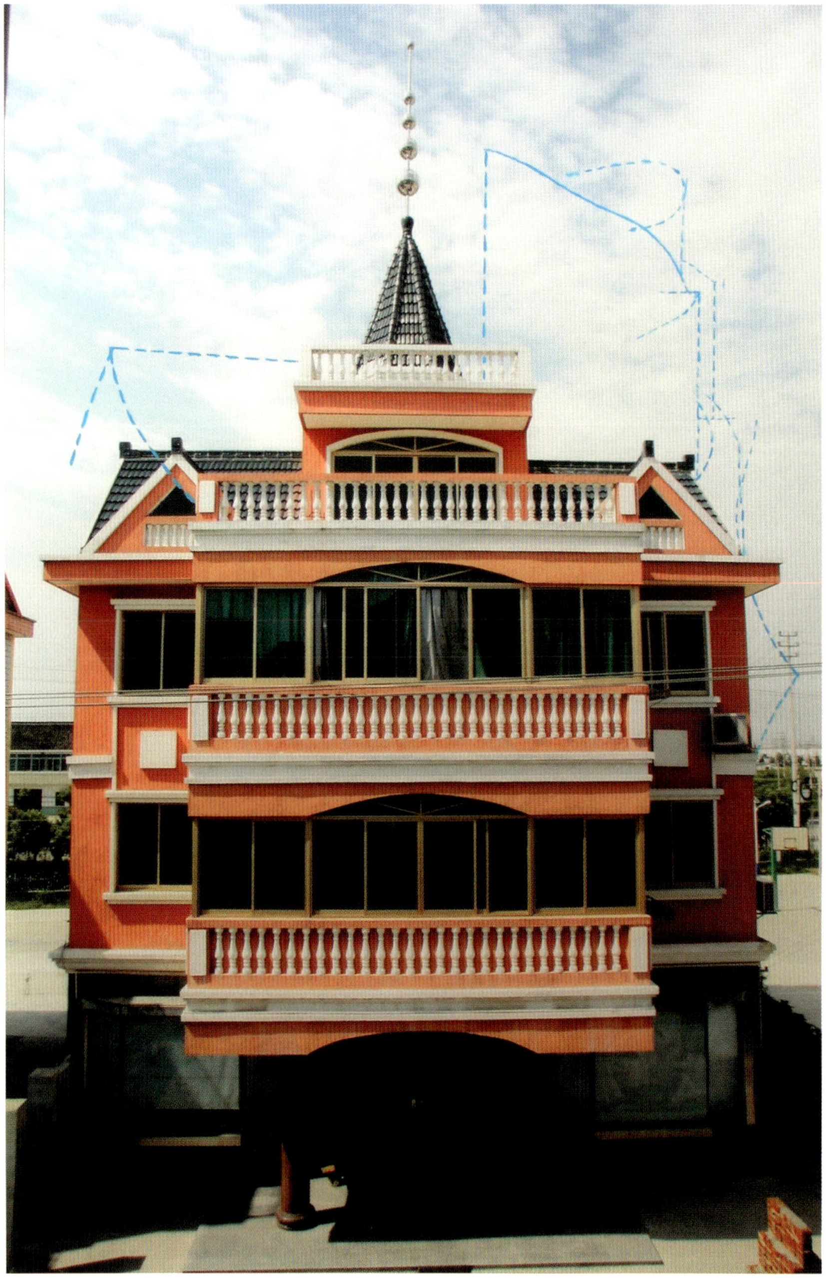

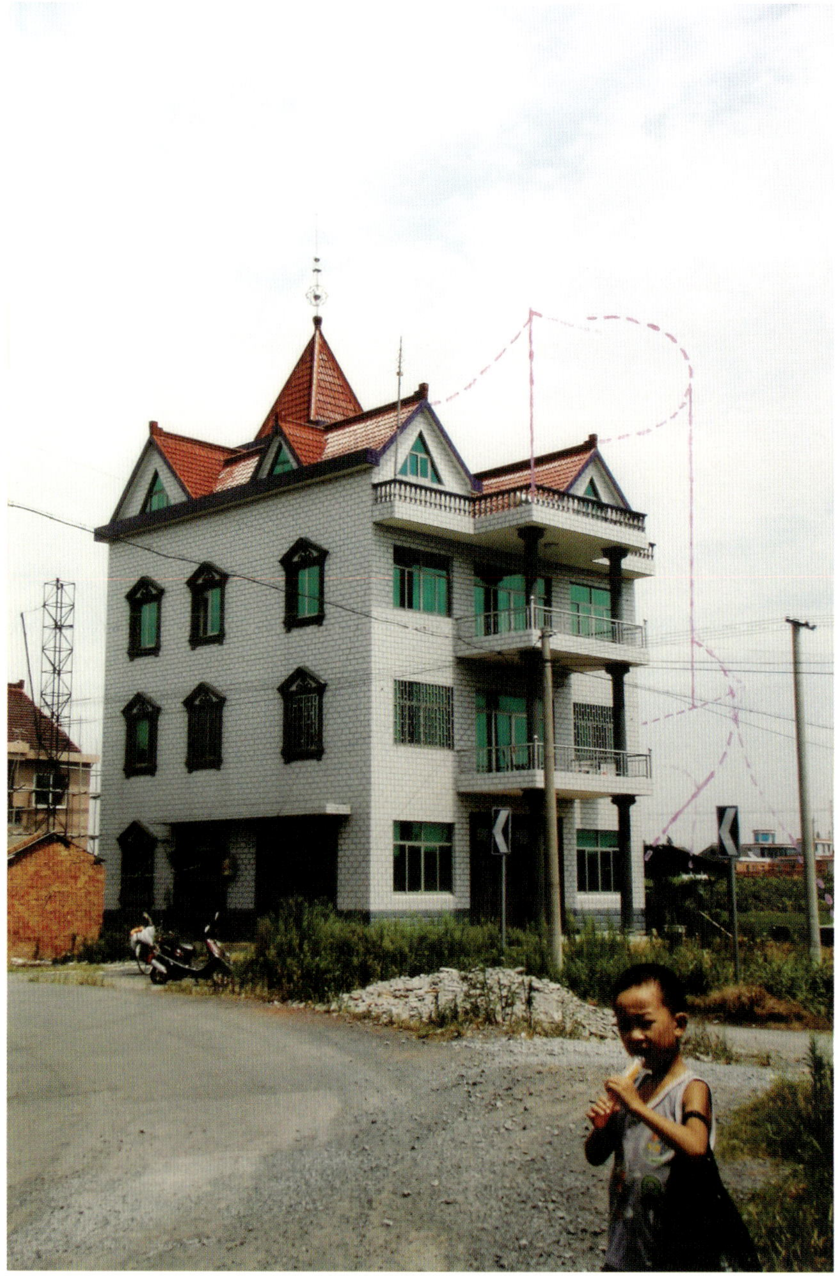

In the China Chapter: New House in an Old Village (2004). Zhang shows how wealthy farmers are able to build cheaply two to four storey houses. To accentuate the weird impact of these houses on the local village scene, Zhang has added brightly color shapes in oil paint, thus enhancing the kitsch aspect of these recently constructed domiciles.

此外，張建君更通過《中國篇：老村庄中的新房》（2004年），顯示富農已有能力廉價建起兩層到四層高的新樓。為了凸顯這些樓房在當地景觀中如何顯得突兀怪異，他還用油彩添加了艷麗的色塊，加深了這些新建居所的庸俗感。

China Chapter: New Village 2006 #3
中國篇：新農村 #3

Oil paint on photo
90 x 60 cm
2006

(left) China Chapter: New Village 2006 #2
中國篇：新農村 #2

Oil paint on photo
90 x 60 cm
2006

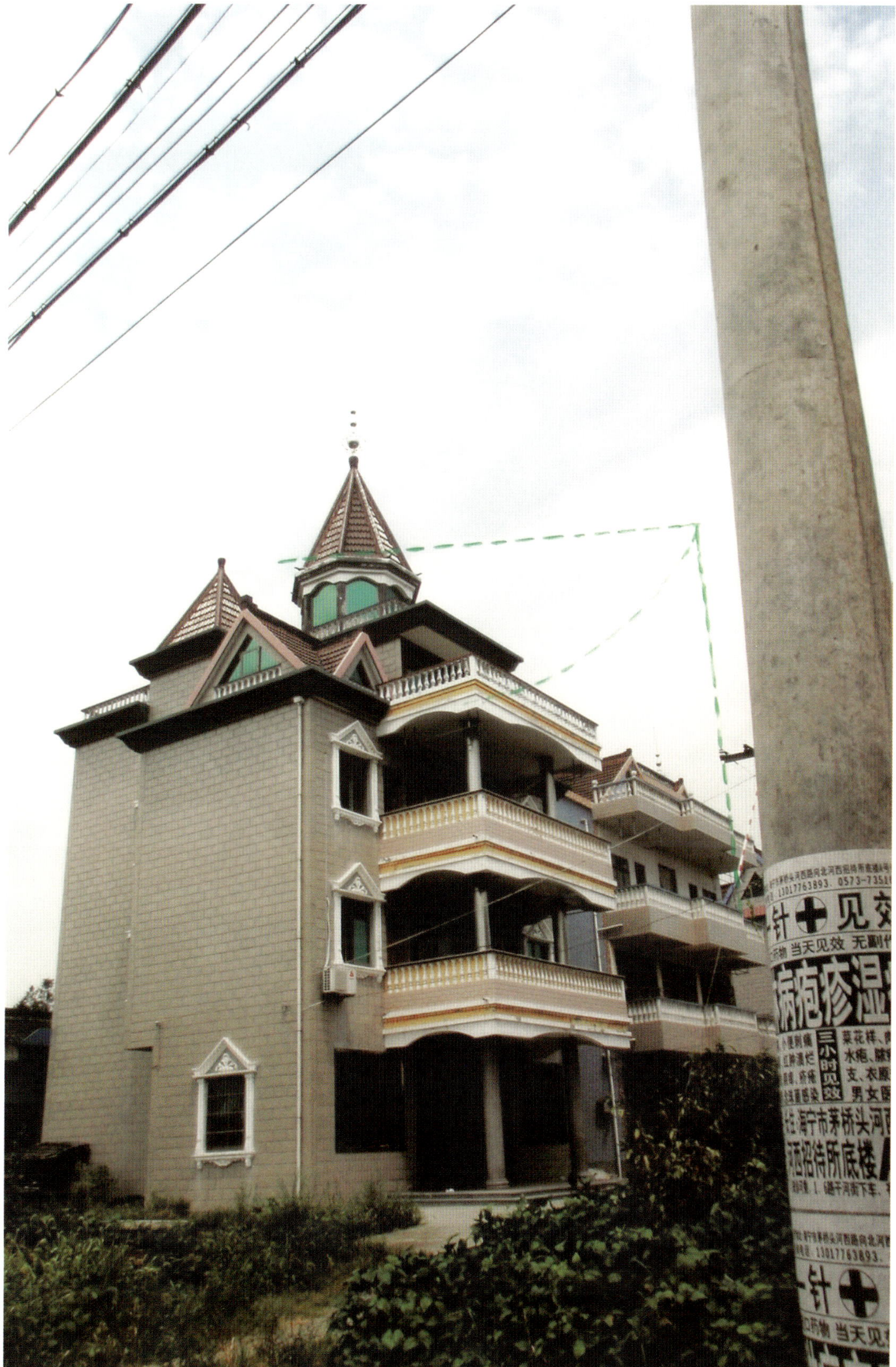

China Chapter: New Village 2006 #5
中國篇：新農村 #5

Oil paint on photo
90 x 60 cm
2006

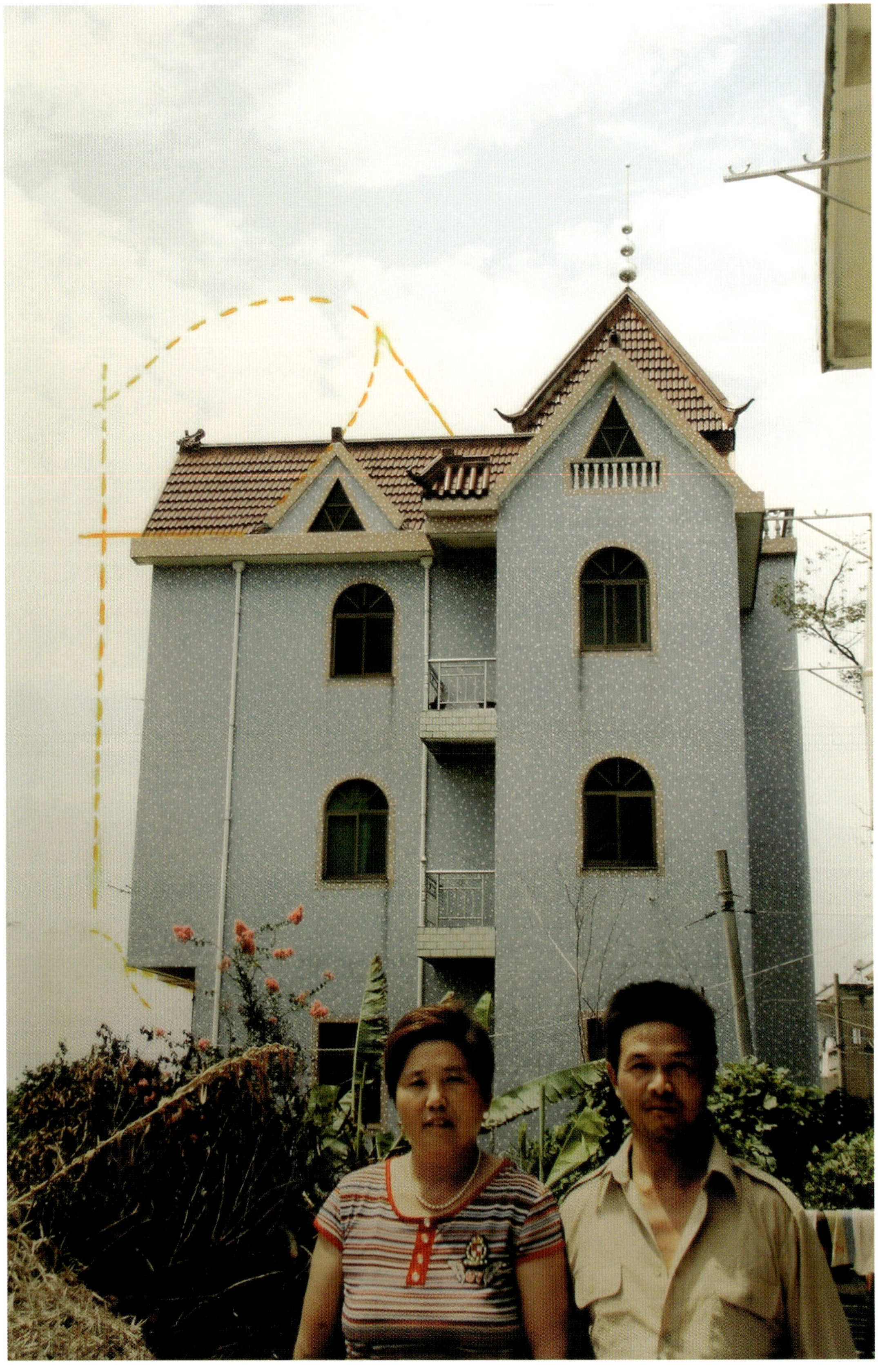

China Chapter: New Village 2006 #6
中國篇：新農村 #6
Oil paint on photo
90 x 60 cm
2006

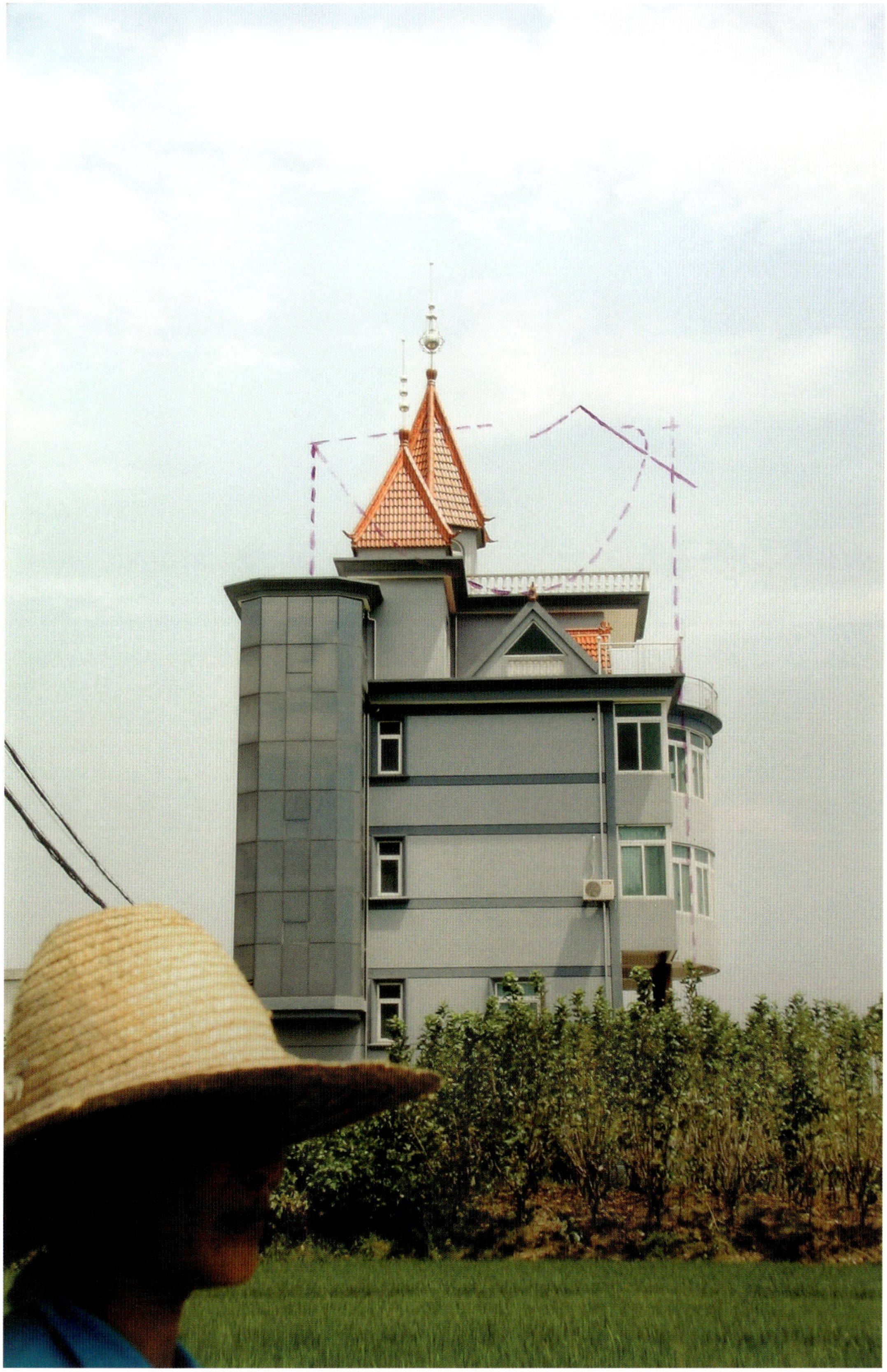

China Chapter: New Village 2006 #7
中國篇：新農村 #7

Oil paint on photo
90 x 60 cm
2006

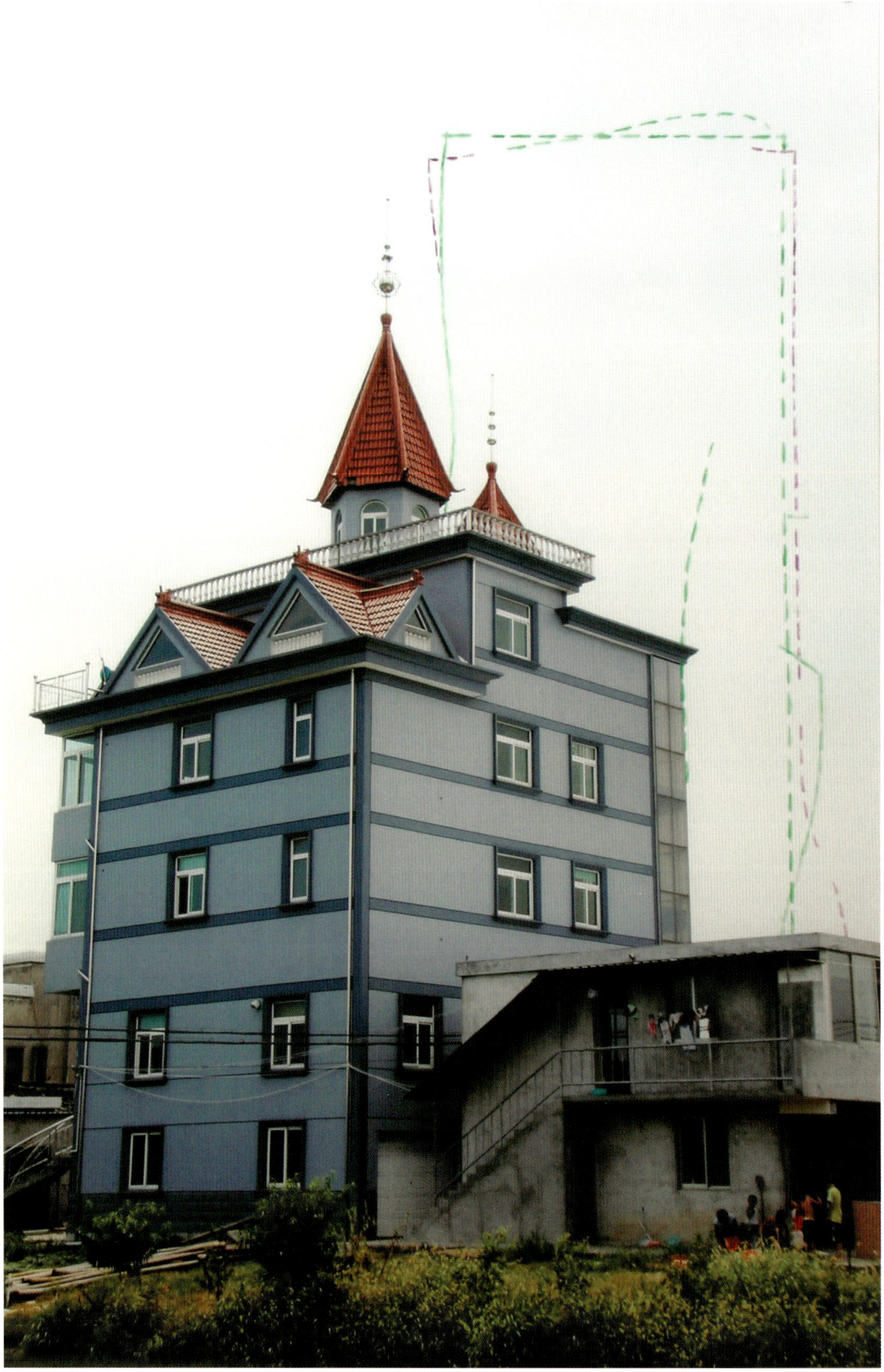

China Chapter: New Village 2006 #8
中國篇：新農村 #8
Oil paint on photo
90 x 60 cm
2006

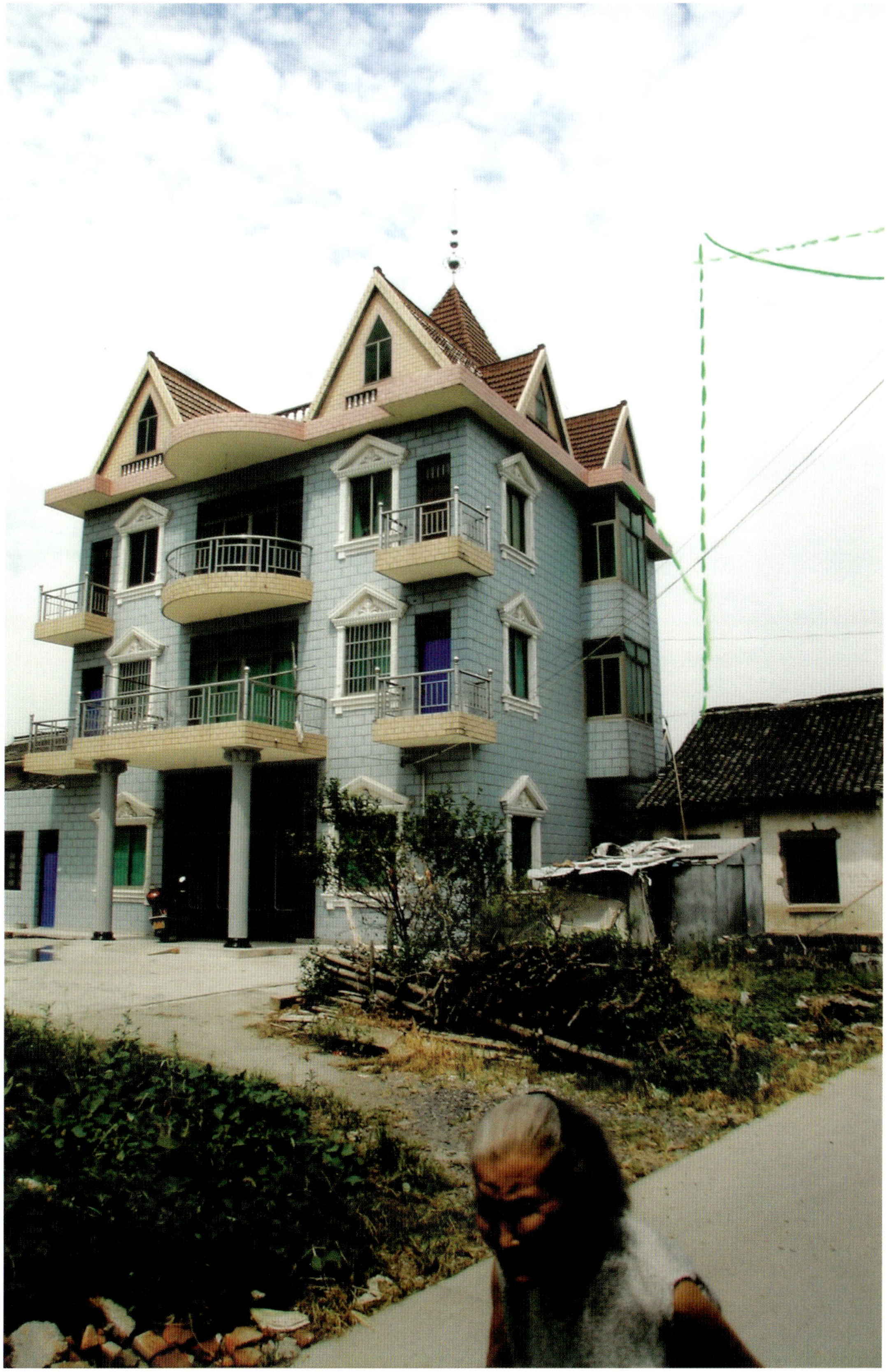

China Chapter: New Village 2006 #9
中國篇：新農村 #9
Oil paint on photo
90 x 60 cm
2006

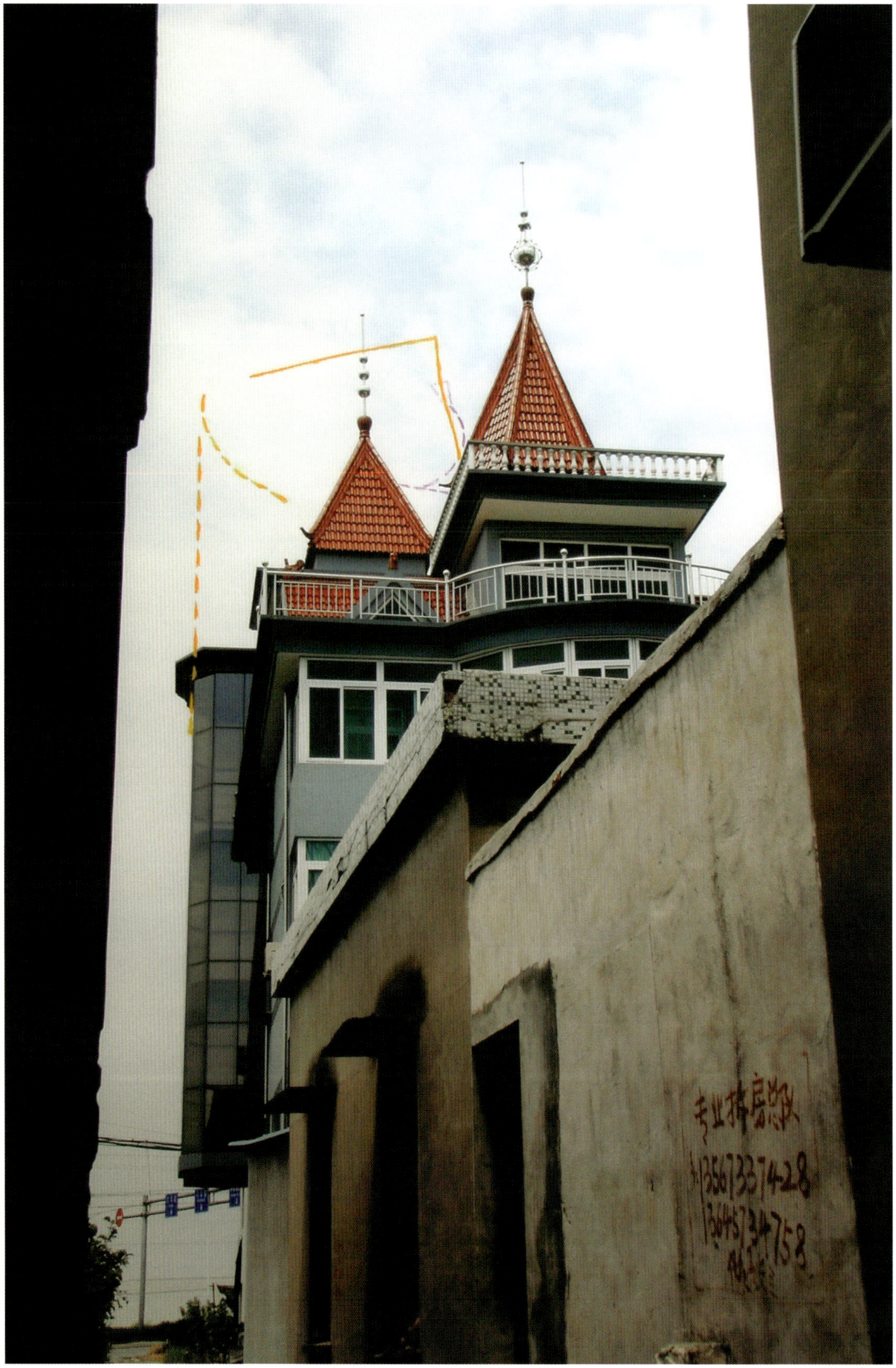

China Chapter: New Village 2006 #10
中國篇：新農村 #10
Oil paint on photo
90 x 60 cm
2006

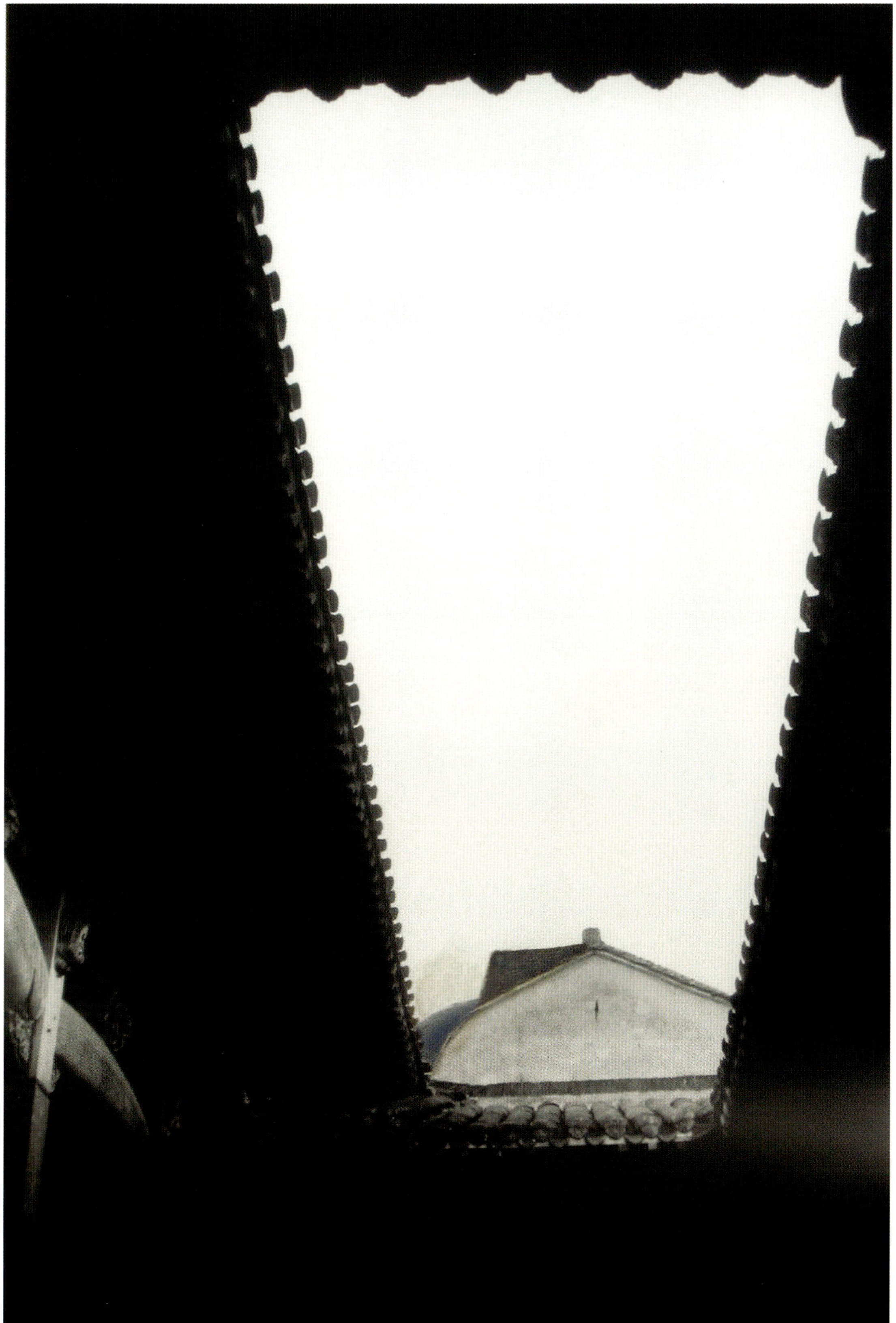

China Chapter: Anhui #1
中國篇：安徽 #1
Oil paint on photo
50 x 34 cm
2002

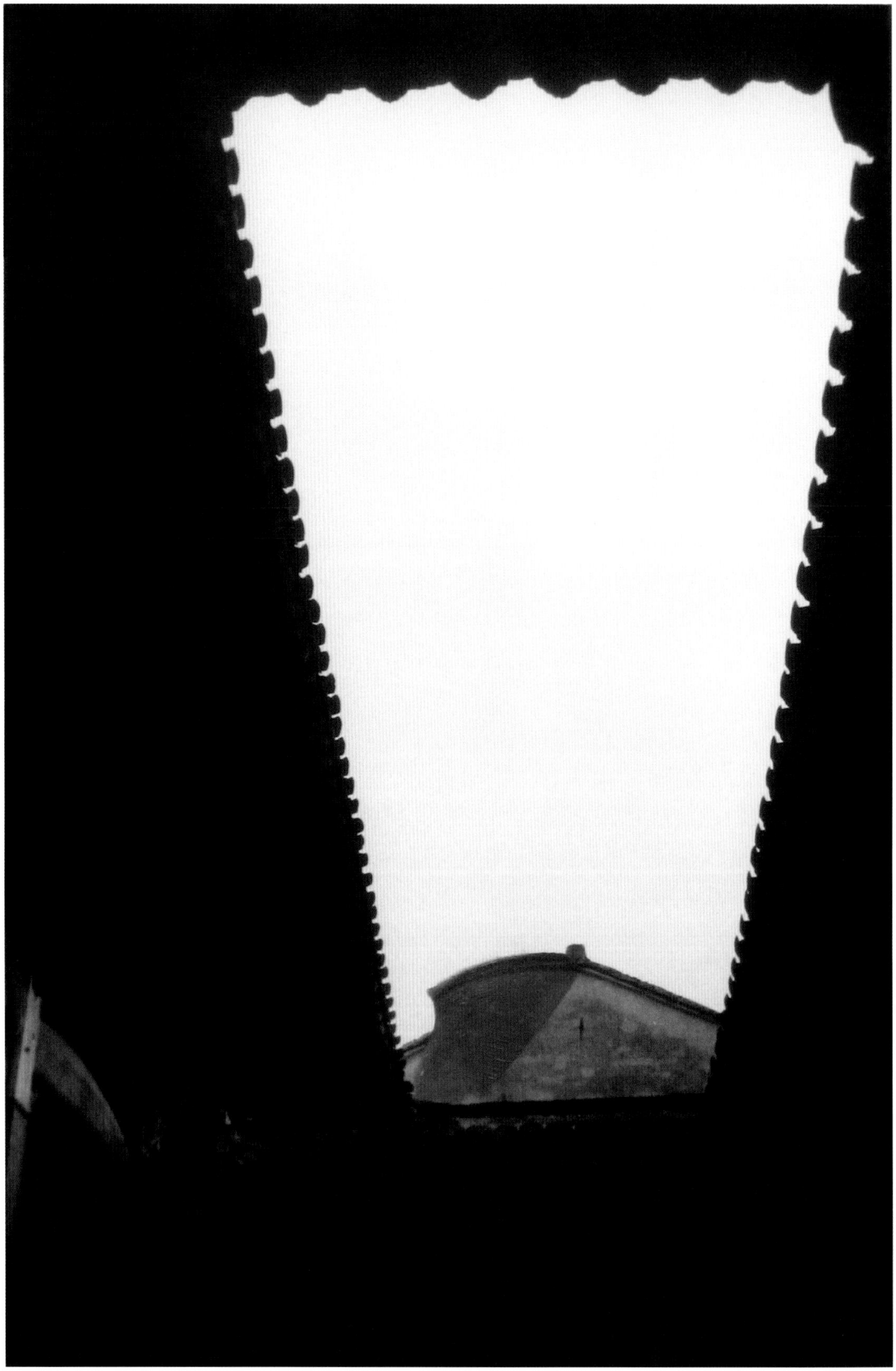

China Chapter: Anhui #2
中國篇：安徽 #2
Oil paint on photo
50 x 34 cm
2002

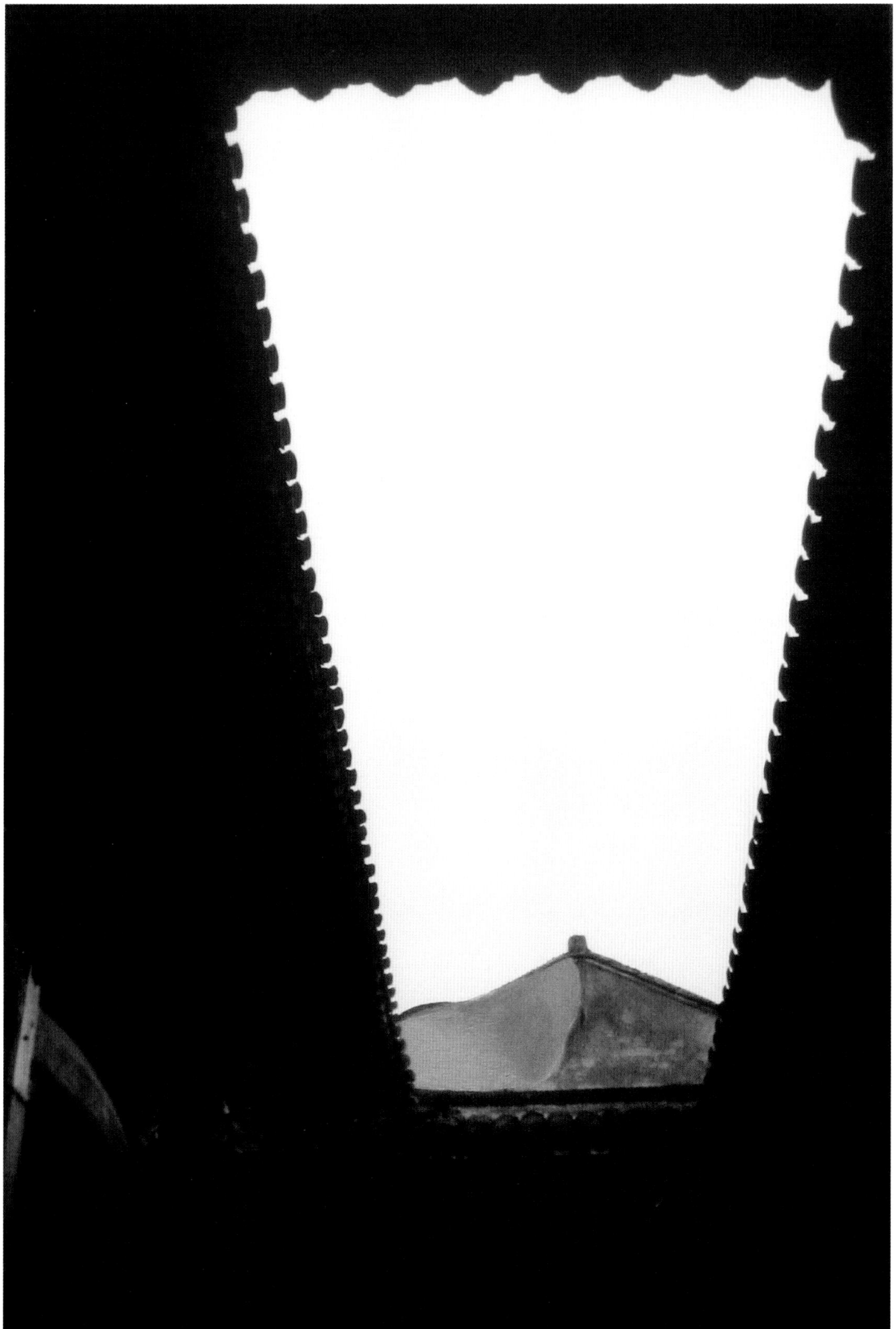

China Chapter: Anhui #3
中國篇：安徽 #3
Oil paint on photo
50 x 34 cm
2002

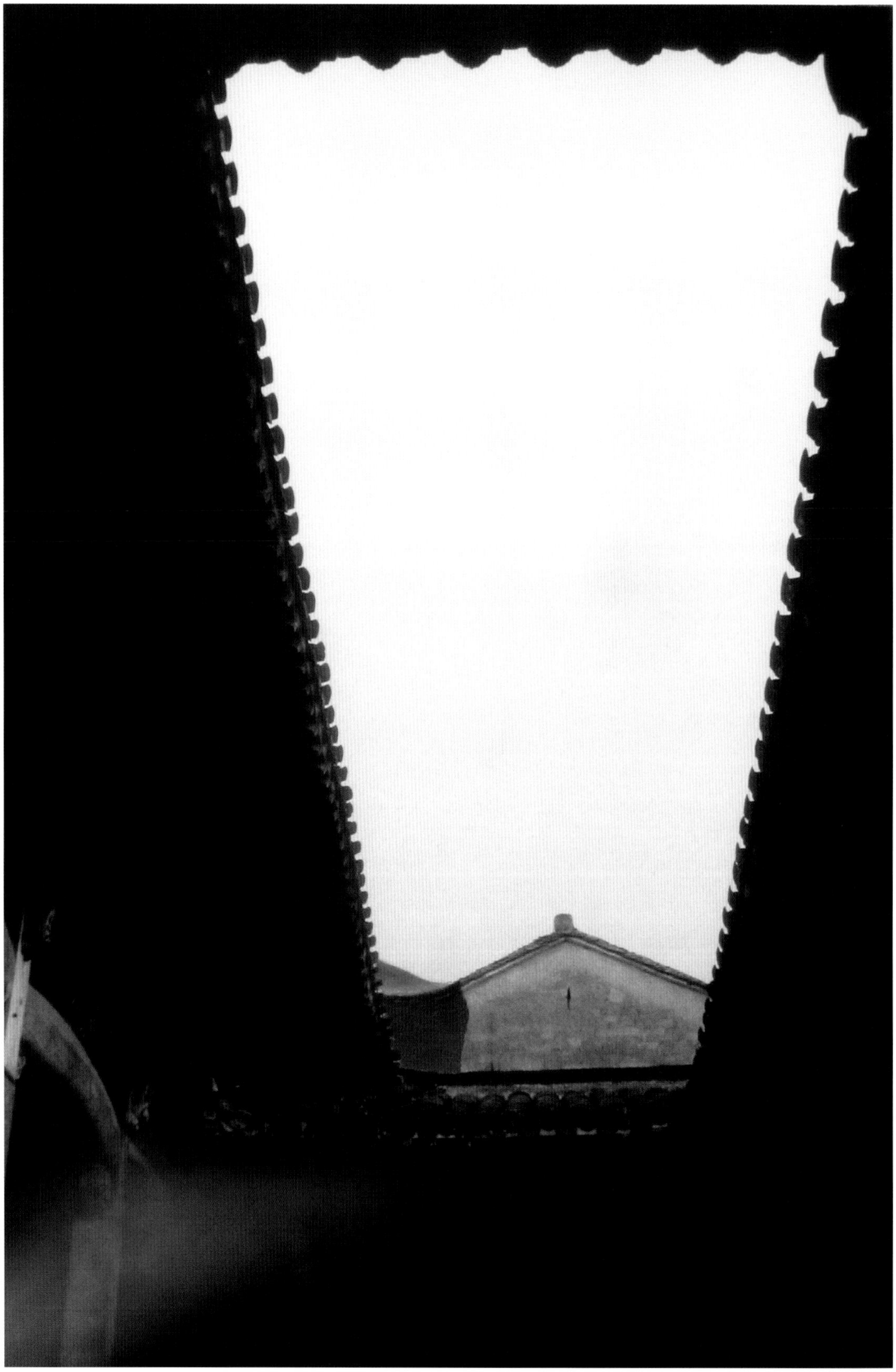

China Chapter: Anhui #4
中國篇：安徽 #4
Oil paint on photo
50 x 34 cm
2002

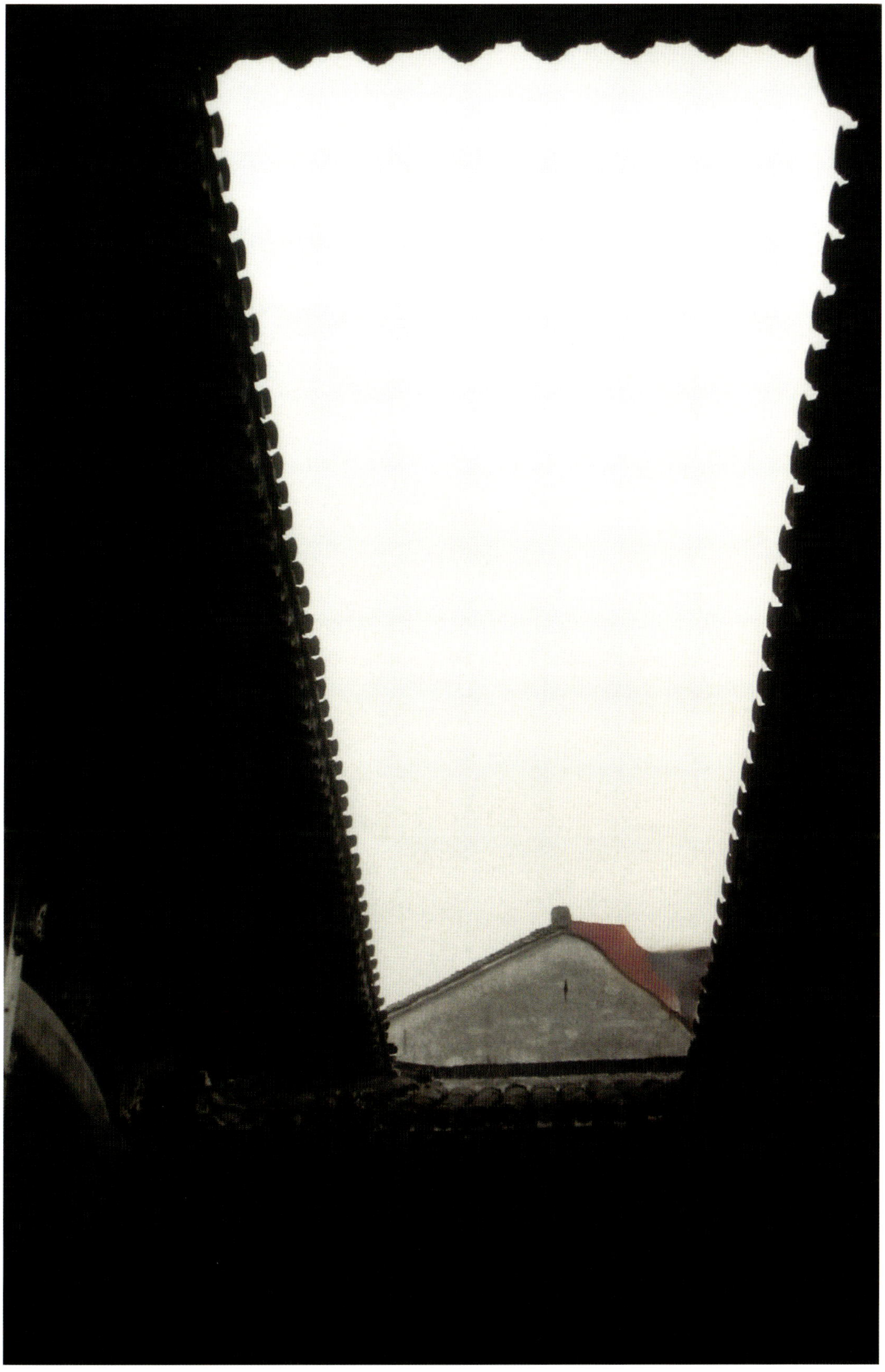

China Chapter: Anhui #5
中國篇：安徽 #5
Oil paint on photo
50 x 34 cm
2002

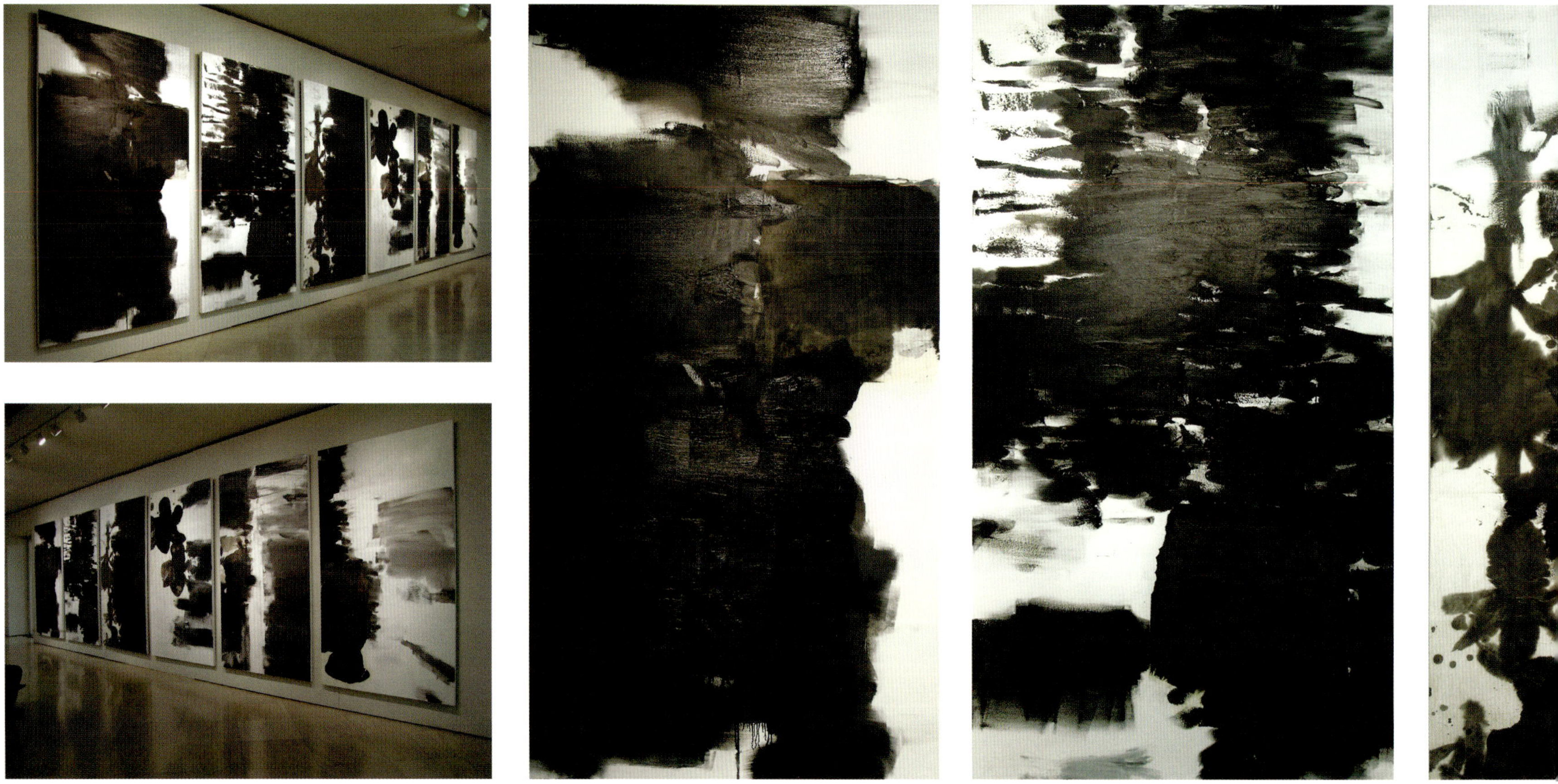

Vestiges of a Process: Water (Part 2) 過程的瞬間：水 （第二部分）, *Oil paint, sumi-ink, rice paper on linen, 260 x 146 cm (each panel), 2005*

Relative to his series of Sumi-Ink paintings and gardens, Zhang recalls his youth when he observed his father practicing calligraphy before going to work. He clearly remembers his father's words that ink – as manifested in the signs of written language – was a true representation of culture and the spiritual consciousness inherent in all human beings. For Zhang, this concept became deeply embedded within him. In Vestiges of a Process: Water (Part 2), one may sense that calligraphy and ink painting is very much within the

在談到自己的水墨畫及庭園系列作品時，張建君記得他兒時觀察父親在外出工作前練習書法的情景。他清楚記得父親曾說過，形諸語言書面符號的墨，是文化以及全人類內在精神意識的真正代表。這個觀念，張建君可是銘記於心的。當我們觀賞《過程的瞬間：水》（第二部分）時，或許能感受到書法和水墨畫是他文化記憶中極為重要的部分。他用油彩和墨在底襯麻

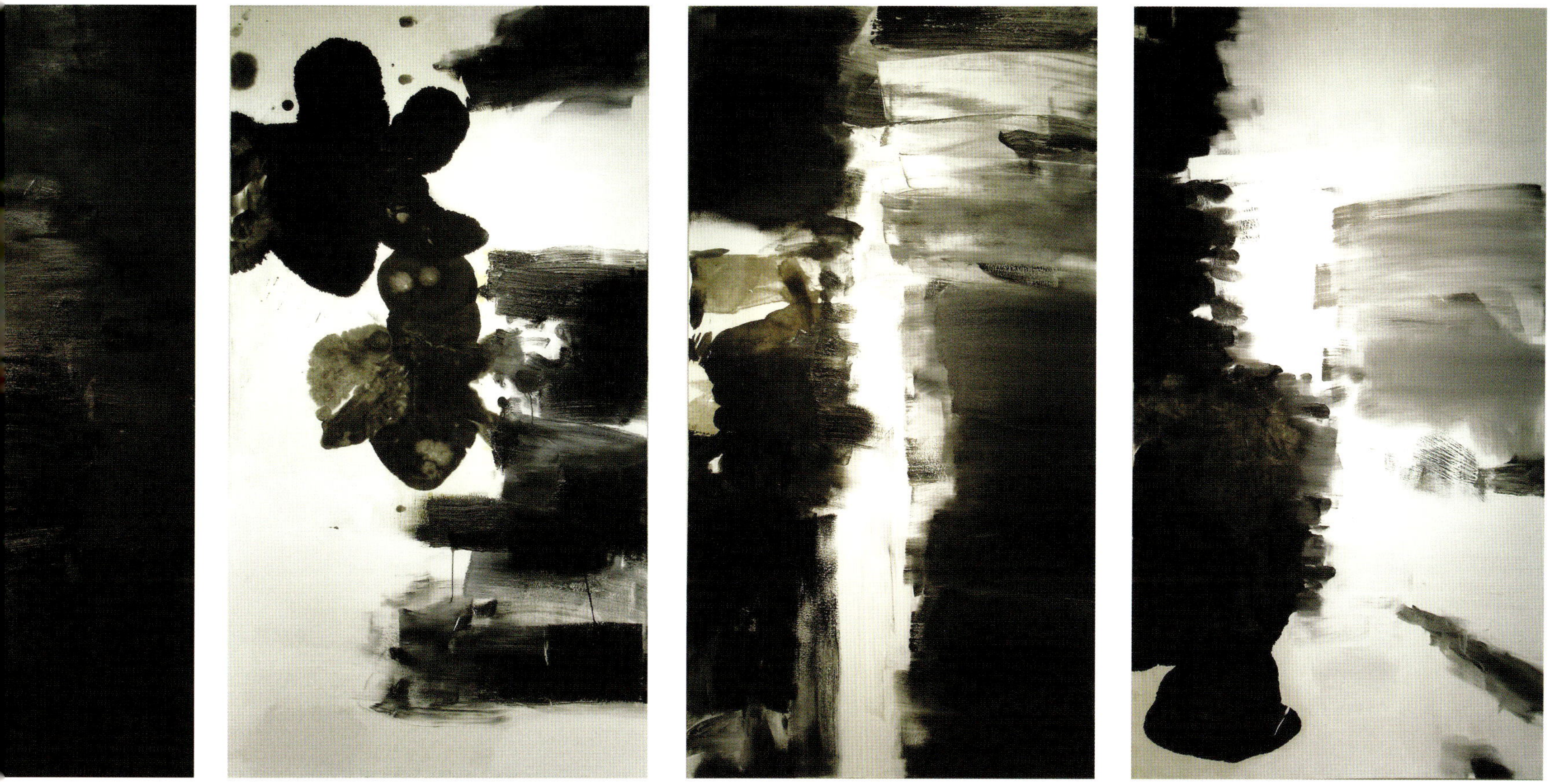

artist's cultural memory. The six large-scale vertical panels, painted in oil and sumi-ink on rice paper over linen, combine a distinct aspect of memory with the process of historical time. We sense the landscape and the presence of water in these paintings, but most of all we are cognizant of the ineluctable visual force of the black ink. These panels were installed in the Shanghai Art Museum in 2005 to accompany Zhang's paintings with water in which he copied images of water (as discussed earlier).

布的宣紙上作畫，畫滿了六個大型的直立畫板，將歷史時間的流逝和記憶的某一鮮明側面結合在一起。畫中的風景和水姑且不論，讓我們感受最深的，其實莫過於黑墨所帶來的、避無可避的視覺沖擊。上述畫板於2005年與張建君以水臨摹經典水畫的畫作（見上文），在上海美術館共同展出。

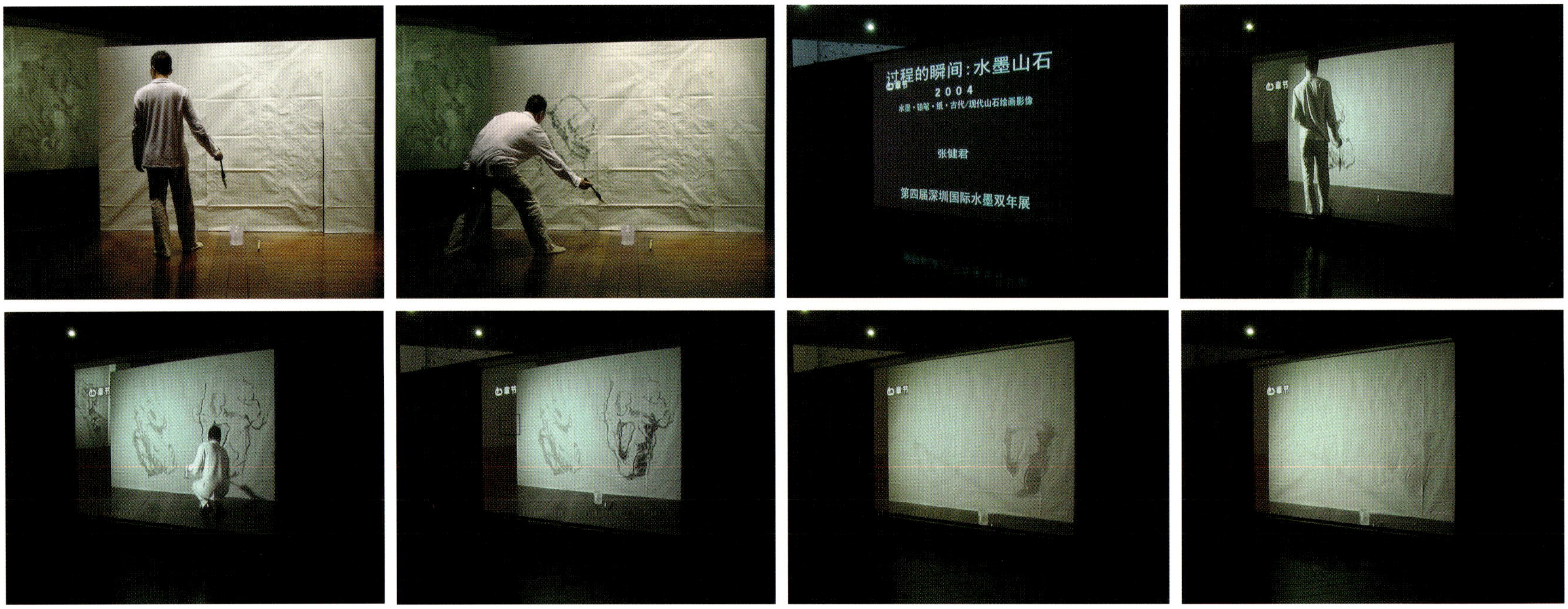

Vestiges of a Process: Sumi-Ink Scholar Rocks (Part 1) 過程的瞬間：水墨山石（第一部分）, *2004 (images from video clip)*

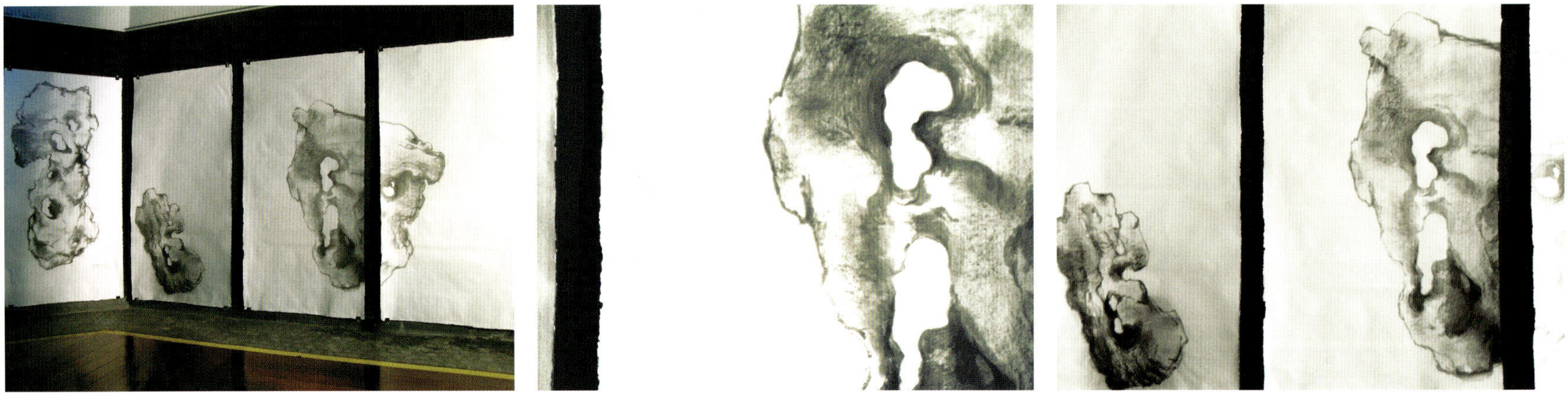

Vestiges of a Process: Sumi-Ink Scholar Rocks (Part 2) 過程的瞬間：水墨山石（第二部分）
Sumi-ink, graphite on rice paper
230 x 125 cm (each panel)
2004

At the Sumi-Ink Space Pavilion of the Fourth Shenzhen International Sumi-Ink Biennale, China.
第四屆深圳水墨雙年展，深圳畫廊

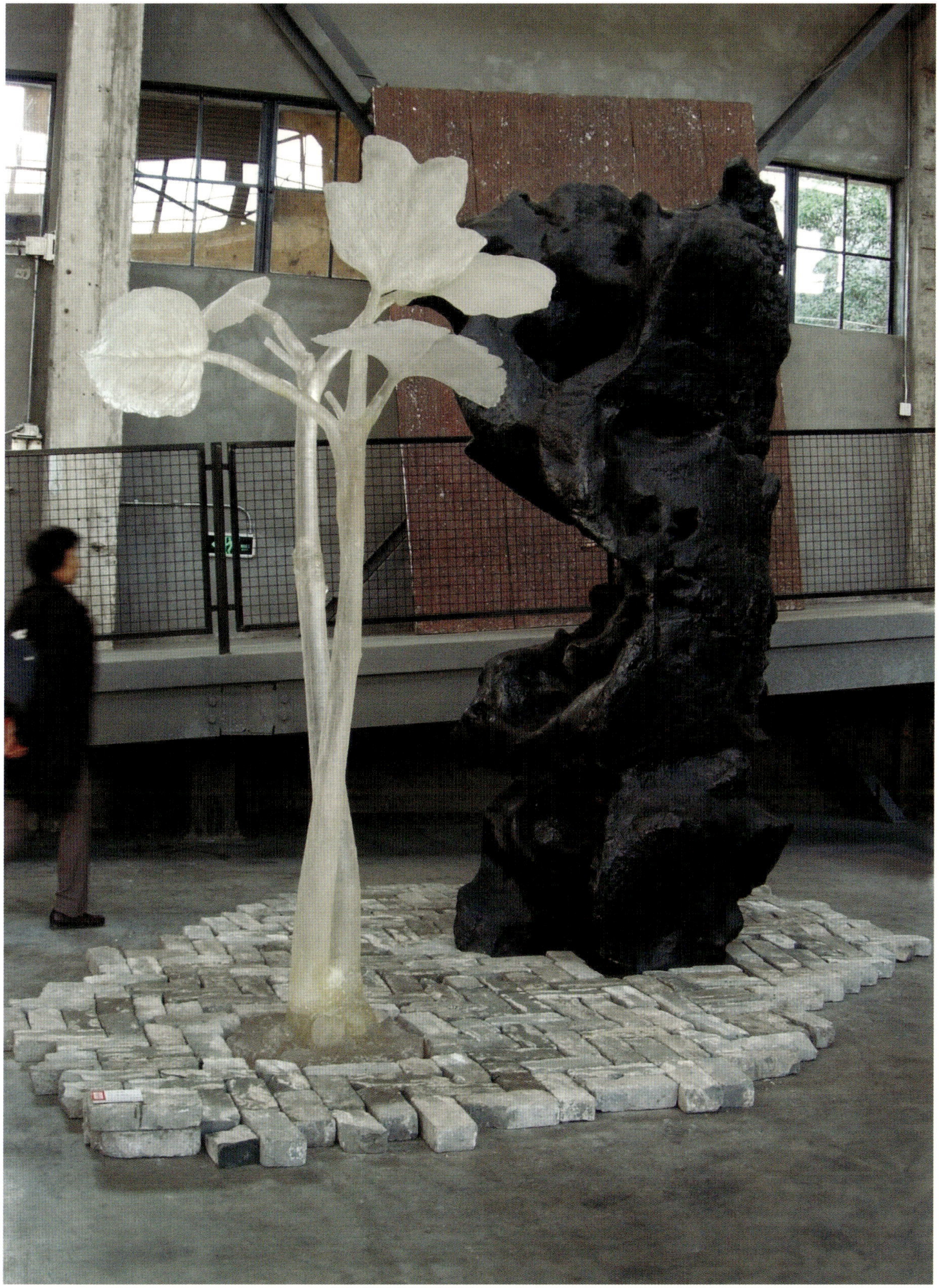

Yi Garden 弈園

Tree: Resin, 275 x 196 x 180 cm
Rock: Sumi-ink, fiberglass, 325 x 140 x 145 cm; old bricks
2005

In collaboration with Barbara Edelstein.
At the Shanghai Sculpture Space, China.
與芭芭拉・艾德斯坦合作
上海雕塑藝術中心

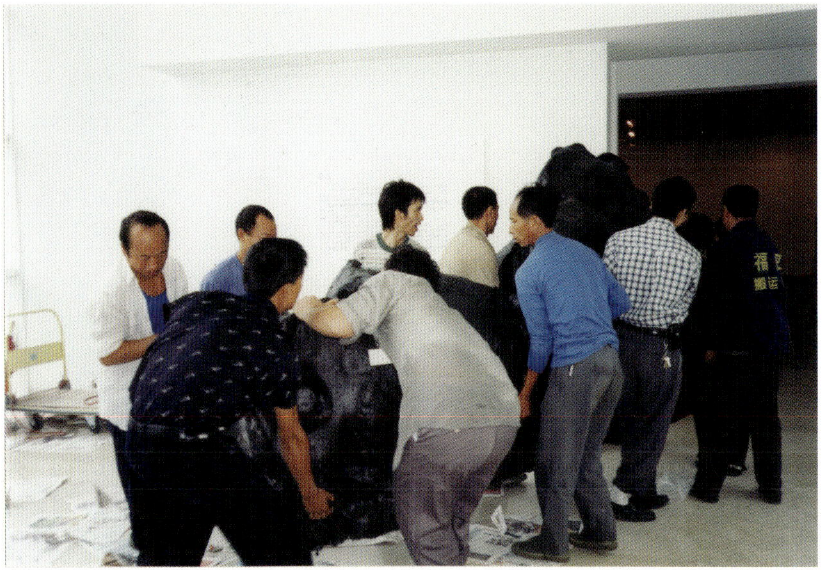

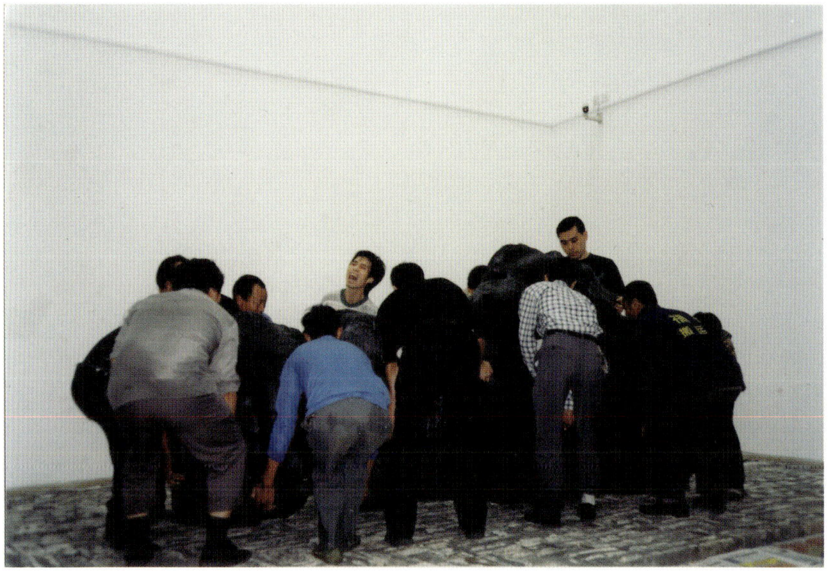

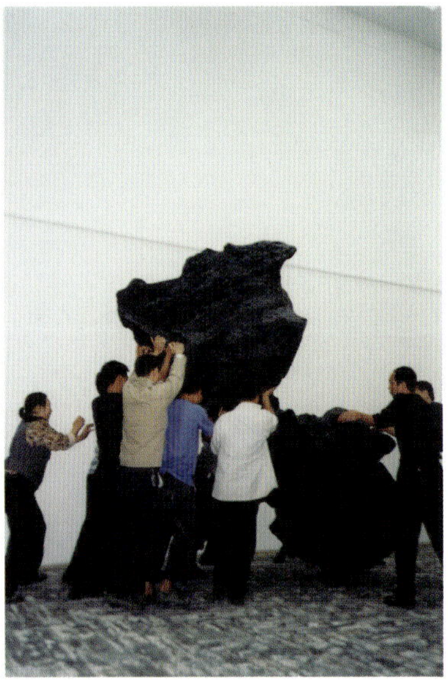

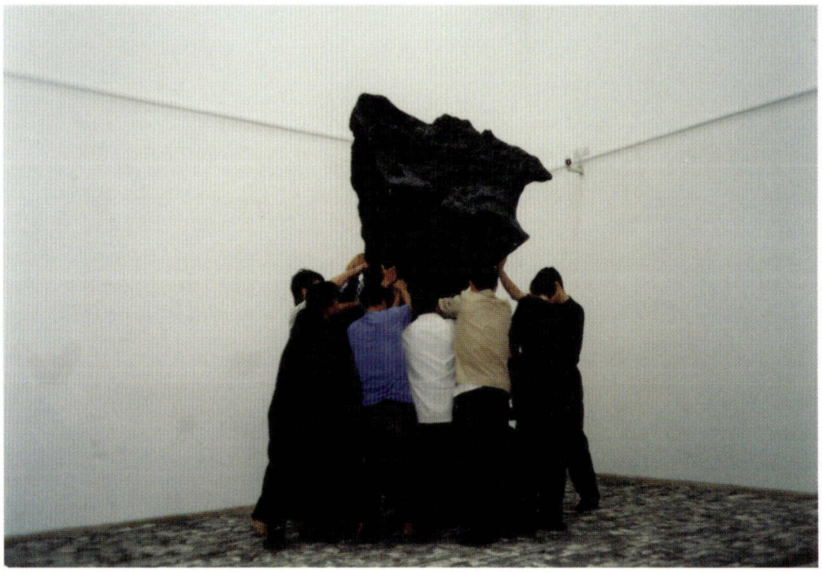

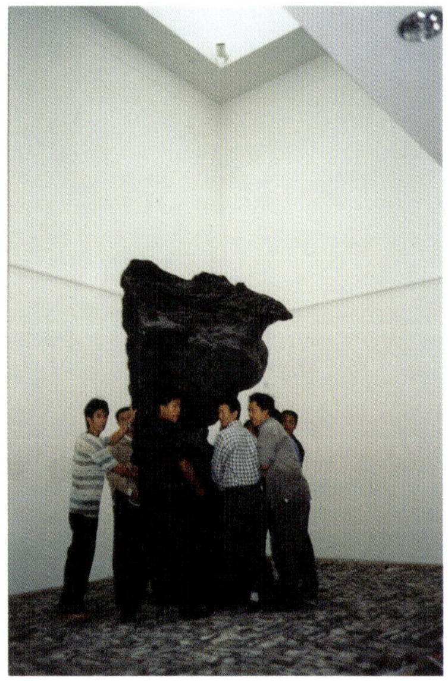

Sumi-Ink Garden of Re-Creation *(Installation)* 墨園，
large sumi-ink rock: 325 x 140 x 145 cm, sumi-ink, old bricks, wood, water, fish, pump system, 2002
At the He Xiangning Museum, Shenzhen, China.

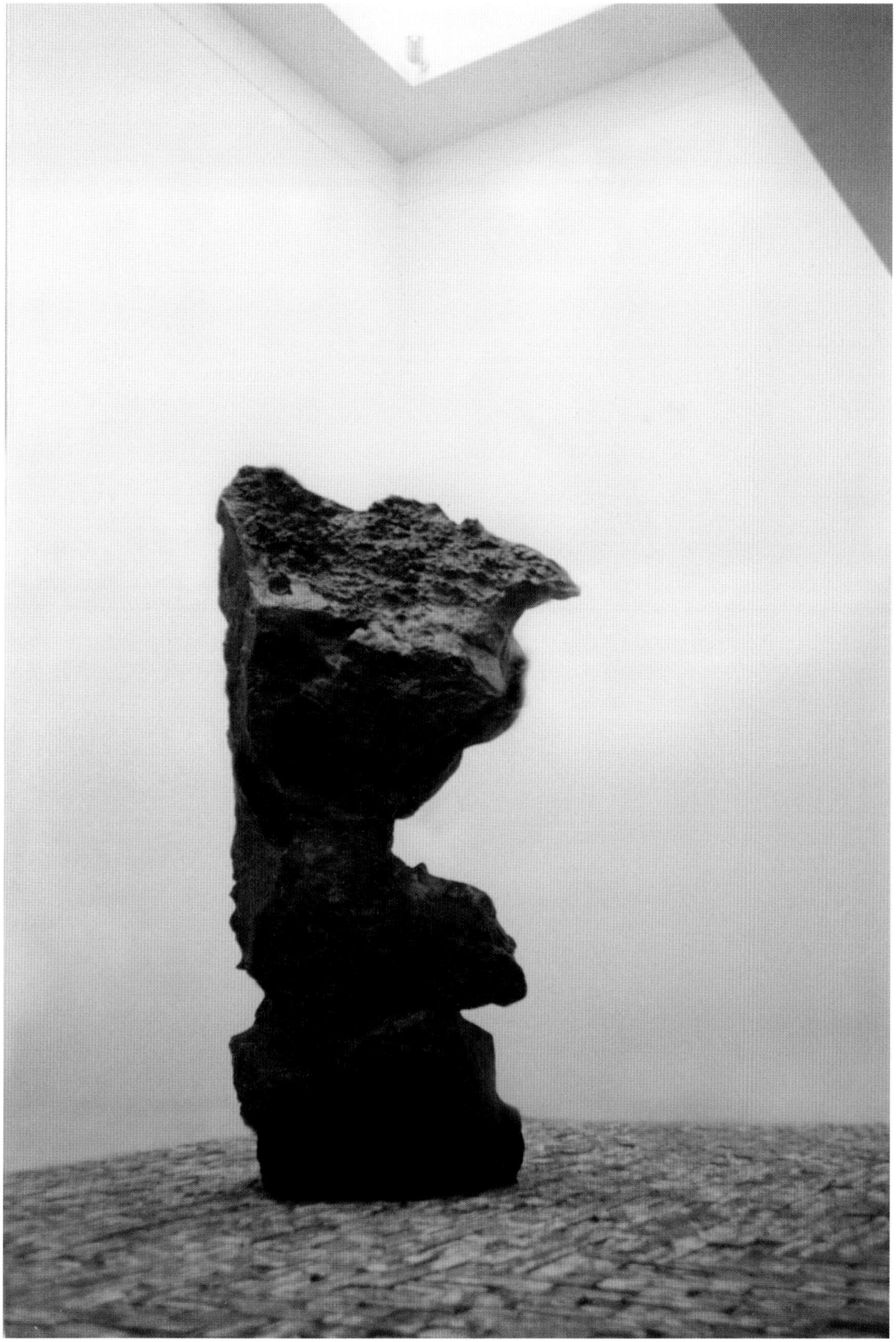

Sumi-Ink Garden of Re-creation (detail)
墨園（局部）

Sumi-ink, old bricks, fiberglass
325 x 140 x 145 cm
2002

At the He Xiangning Museum, Shenzhen, China.

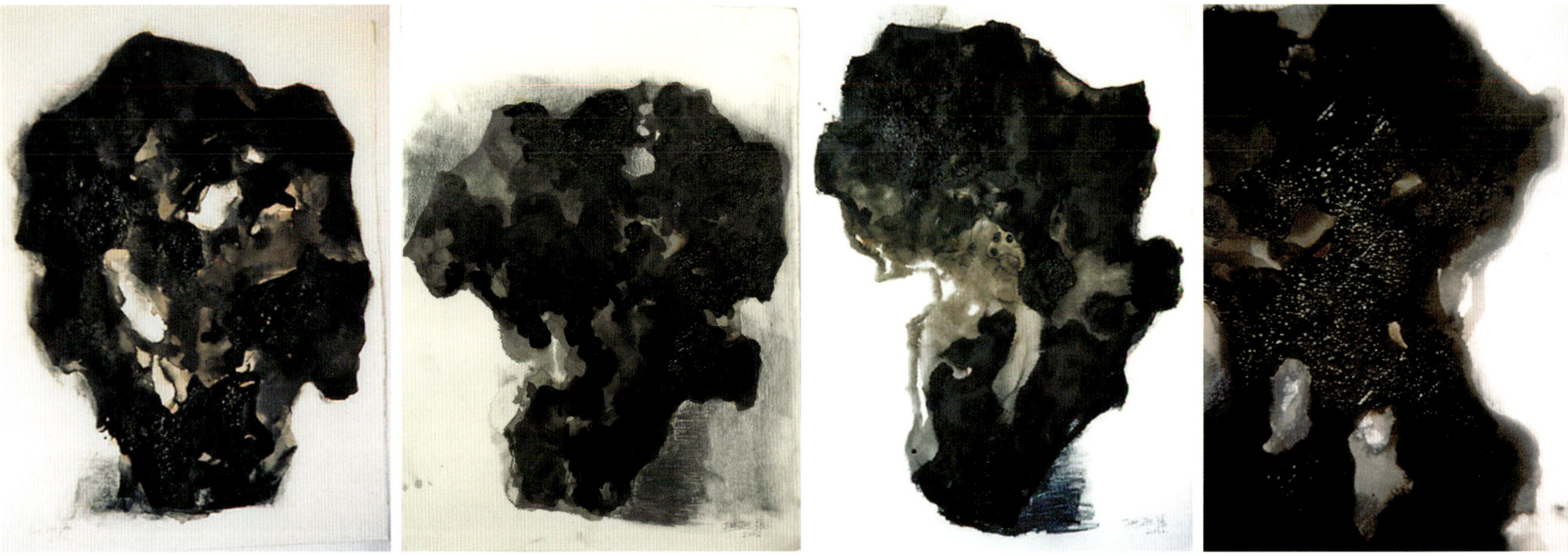

Ink Rock Series 墨石系列, *Sumi-ink on paper, 76 x 56 cm, 2002*
At the He Xiangning Museum, Shenzhen, China.

Other eminent works involving the use of ink were shown in two exhibitions that opened respectively in October and November 2002. The first was held at the He Xiangning Museum of Art in Shenzhen (a solo exhibition) and the second was at the Fourth Shanghai Biennale in Shanghai. Each installation shared the same title: Sumi-Ink Garden of Re-Creation. Given Zhang's persistent interest in the use of materials - whether traditional or industrial, natural or synthetic - the Sumi-Ink Garden simulated the appearance and volume of Tai-Hu rocks through the manipulation of solidified sumi-ink. Three of the rocks were placed in glass containers with water fed through a pump system. Gradually the ink would erode

至於張建君其他用上墨的名作，則是在另外兩個分別於2002年10月及11月開幕的藝展中亮相的。首先是在深圳何香凝美術館所舉辦的個展，其次是上海的第四屆上海雙年展。這兩件裝置藝術品共用同一名稱：《墨園》。顯然，張建君始終熱衷於運用各種不同的材質；無論是傳統或工業的、自然或人造的，皆無所不可。他在《墨園》中巧妙運用了固態的中國墨來模擬太湖石，其外觀與大小均堪稱逼真。其中有三塊“墨石”被放置在玻璃容器裡，用泵引水從當中流出。墨逐漸溶化以後，遂

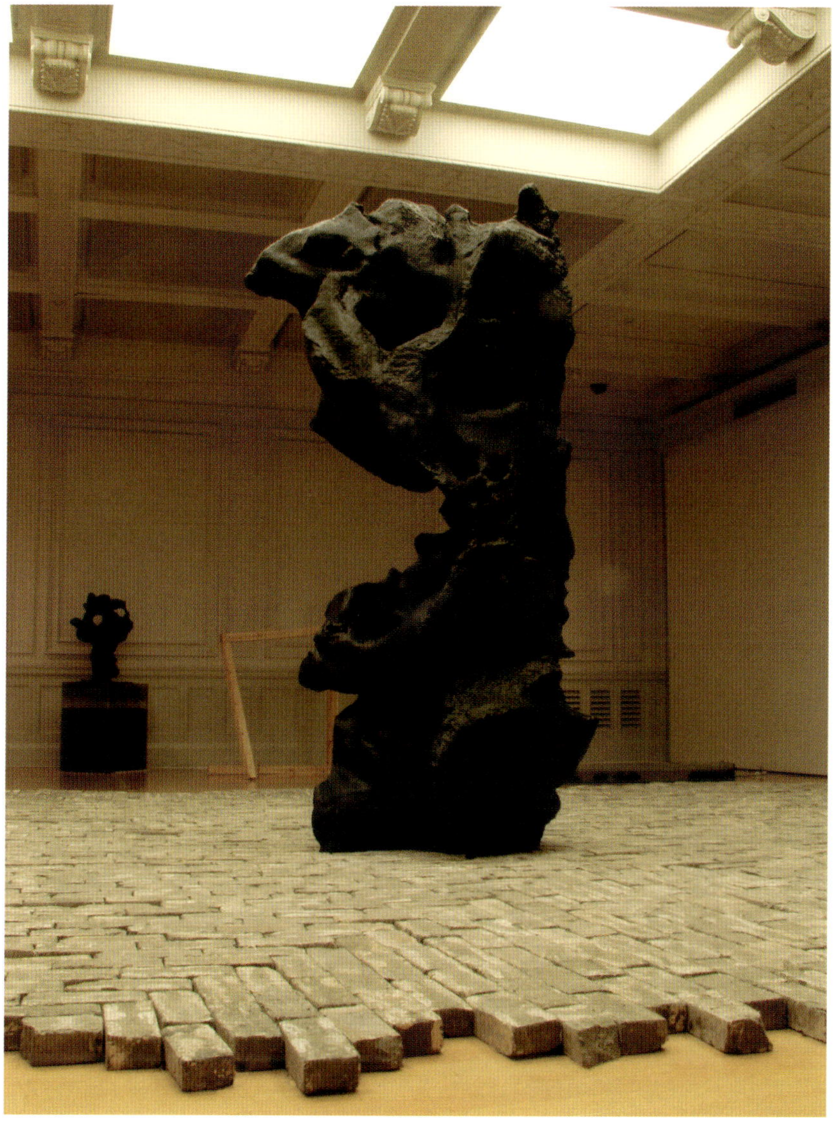

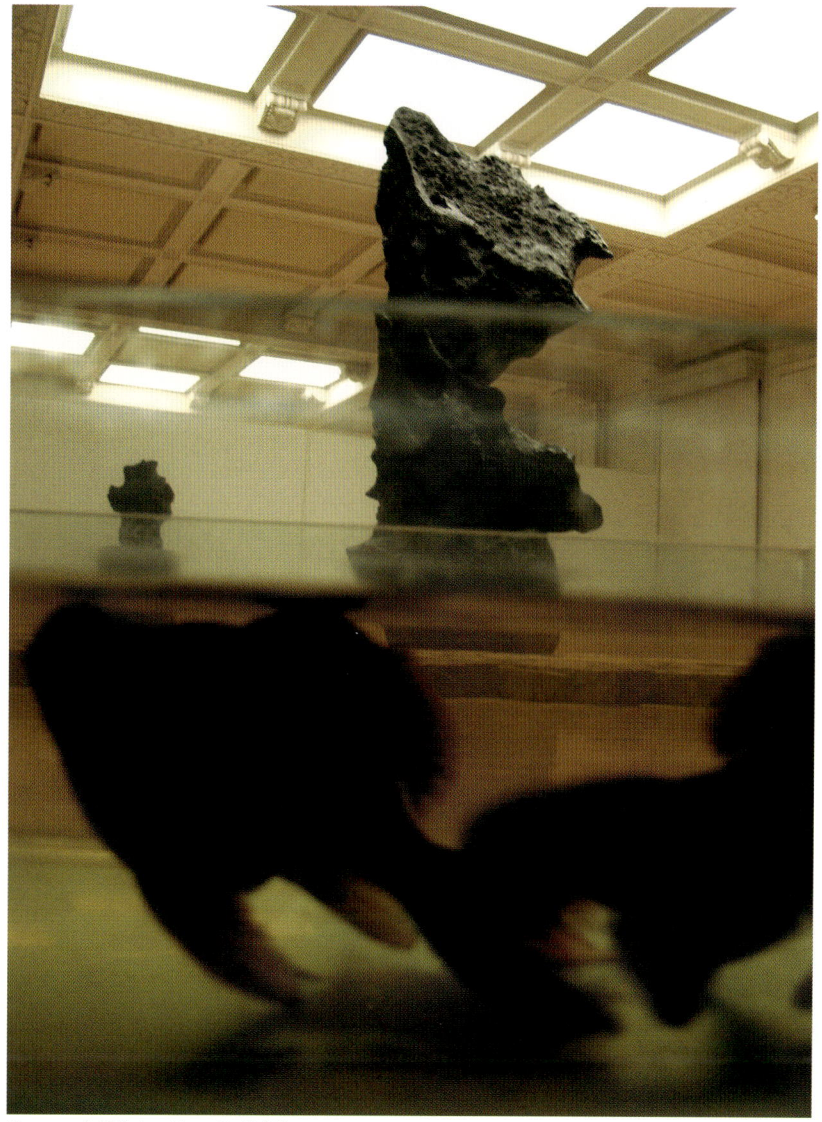

Photograph攝影：Luo Yong Jin 羅永進

Sumi-Ink Garden of Re-Creation *(Installation)* 墨園，
large sumi-ink rock: 325 x 140 x 145 cm, sumi-ink, old bricks, wood, water, fish, pump system, 2002
At the Fourth Shanghai Biennale, Shanghai Art Museum, China.

and blacken the water. There was also a glass water pond that contained five black goldfish. A platform constructed of three hundred year old bricks was placed around the pond on which the larger majestic scholars' rocks were situated. In Sumi-Ink Garden, the presence of ink as a transmutable organic substance laden with historical and cultural references plays a dominant role in the installation. Zhang's introductory comments for this work state the following: "The form of human culture changes in response to the evolving times, ideology, and global politics. The present continually wears away, and is replaced by the new. At the same time, a portion of the old is retained but it assimilates with its replacement to form something innovative with a touch of tradition."

將水染黑。此外，另有一個玻璃池塘，內有五尾黑金魚。圍繞池塘的，是一個用三片百年老青磚砌成的平台，上面擺放著較大、較壯觀的太湖石。作為有機可變物質的墨，背負著大量的歷史和文化指涉，因此在此作品中扮演了舉足輕重的角色。張建君在介紹這件作品時說："人類的文化形態會隨著時代、意識形態及全球政治的變化而轉變。逝者如斯夫，不舍晝夜一總有新事物取而代之。然而，舊的東西也總有一部分保留下來，與替代者彼此融合，形成既創新又帶點傳統色彩的東西。"

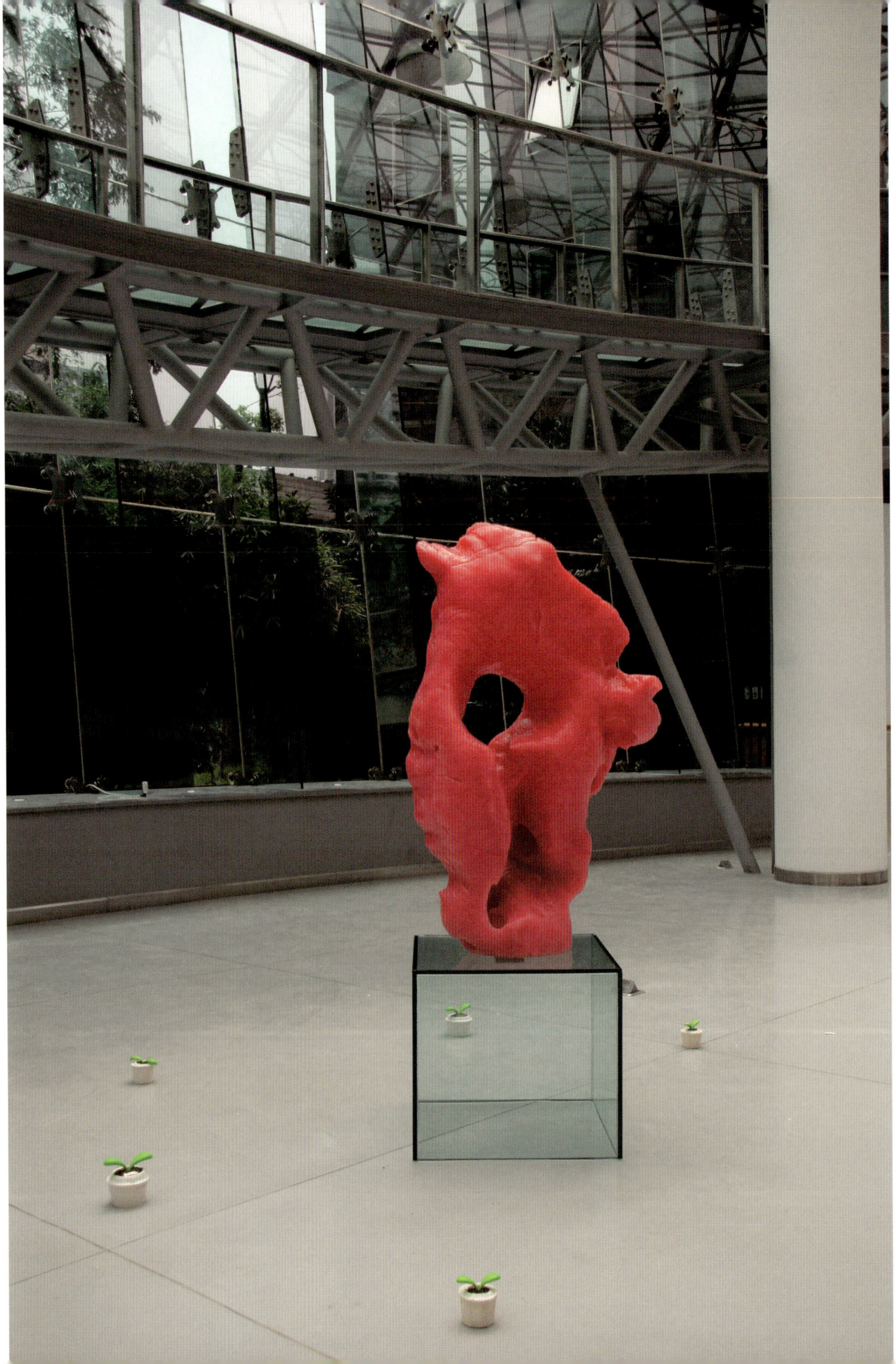

Mirage Garden Part 1 幻園

Silicone rubber, solar-powered leaves
125 x 84 x 65 cm
2006

At the Museum of Contemporary Art, Shanghai, China.
上海當代美術館

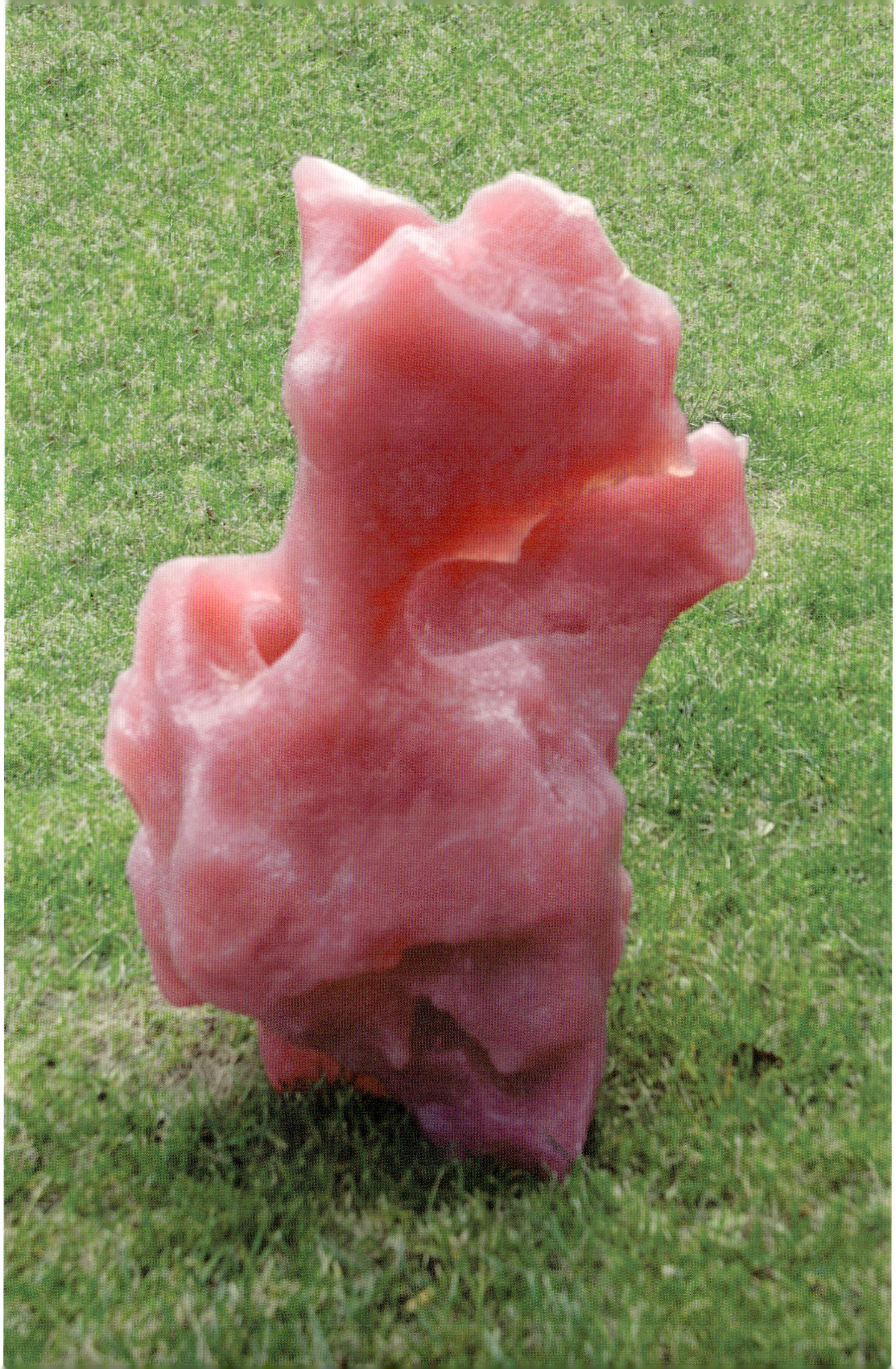

Mirage Garden Part 3 幻園 #3
Silicone rubber
69 x 38 x 55 cm
2006

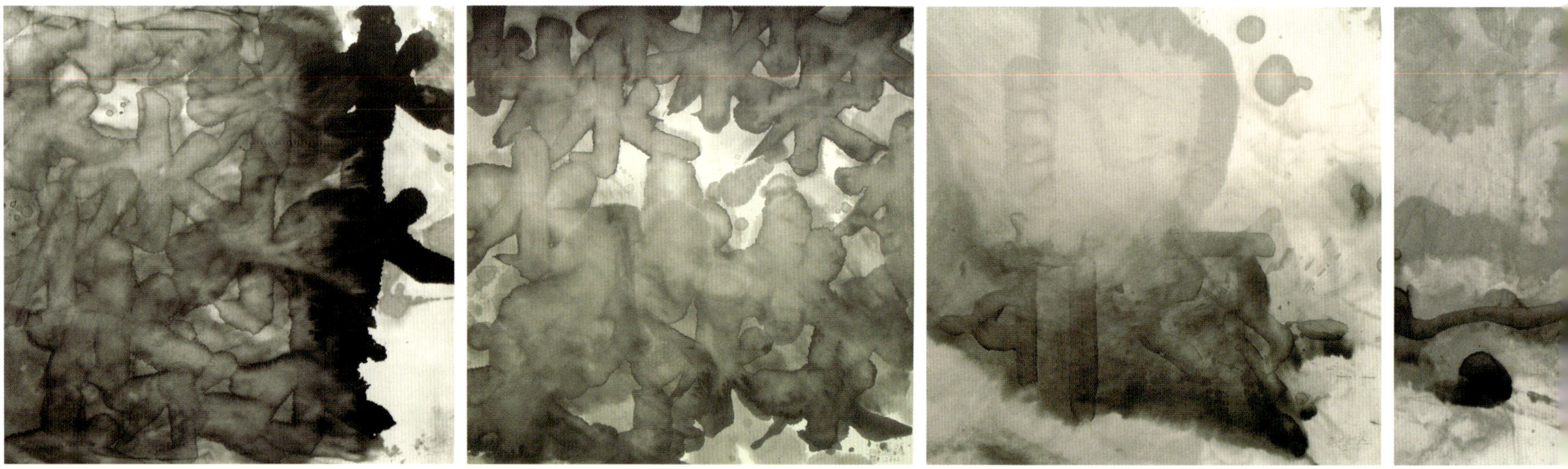

River *(in various languages, total 36 panels)* 山・水（局部）
Sumi-ink on rice paper
68.5 x 68.5 cm
2003

At the Barbara Davis Gallery, Houston, Texas, USA.
芭芭拉・戴維斯畫廊

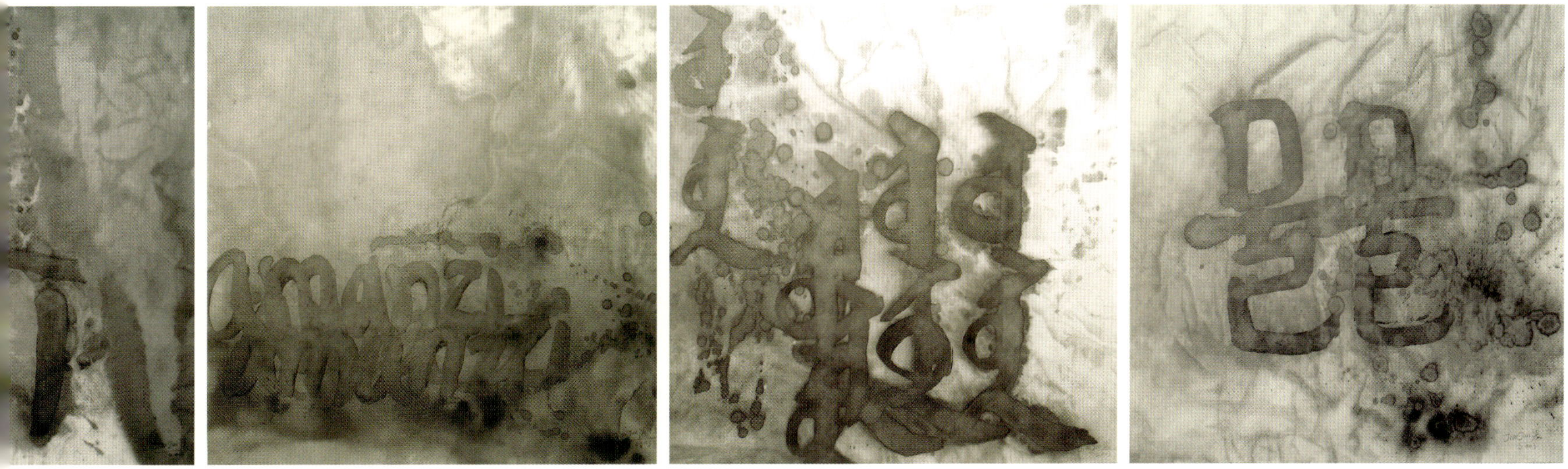

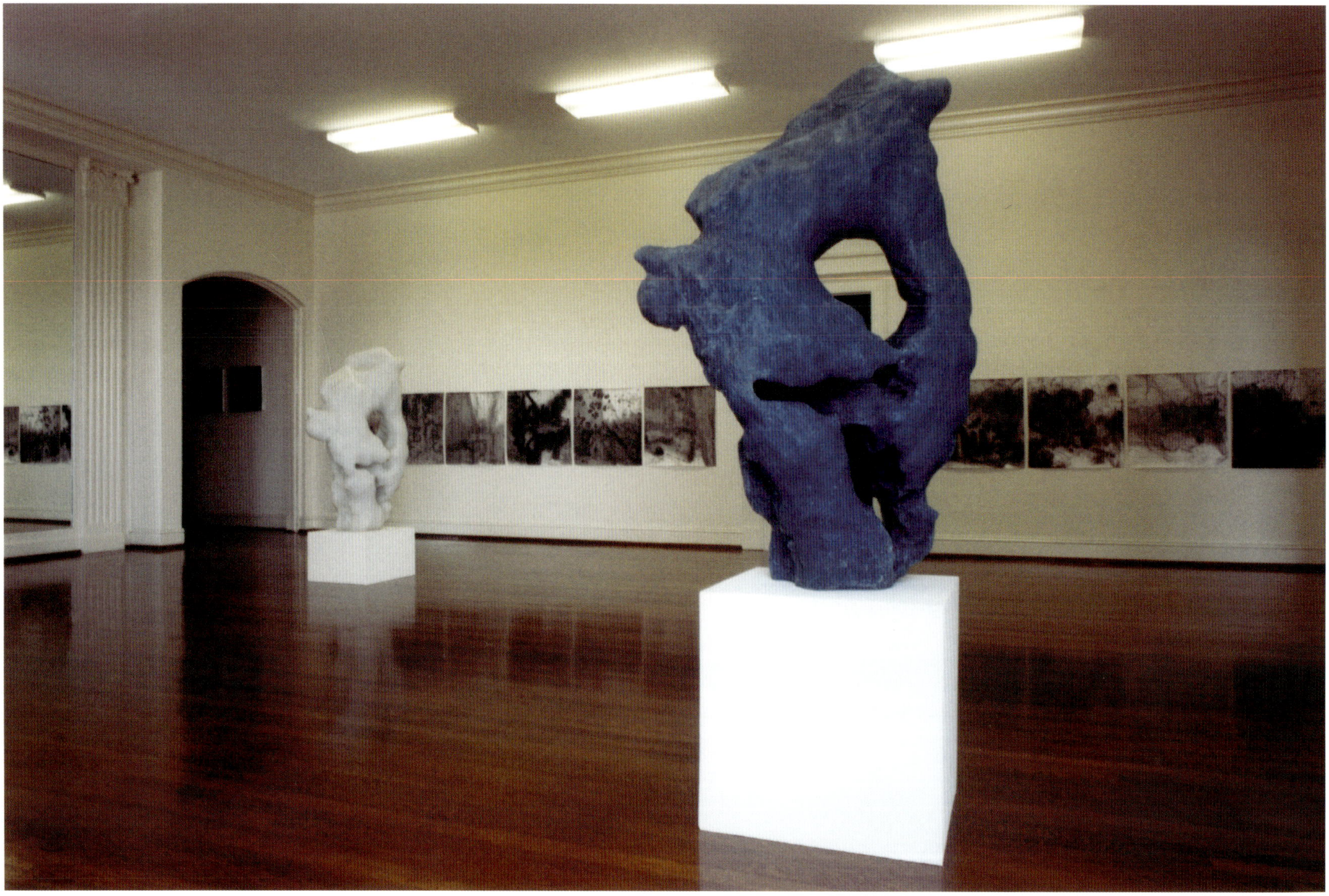

Mountain and River 山・水, *2003*

At the Barbara Davis Gallery, Houston, Texas, USA.
芭芭拉・戴維斯畫廊

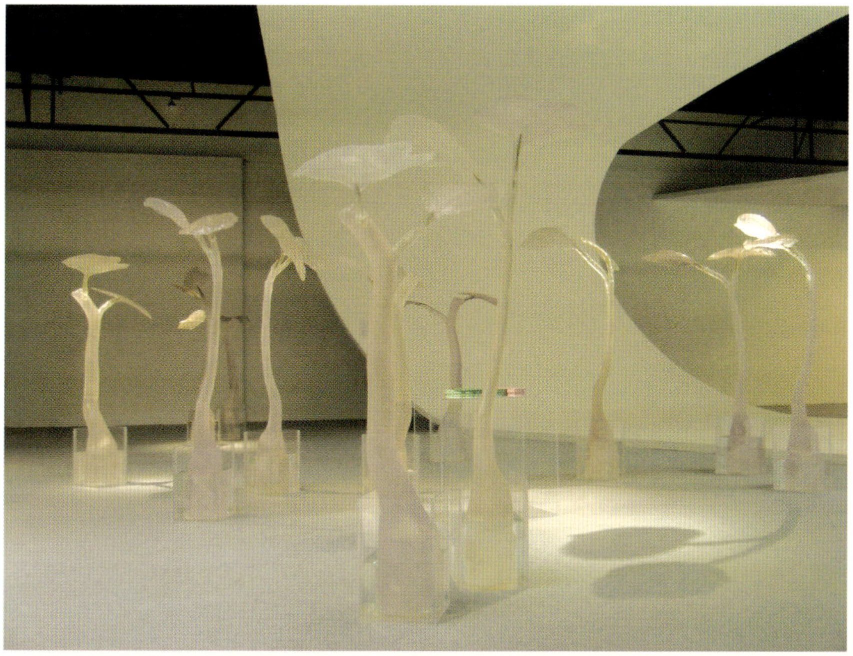
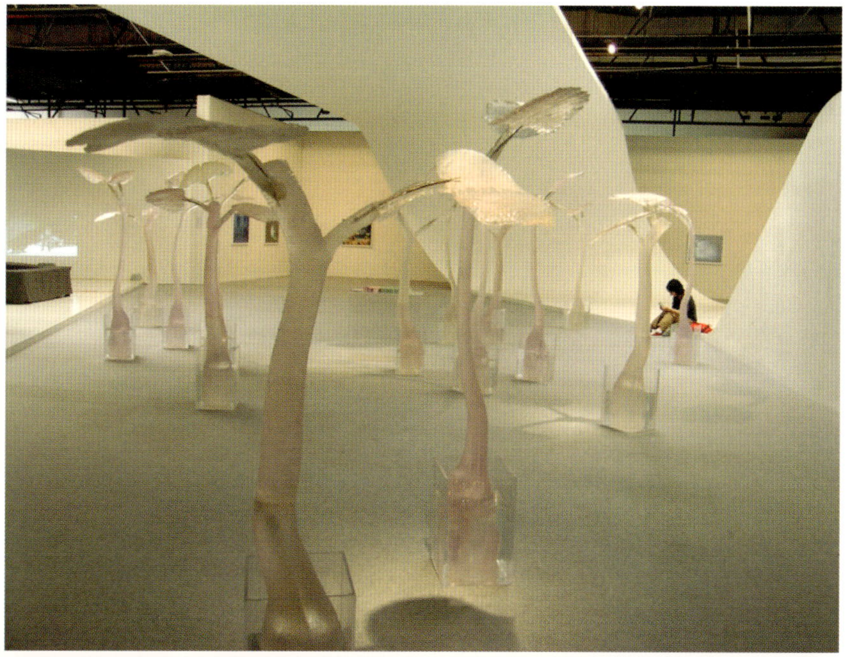
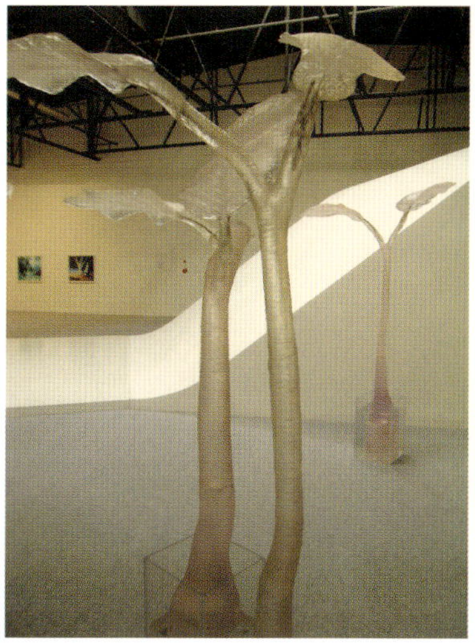
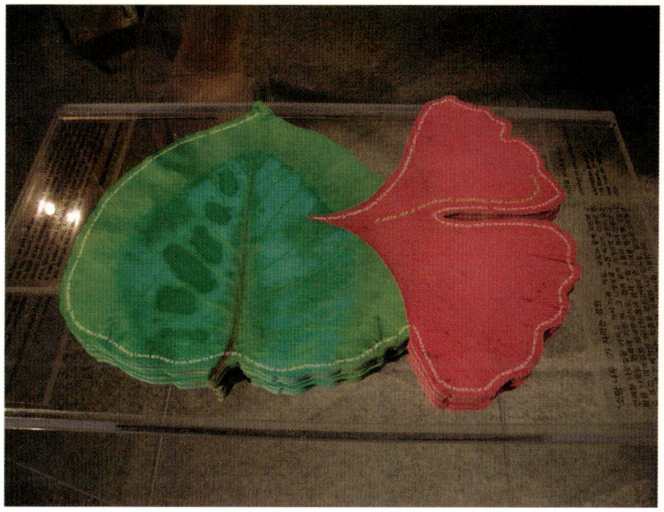
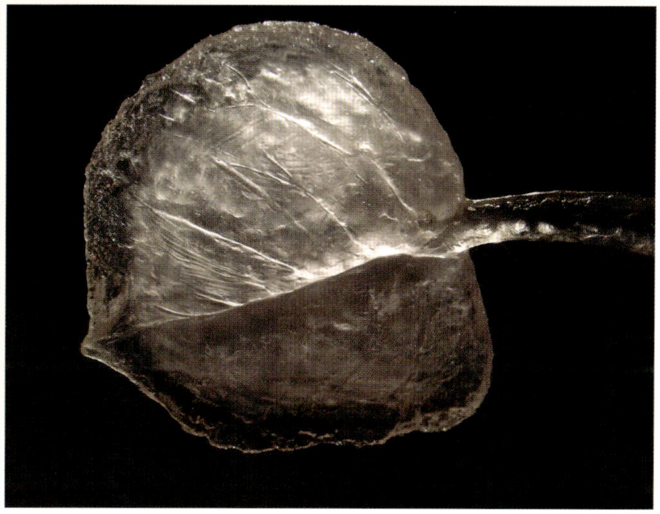

Garden of Wishing Trees 願望樹

Resin, water, plexiglas, print
Installation: 231 x 1280 x 975 cm
Poster: 41 x 56 cm
2004

In collaboration with Barbara Edelstein.
At the Fifth Gwangju Biennale: A Grain of Dust A Drop of Water, Korea.
與芭芭拉艾德斯坦合作。
第四屆光洲雙年展。

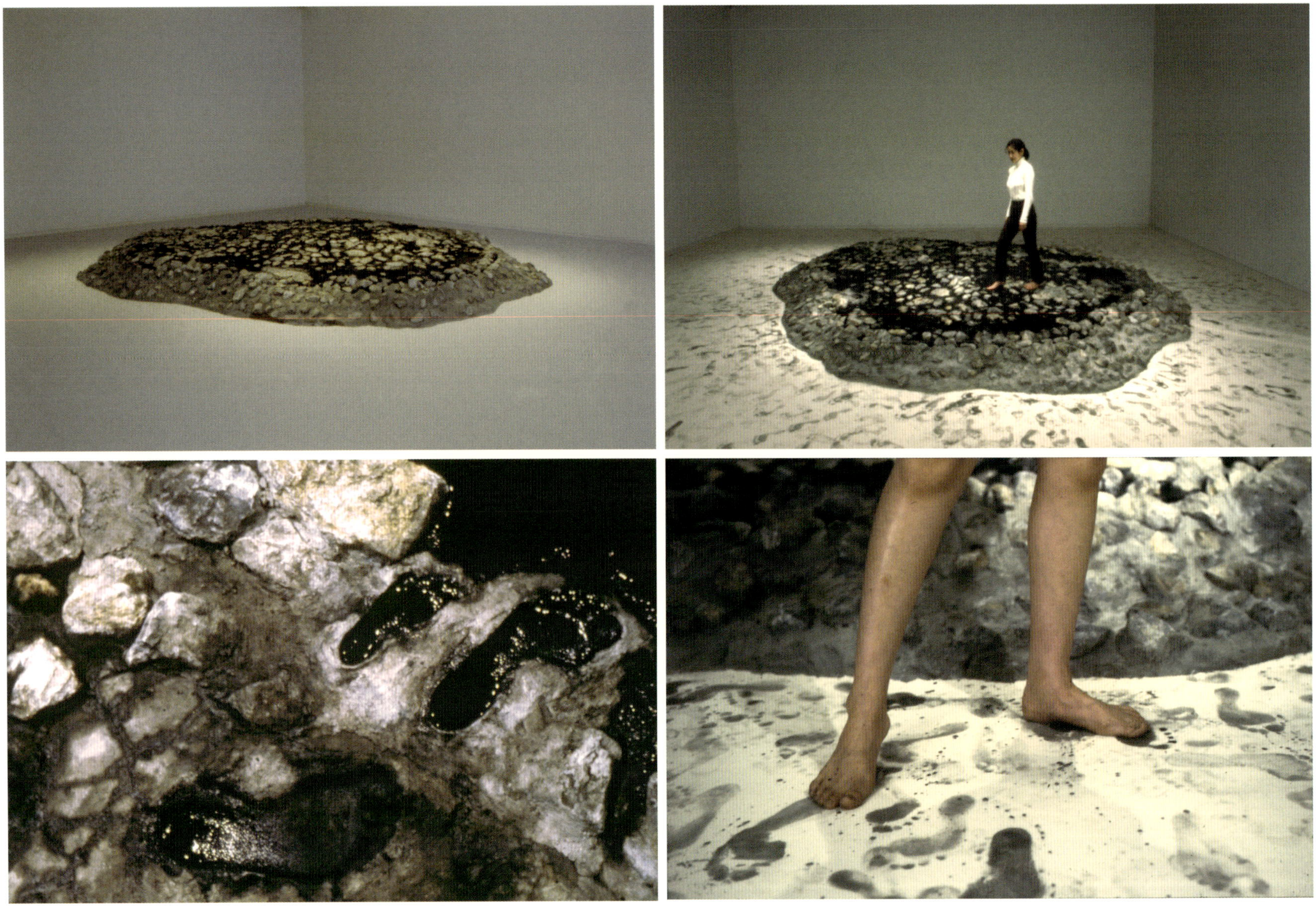

Footprint 足跡

Time, stone, cement, water, sumi-ink, canvas, pump system
76 x 1500 x 1000 cm
1997

At the Galerie Deux, Tokyo, Japan.
Galerie Deux 畫廊，日本東京

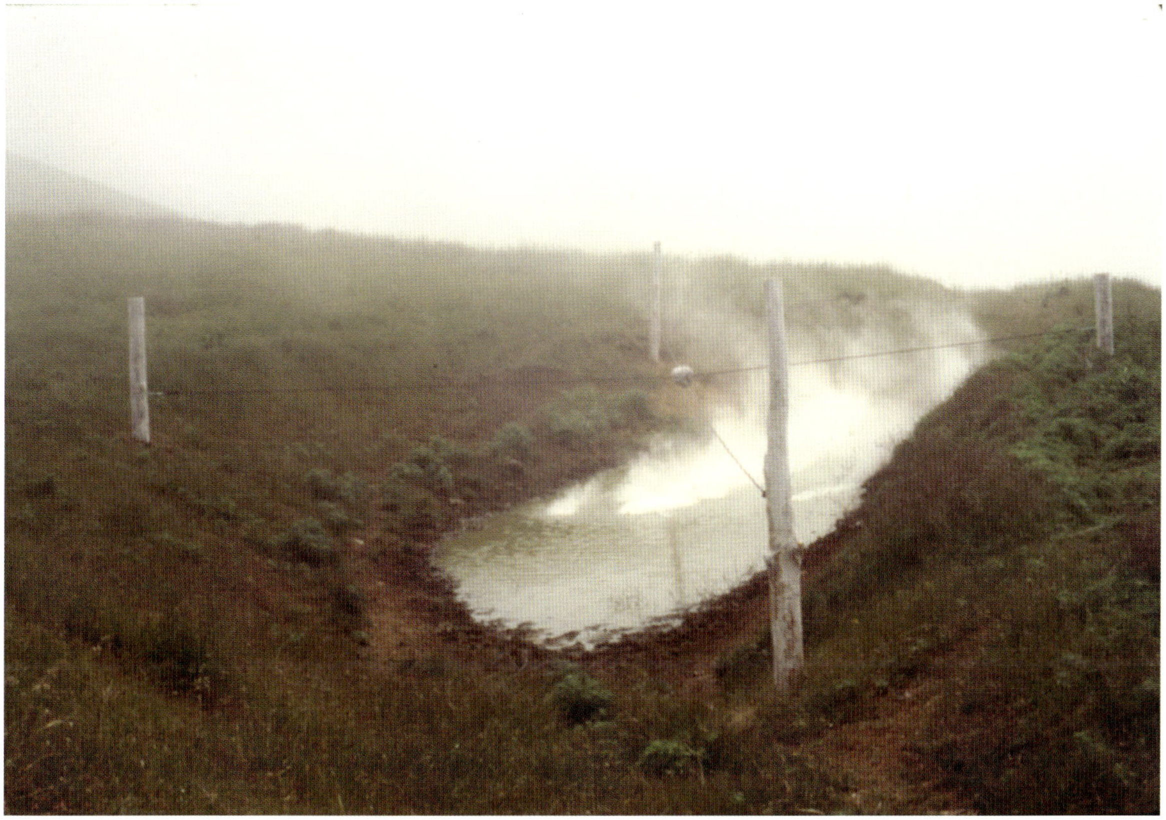

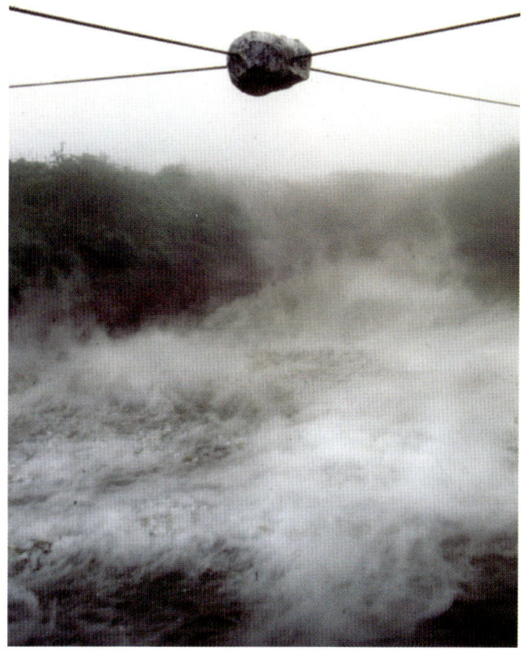

To Fuse 融

Stone, wood, rice paper, water, fog, dry ice, sumi-ink
300 x 5000 x 2700 cm
1994

At the Djerassi Sculpture Park, California, USA.
Djerassi雕塑公園，美國加洲

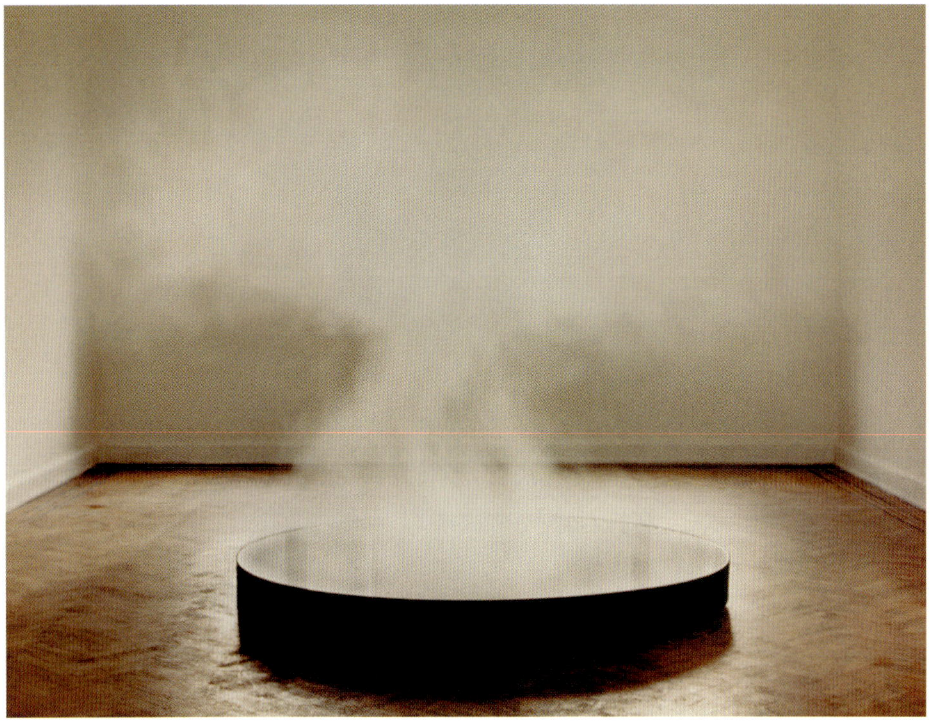

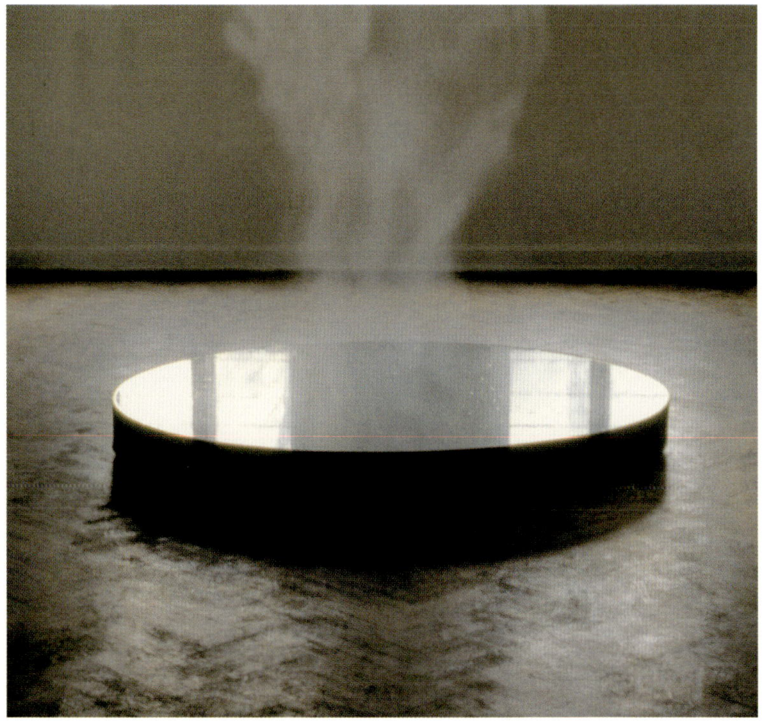

Fog Inside 內在的霧

Steel, water, sumi-ink, heating system
Steel pool: 20 x 200 x 200 cm
1992

At the Artists' Museum, Lodz, Poland.
藝術家美術館，波蘭，羅茲

Indeed, Zhang's statement is far-reaching, stretching beyond pure painting into the function of ink as a metaphor of Chinese culture. Back in 1993, he constructed a circular black metal pool, entitled Fog Inside (1993), in which he placed water and ink. By heating the pool, the temperature of the ink-water rose, becoming steam, and soon dissipated into the atmosphere. While both installations have translated the tradition of ink into contemporary form in different ways, the focus of the works becomes a basis for experimentation and, to some extent, provocation. The metaphorical connection is directly related to Renato Poggiolo's concept of the avant-garde. In his book,"The Theory of the Avant Garde," Poggiolo talks of lingering traces of the past that somehow persist into the present, thus invoking time as a continuum on which art marks the place where true advances are made and eventually assimilated into human consciousness.

張建君的這個說法無疑具有深遠的意義。它超越了單純的繪畫，觸及了墨對於中國文化的隱喻功能。他早在1993年就造了一個黑色的圓形金屬池，名為《內在的霧》（1993年），裡面灌入墨和水。藝術家將池水加熱，使墨汁化為蒸汽，並逐漸消散於空氣之中。《內在的霧》及《墨園》其實各以不同的方式，將墨的傳統轉化成當代形式，而作品的焦點既是試驗的基礎，在一定程度上也成為了得以刺激觀畫者的基礎。這裡頭的隱喻關聯，與雷納托 · 波吉奧利（Renato Poggioli）關於前衛派的觀念直接相關。波吉奧利的著作《前衛藝術的理論》談到，有些歷史的殘跡延續至今，向我們提示了一點：時間是一個連續體，藝術在當中標示了真正的進步發生於何處，並且又於何處最終為人類的意識所吸收。

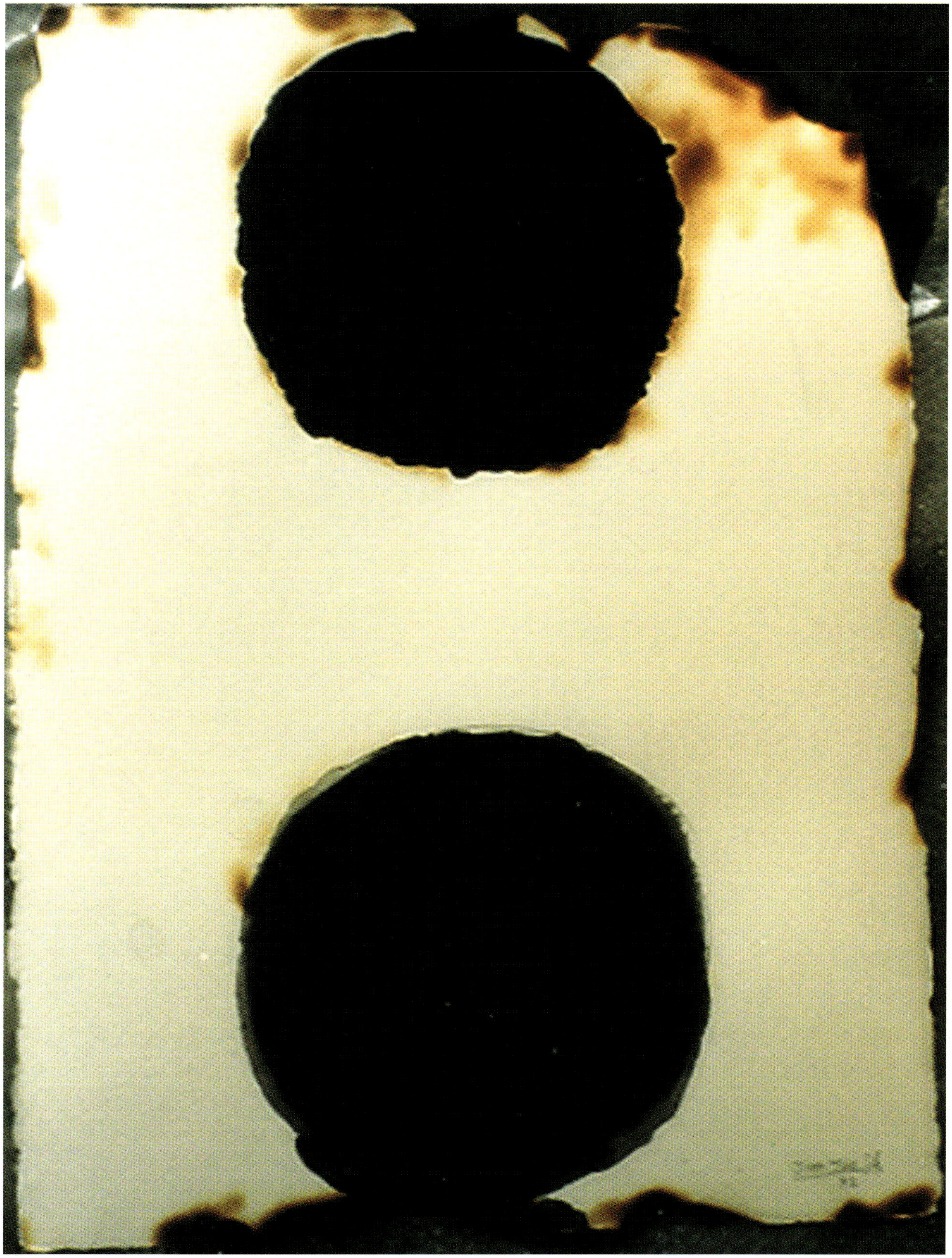

Water & Fire 水・火
Sumi-ink on paper
76 x 56 cm
1992

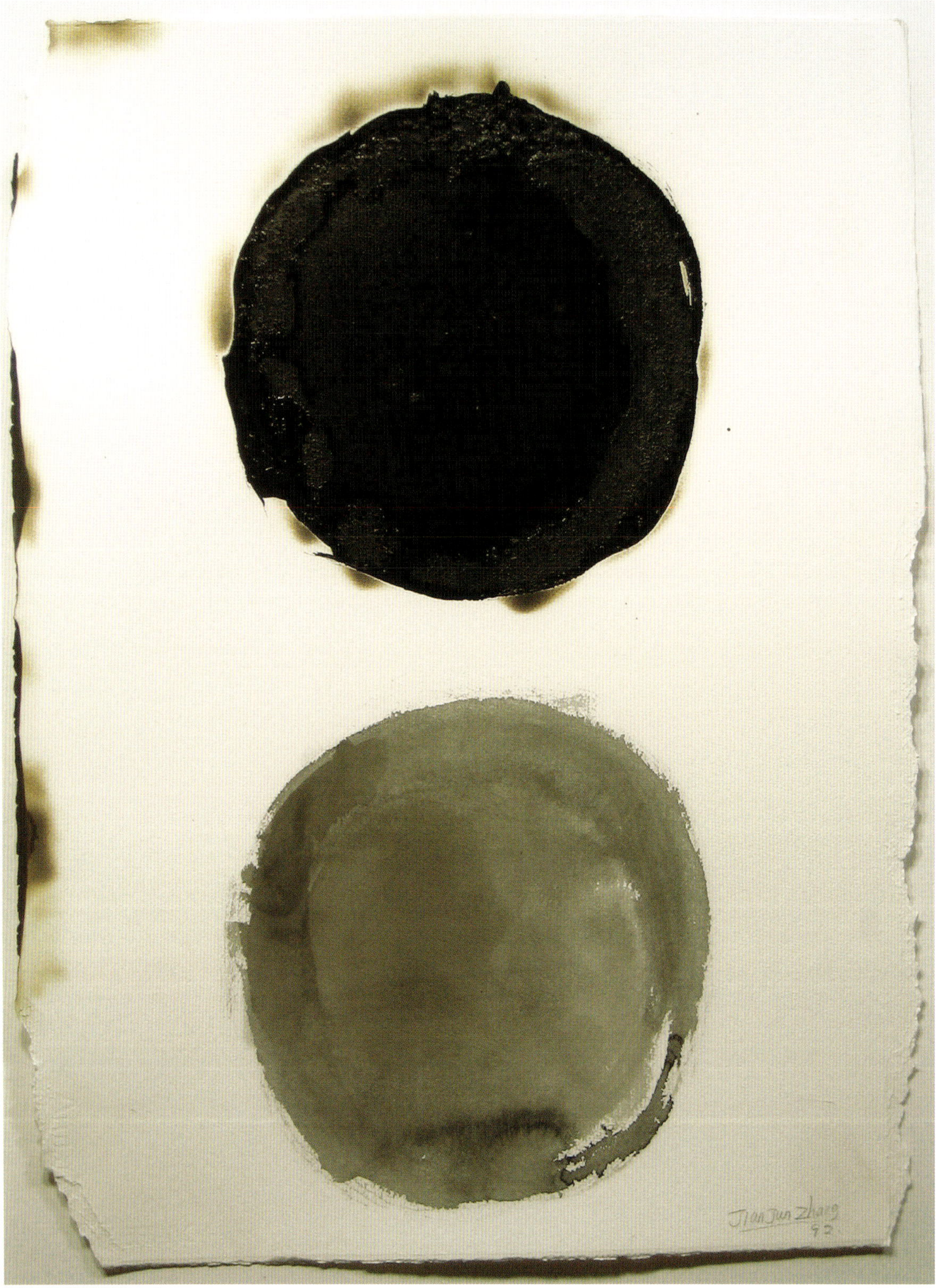

Water & Fire 水・火

Sumi-ink on paper
76 x 56 cm
1992

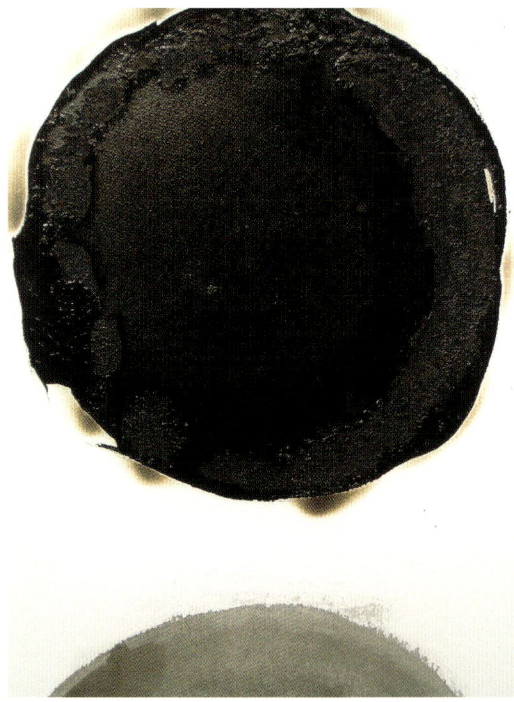

Water & Fire (detail) 水・火（局部）

Sumi-ink on paper
76 x 56 cm
1992

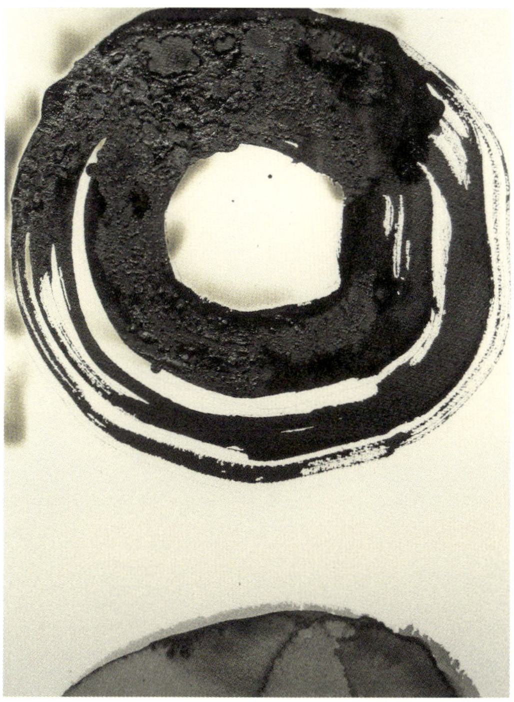

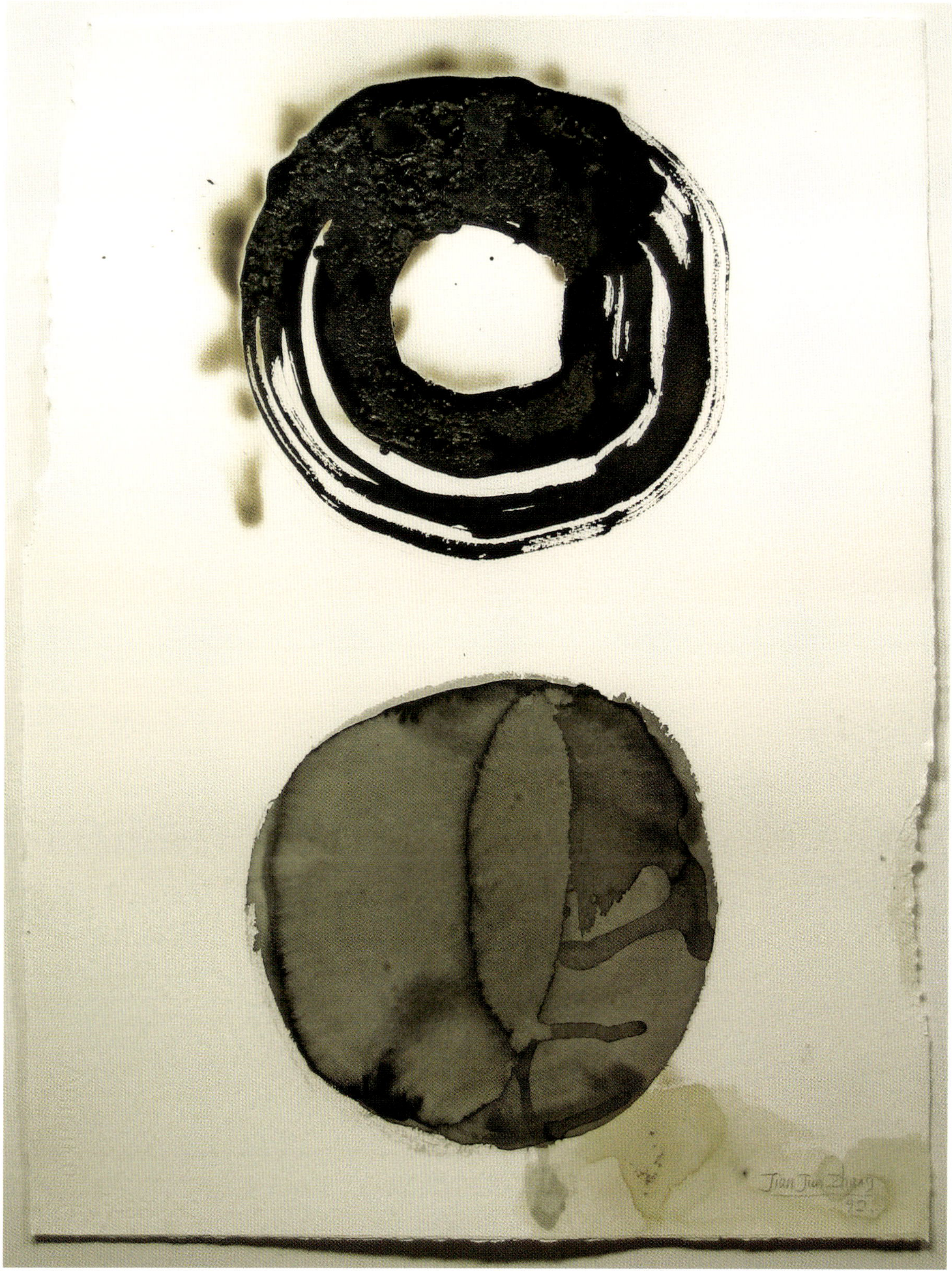

Water & Fire (detail) 水・火（局部）
Sumi-ink on paper
76 x 56 cm
1992

Water & Fire 水・火
Sumi-ink on paper
76 x 56 cm
1992

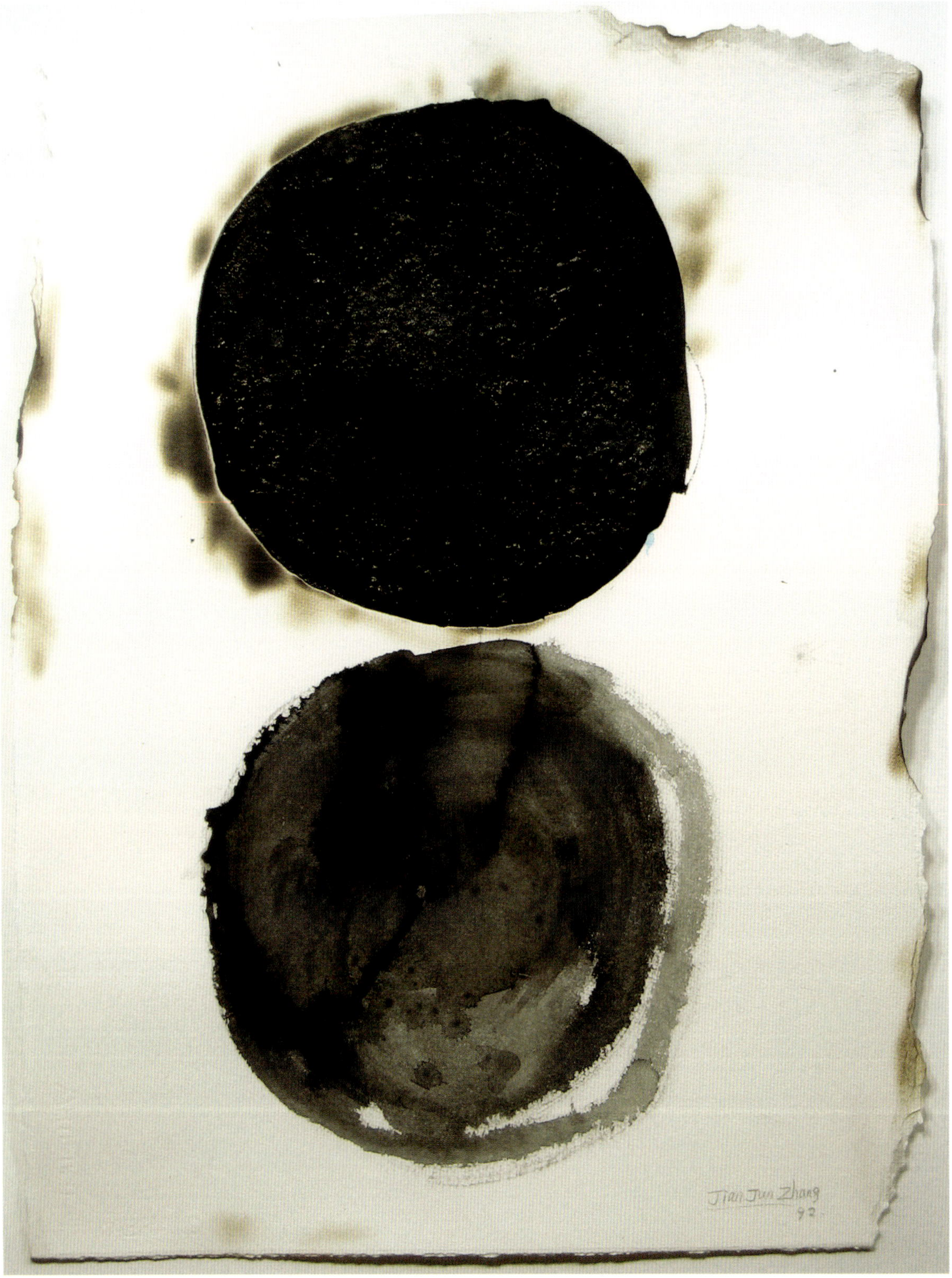

Water & Fire 水・火
Sumi-ink on paper
76 x 56 cm
1992

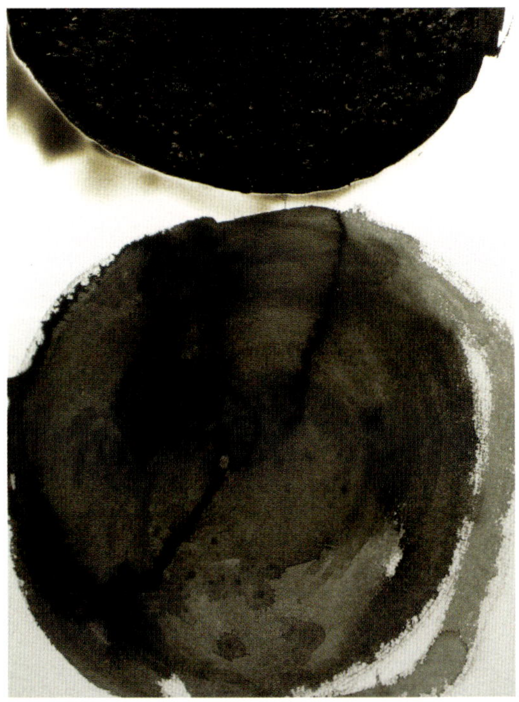

Water & Fire (detail) 水・火（局部）
Sumi-ink on paper
76 x 56 cm
1992

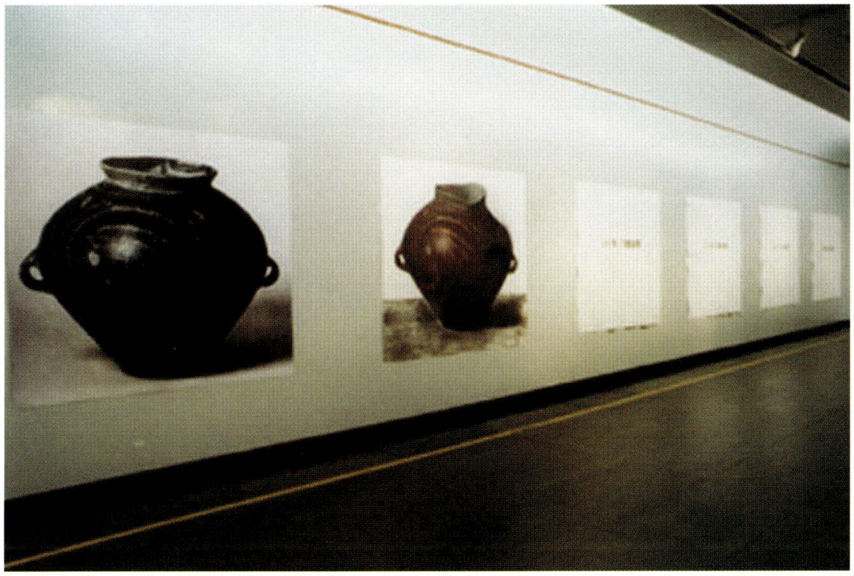

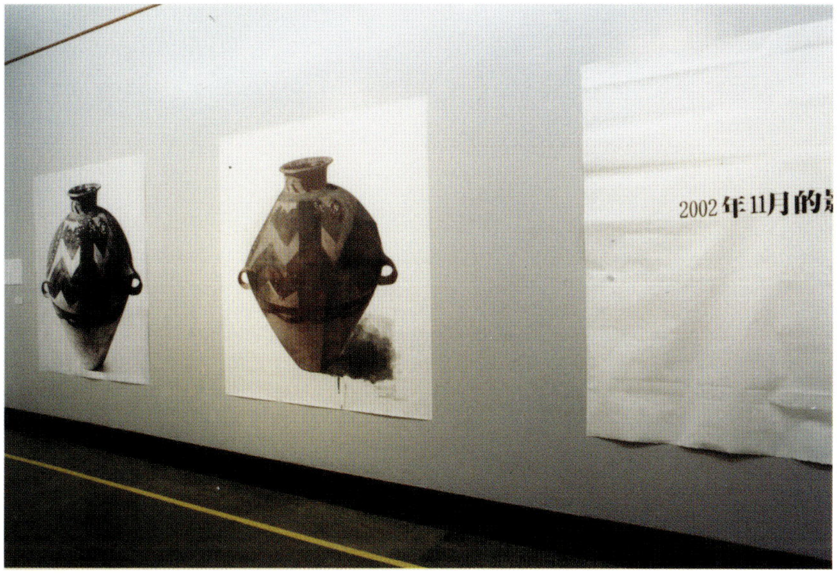

Vestiges of a Process: China Project 過程的瞬間：中國篇 2002-2102

Oil paint, graphite, photo emulsion on rice paper, time
200 x 180 cm (each panel)
2002 - 2102

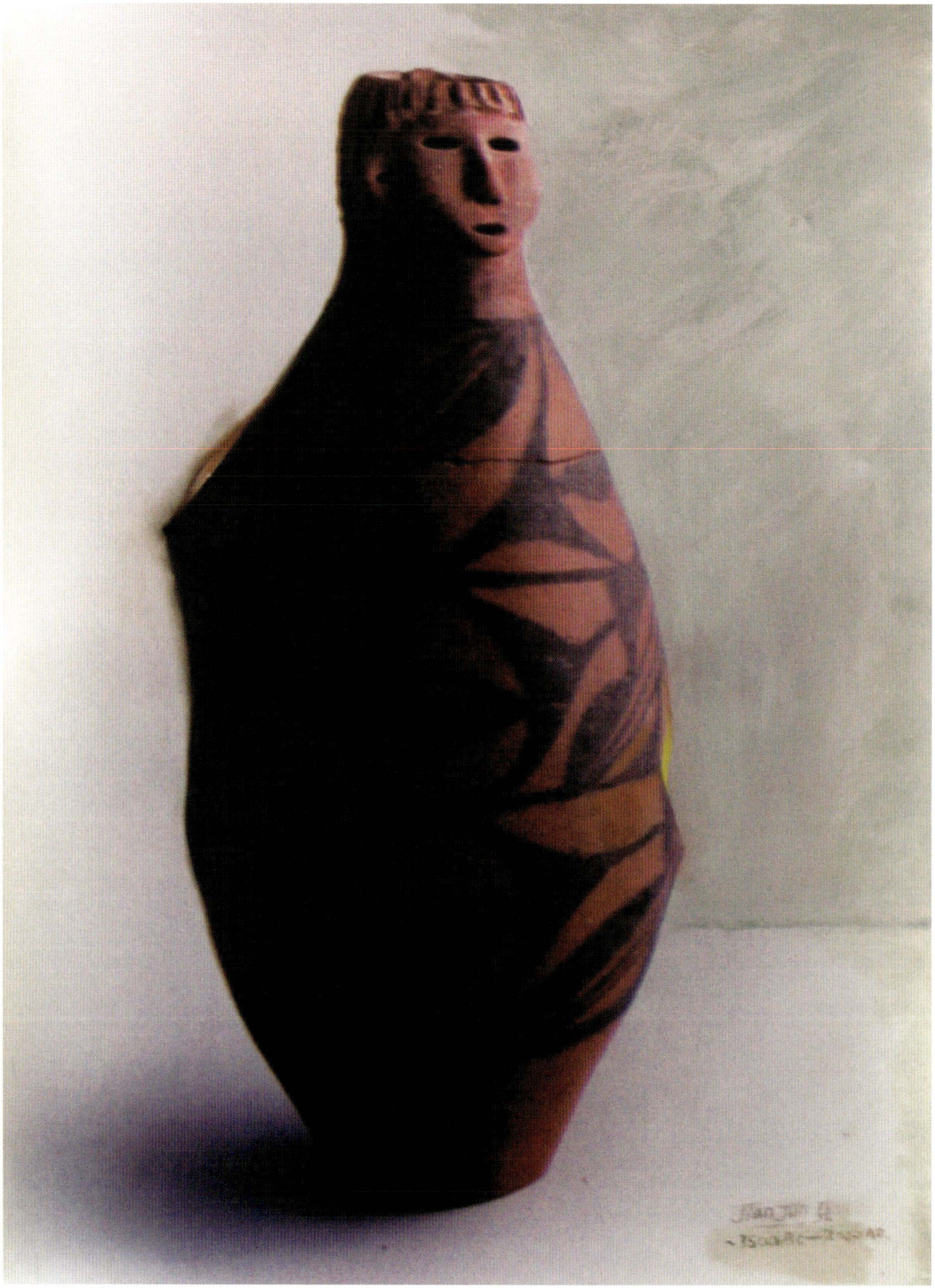

China Chapter
“中國篇”系列
Oil paint on photo
102 x 76 cm
2000

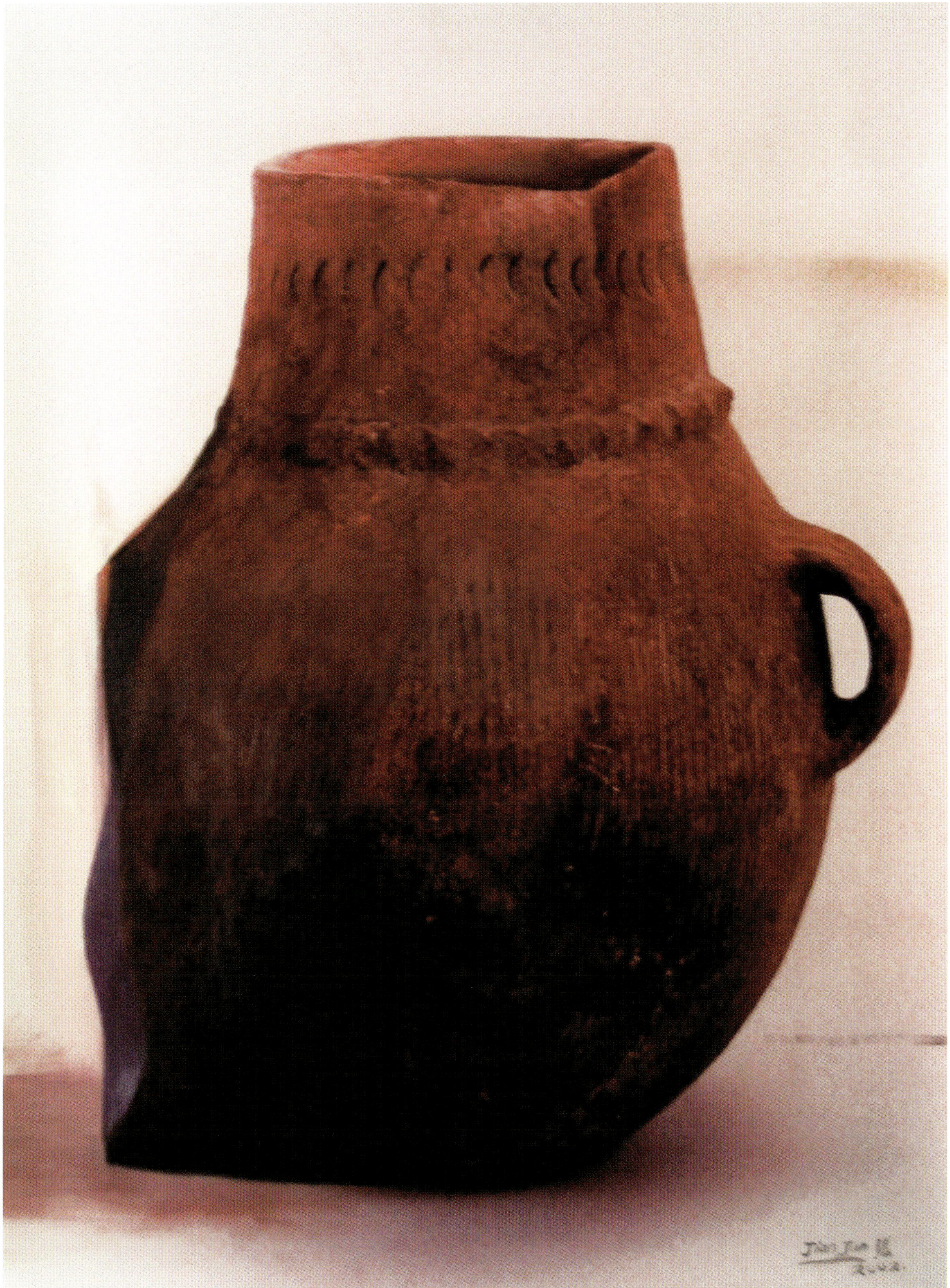

China Chapter #25
中國篇 #25
Oil paint on photo
102 x 76 cm
2002

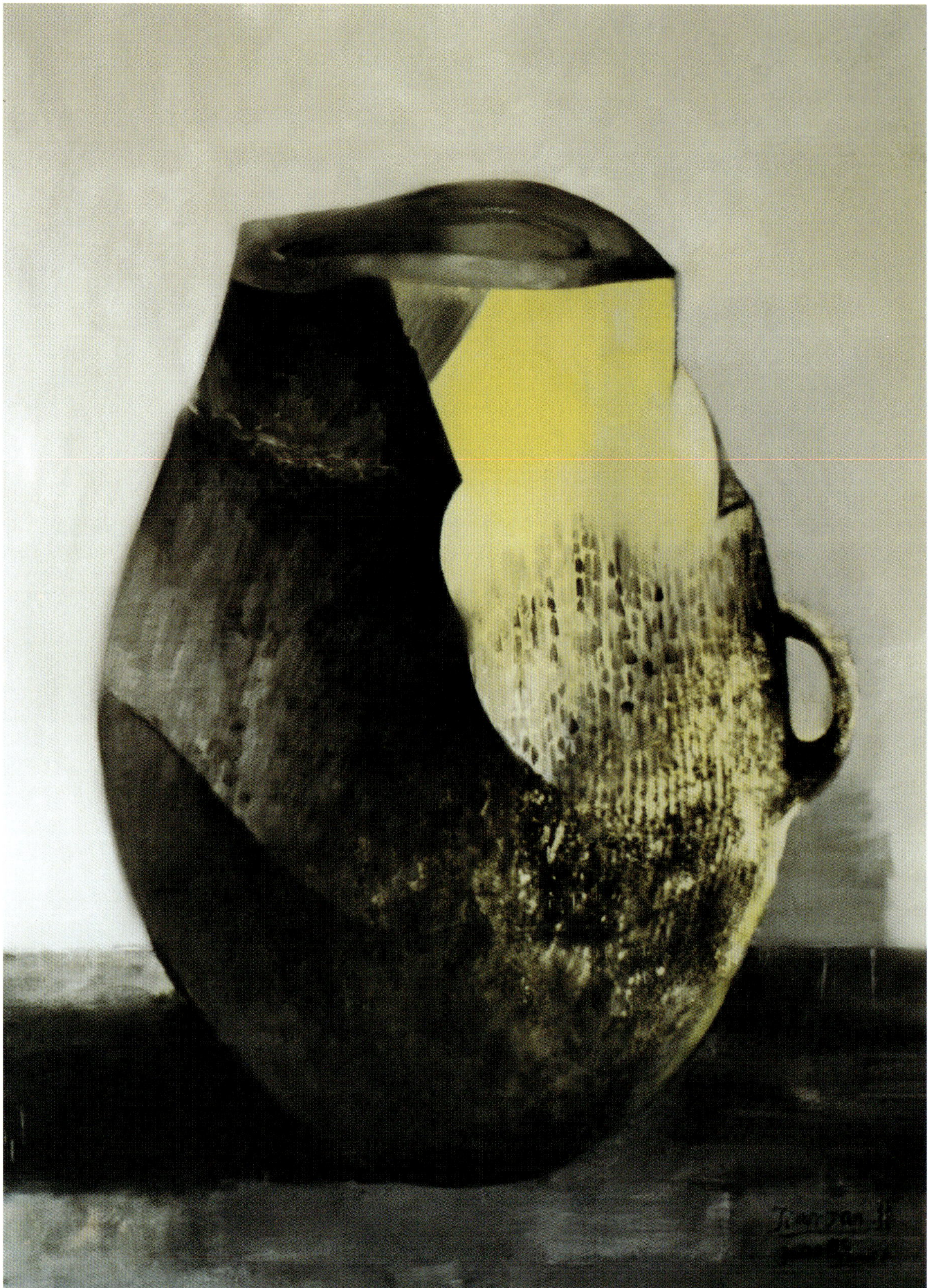

China Chapter #53 中國篇 #53

Photo emulsion and oil paint on canvas
158 x 117 cm
~3500 BC - 2001 AD

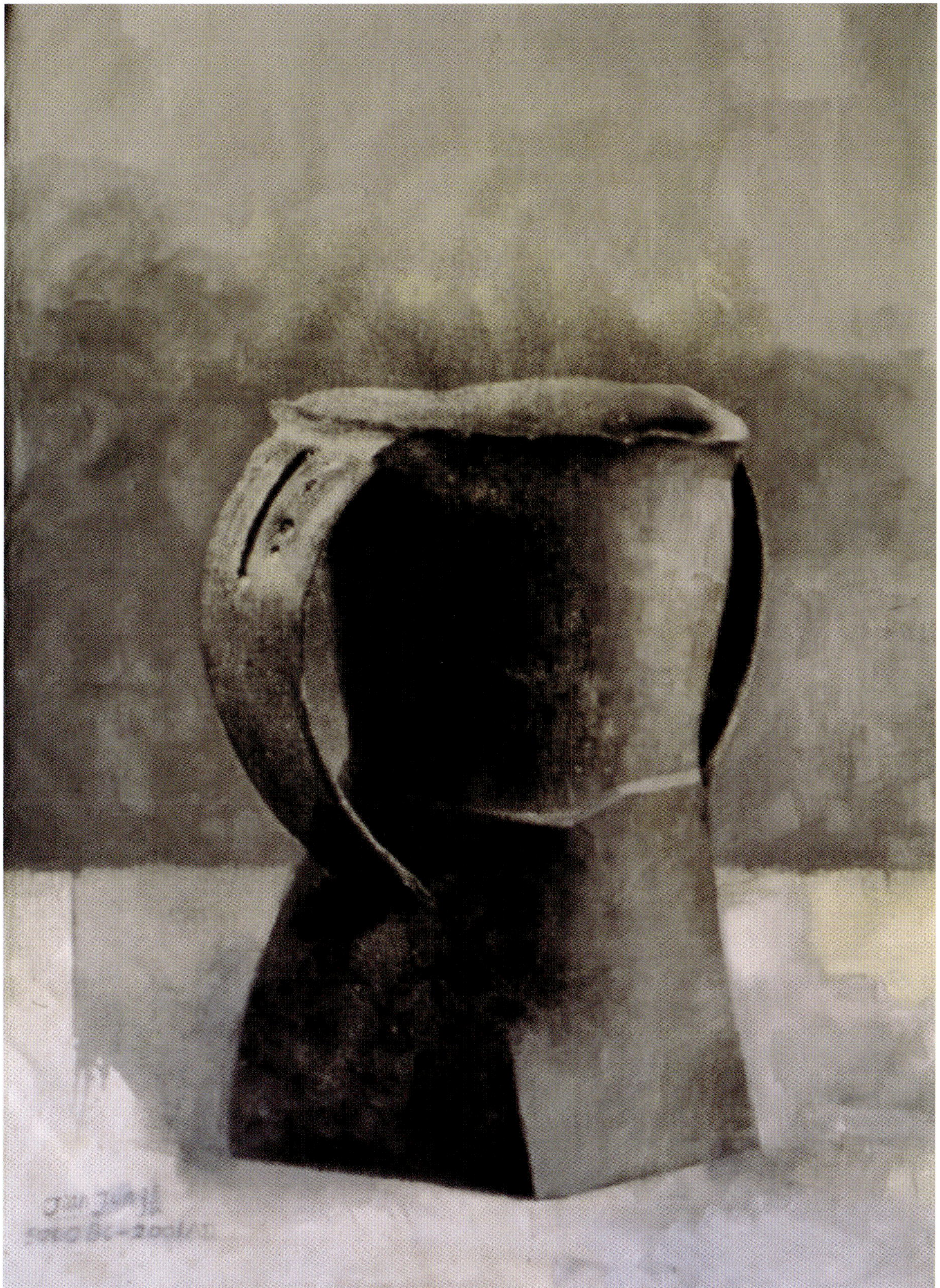

China Chapter #62 中國篇 #62

Photo emulsion and oil paint on canvas
158 x 117 cm
~3500 BC - 2001 AD

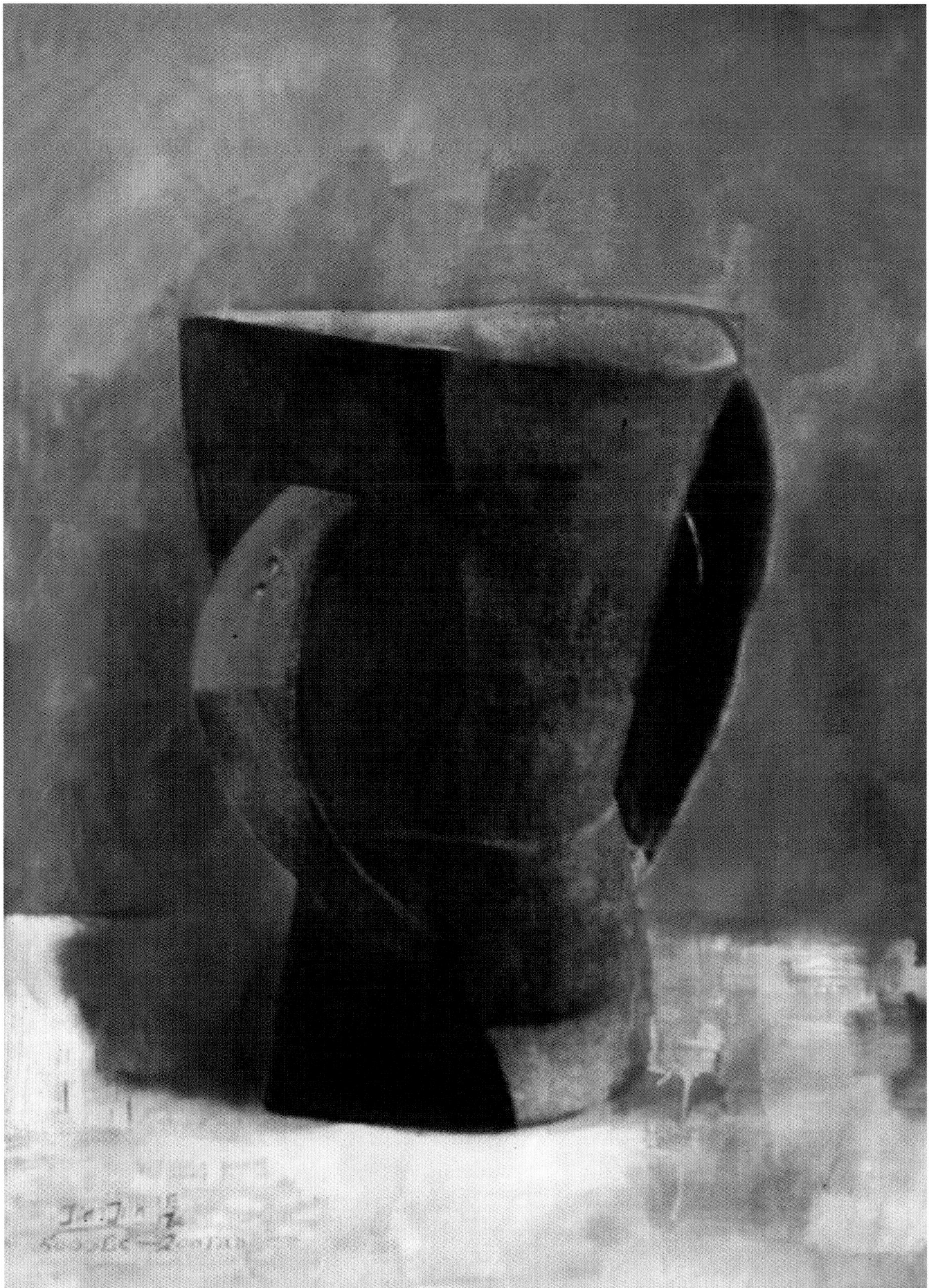

China Chapter #63 中國篇 #63

Photo emulsion and oil paint on canvas
158 x 117 cm
~3500 BC - 2001 AD

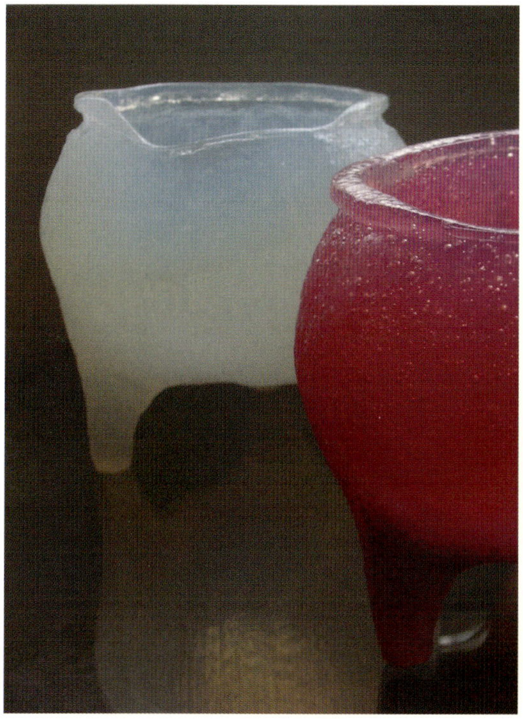
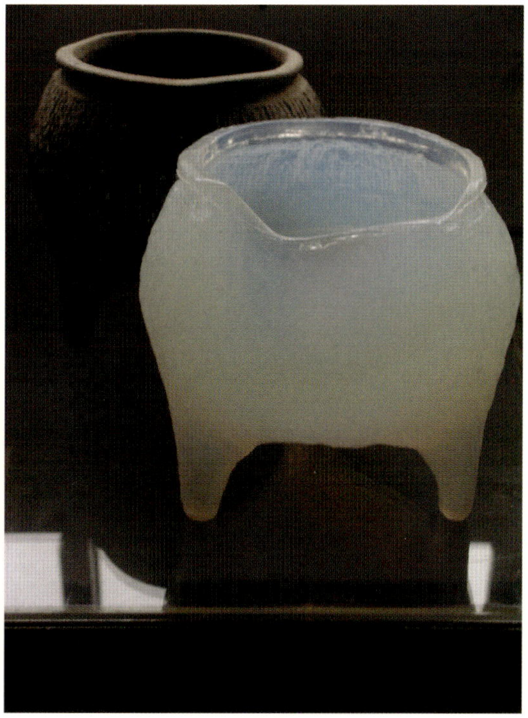
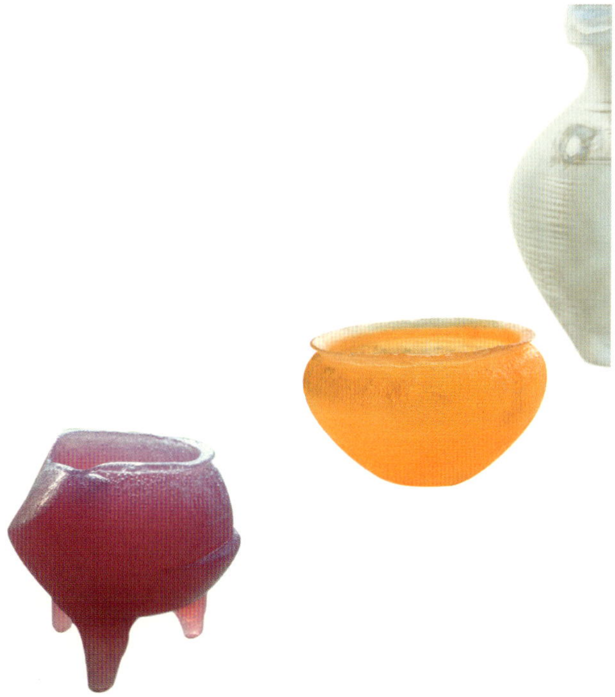

China Chapter: New Antique Vase 中國篇：新古董

Silicone rubber
14 x 15.5 x 16.5 cm
2006 - 2007

For Poggioli, the avant-garde is divided between historical phenomena and on-going experimentation. This model could be no more apparent than in Zhang's recent scholar's rocks and antique vessels, both cast in silicone rubber and mixed with bright phosphorescent dry pigments. Again, the artist's interest in materials comes to the foreground of attention. To place these silicone rubber objects in a traditional setting suggests an updating of historical phenomena. Rather than existing separately from nature, they become natural. Their formal appearance moves into a present-day context, thus attributing them with special meaning. As signs and symbols of the past, they still exist but not as time-worn objects. Rather they have become prototypes that may be crafted or manufactured in terms of the multiple. Their special meaning is no longer about fetishizing the object into something purloined from the distant past, but about deciphering a concept of form intrinsic to these objects that is conceptually transmitted from the past to the present. The new materials – silicone rubber and phosphorescent color – extend their meaning apart from mundane utility and into the language of art. One can speak about a system of objectification in these rocks and vessels that places these works in a trajectory beginning with Duchamp and Koons, and finally updated in recent works by such artists as Zhan Wang and Zhang Jian-Jun.

對波吉奧利而言，前衛表現分為歷史現象和進行中的實驗兩類。這一模式最明顯的表現，莫過於張建君近期創作中所運用的觀賞石和古器皿。兩者都以硅膠鑄成，摻合色彩鮮艷的干磷光顏料。在這裡，張建君對材質的濃厚興趣又再度引人注目。他把硅膠物件安置在傳統場景中，顯示了對歷史現象的一種更新。這些物件不再是脫離大自然的，而是已自然化了。它們的形態因為轉移到現代語境中的關系，獲得了特殊的意義。它們仍作為過往的符號和象征而存在，但已不再是經過時間腐朽的物件。相反的，它們變成了能夠被大量塑造或制造的原型。其特殊意義，不復在於把物體力捧為偷取自遠古時代的什麼寶物，而是在於對物件內在形式概念的破譯，也就是對從過去流傳到現在的概念的破譯。硅膠和磷光色料等新材質的意義，遂從普通日常功能的領域延伸出去，進入了藝術語言。我們可以說，這些石頭和器皿上面有一套物化體系。它把張建君的這類作品納入了一條特定的發展軌跡；這條軌跡始於杜尚與昆斯，一直到展望與張建君等藝術家的近作上，才終於獲得了更新。

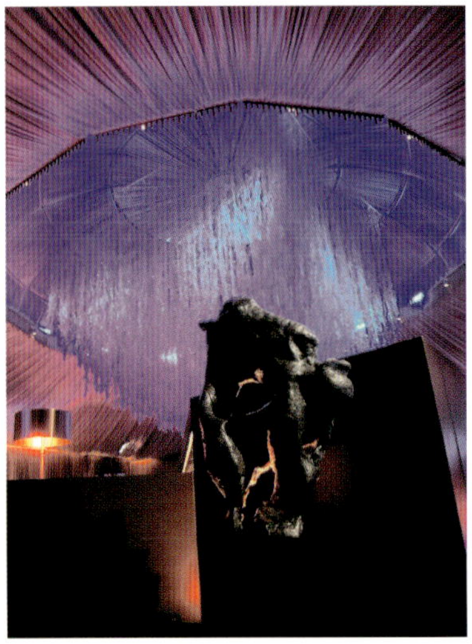

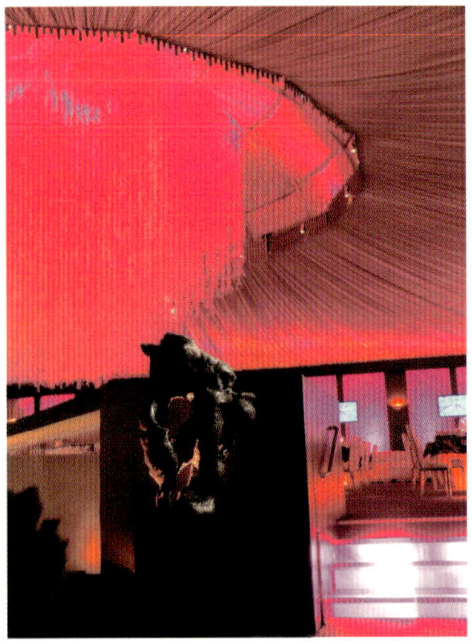

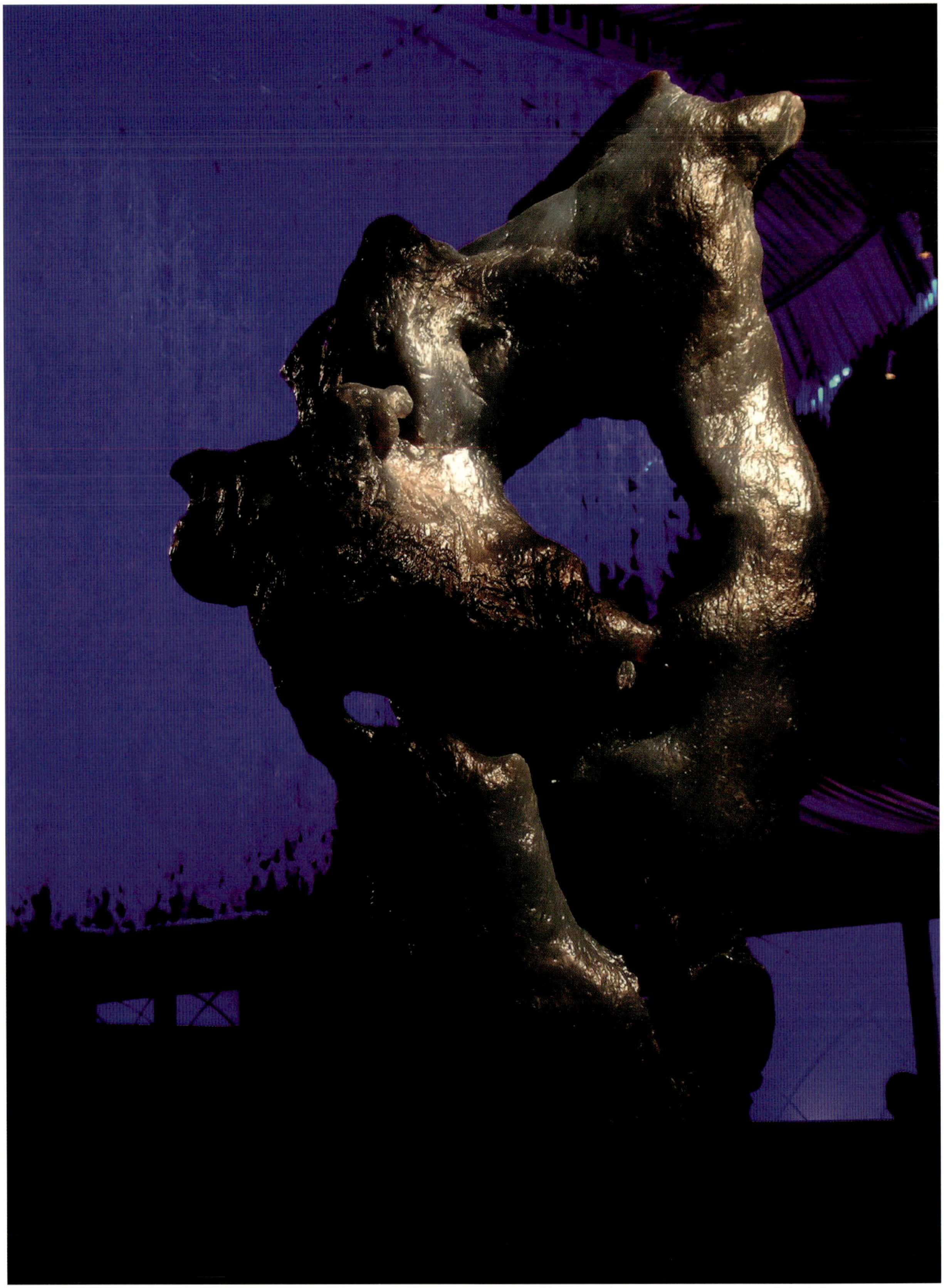

Mirage Garden #5 幻園 #5

Silicone rubber
125 x 84 x 65 cm
2007

At the 2007 Golden Globe Party

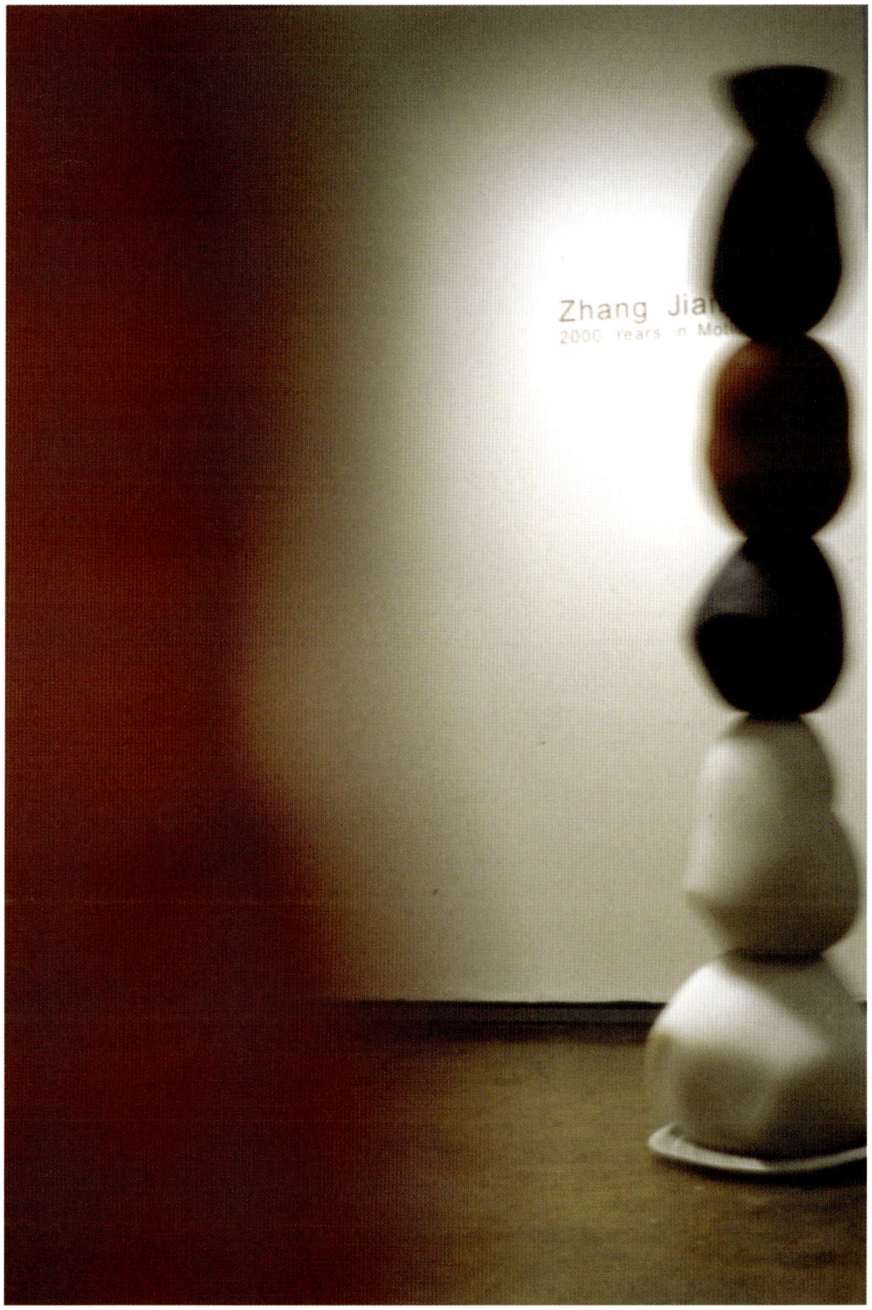

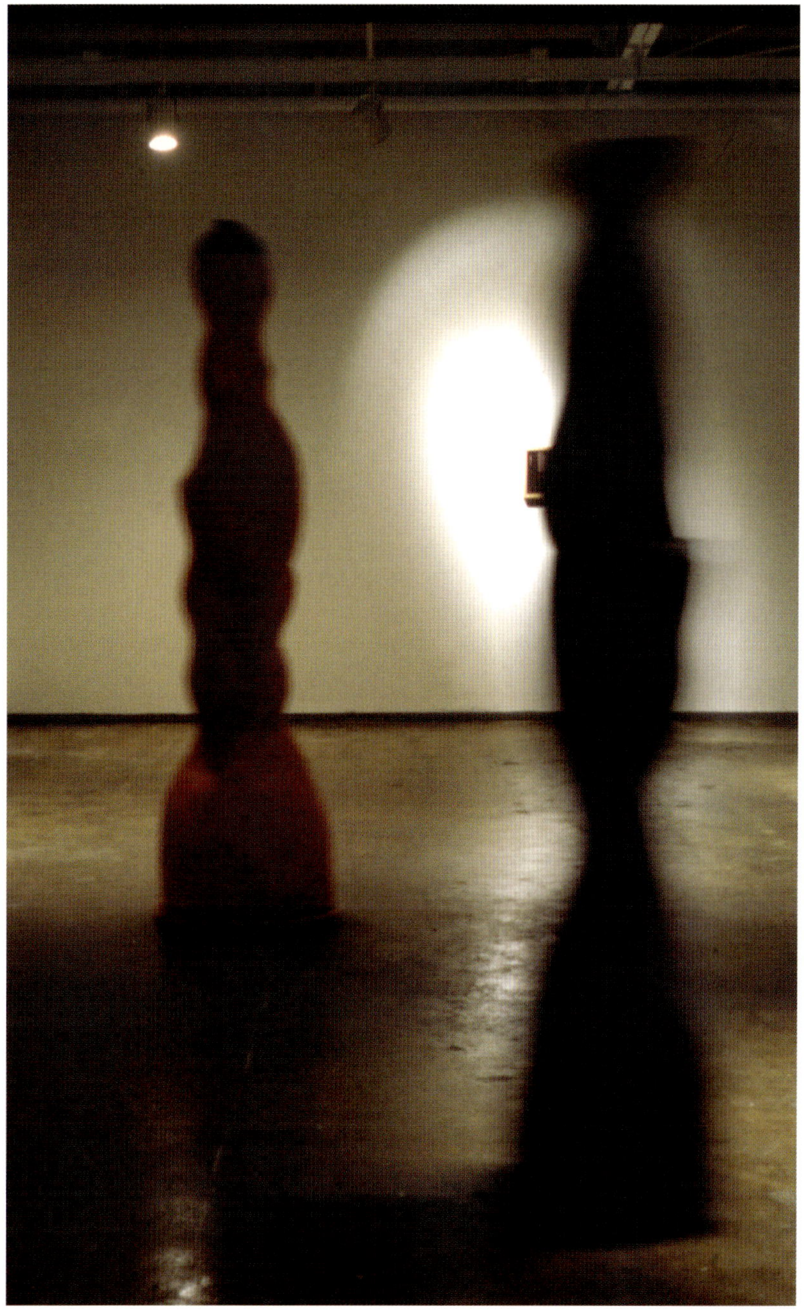

2000 Years in Motion 行進中的2000年

Antique vessel, silicone rubber, machine
~200 BC - 2003 AD

At DiverseWorks, Houston, Texas, USA.
Diverse當代藝術中心，美國

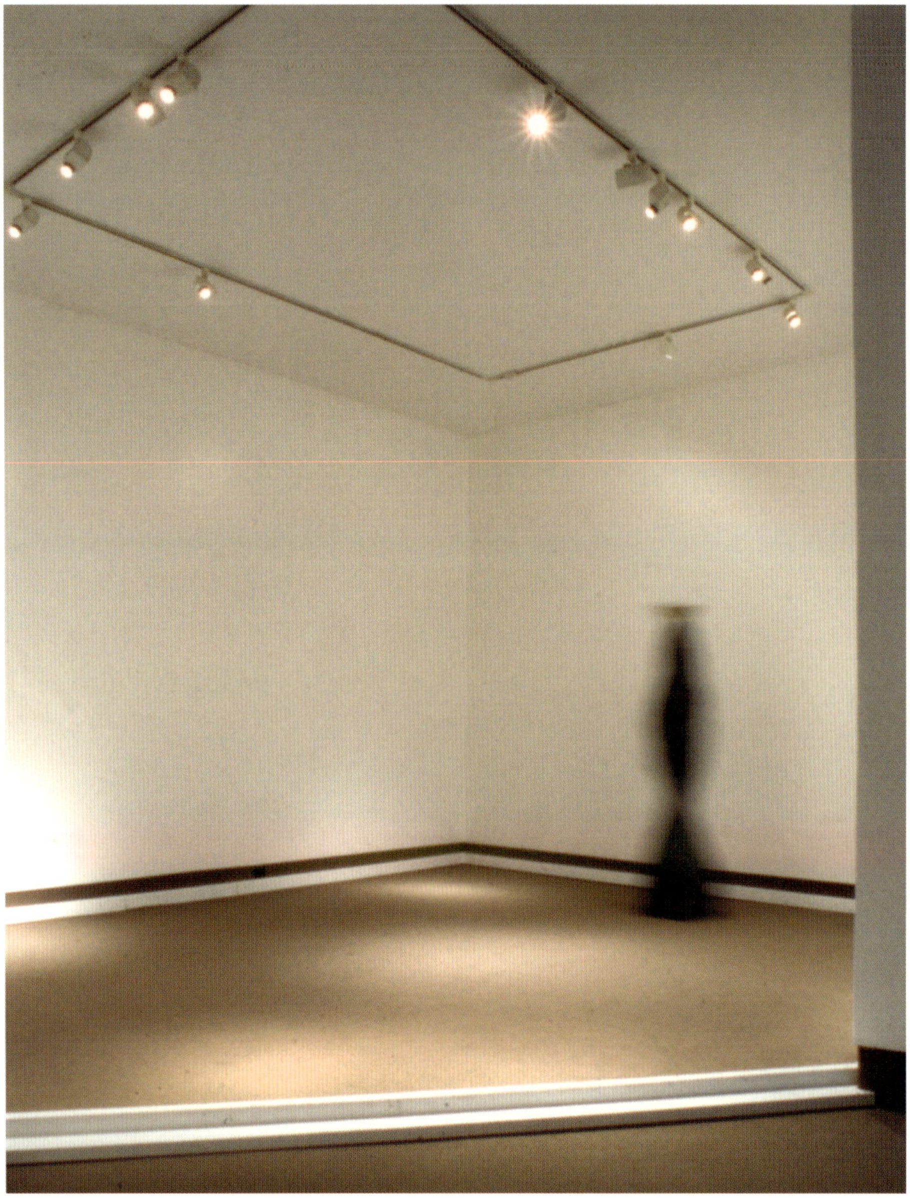

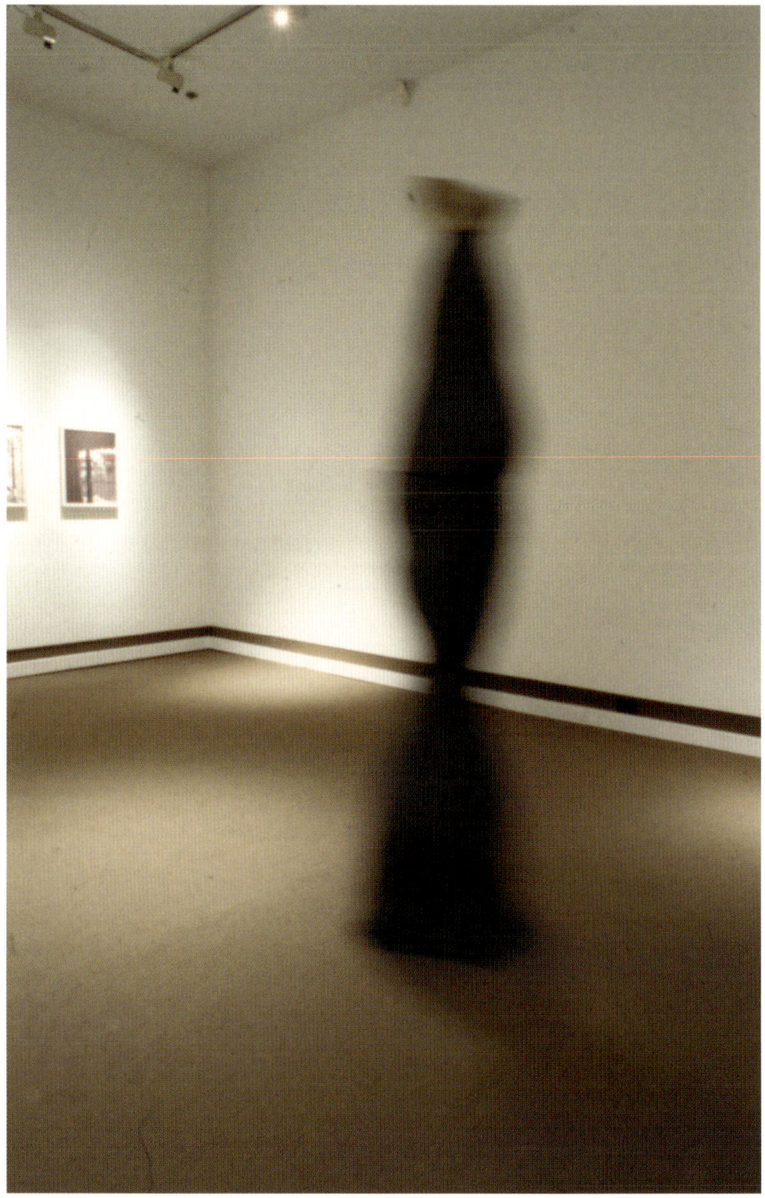

2000 Years in Motion 行進中的2000年

Antique vessel, silicone rubber, machine
~200 BC - 2003 AD

At the New York University Gallery, New York, USA
紐約大學畫廊，美國

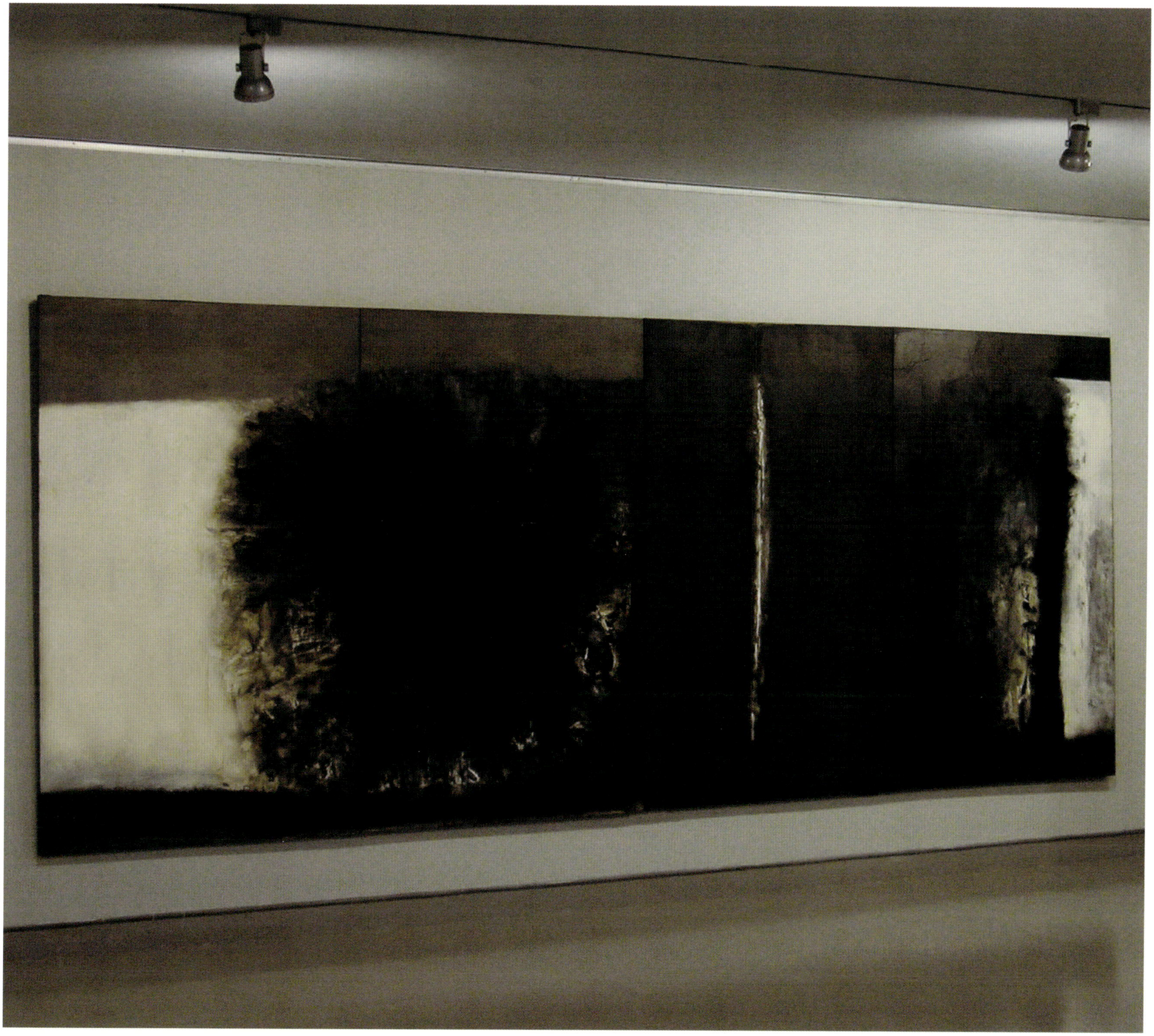

Existence #115 "有" #115

Oil paint on canvas
200 x 500 cm
1985 - 1986

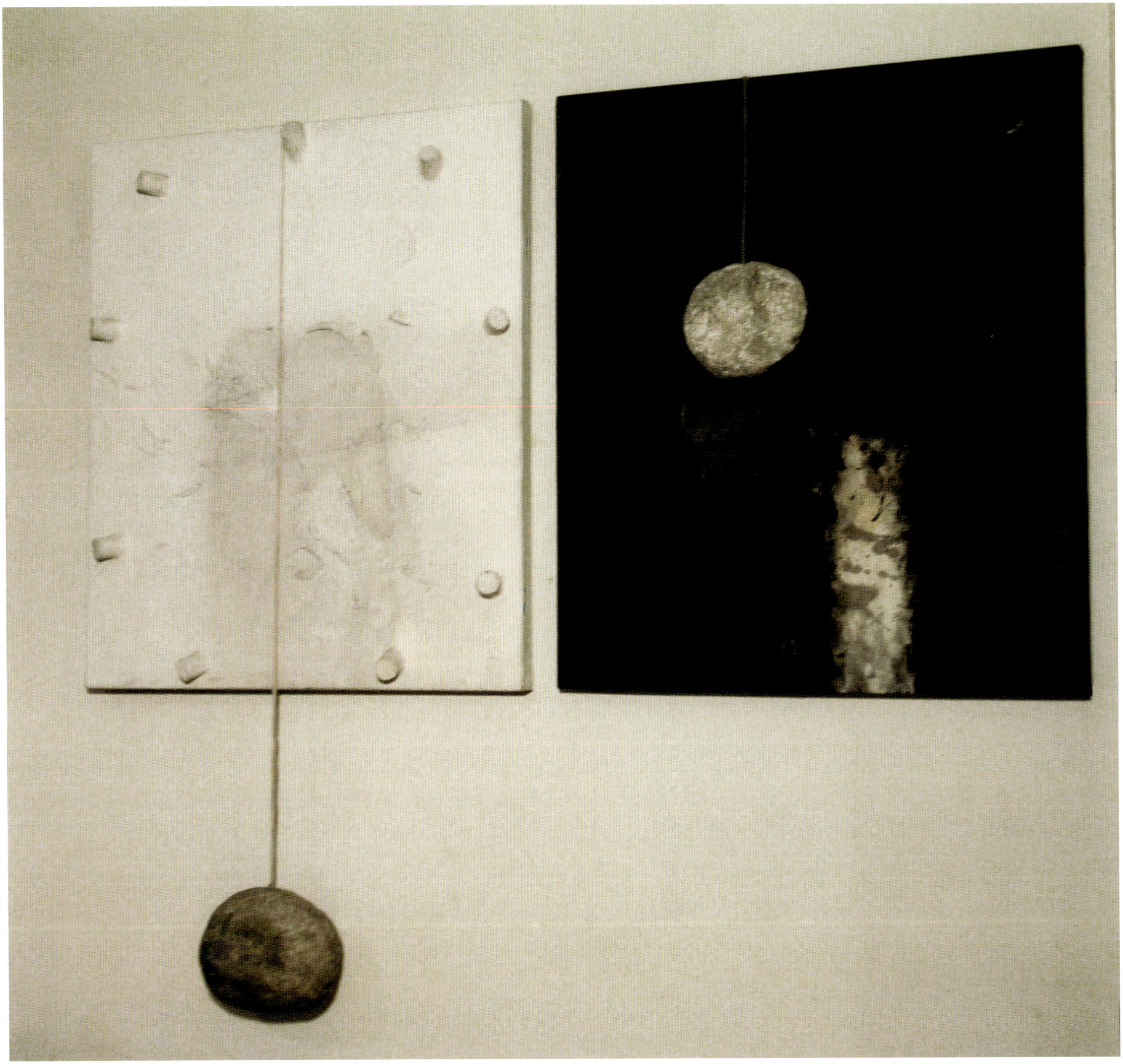

Existence Series “有”系列

Oil paint, acrylic, rice paper, wood on linen with stone, papier mache
86.5 x 76 cm
1987

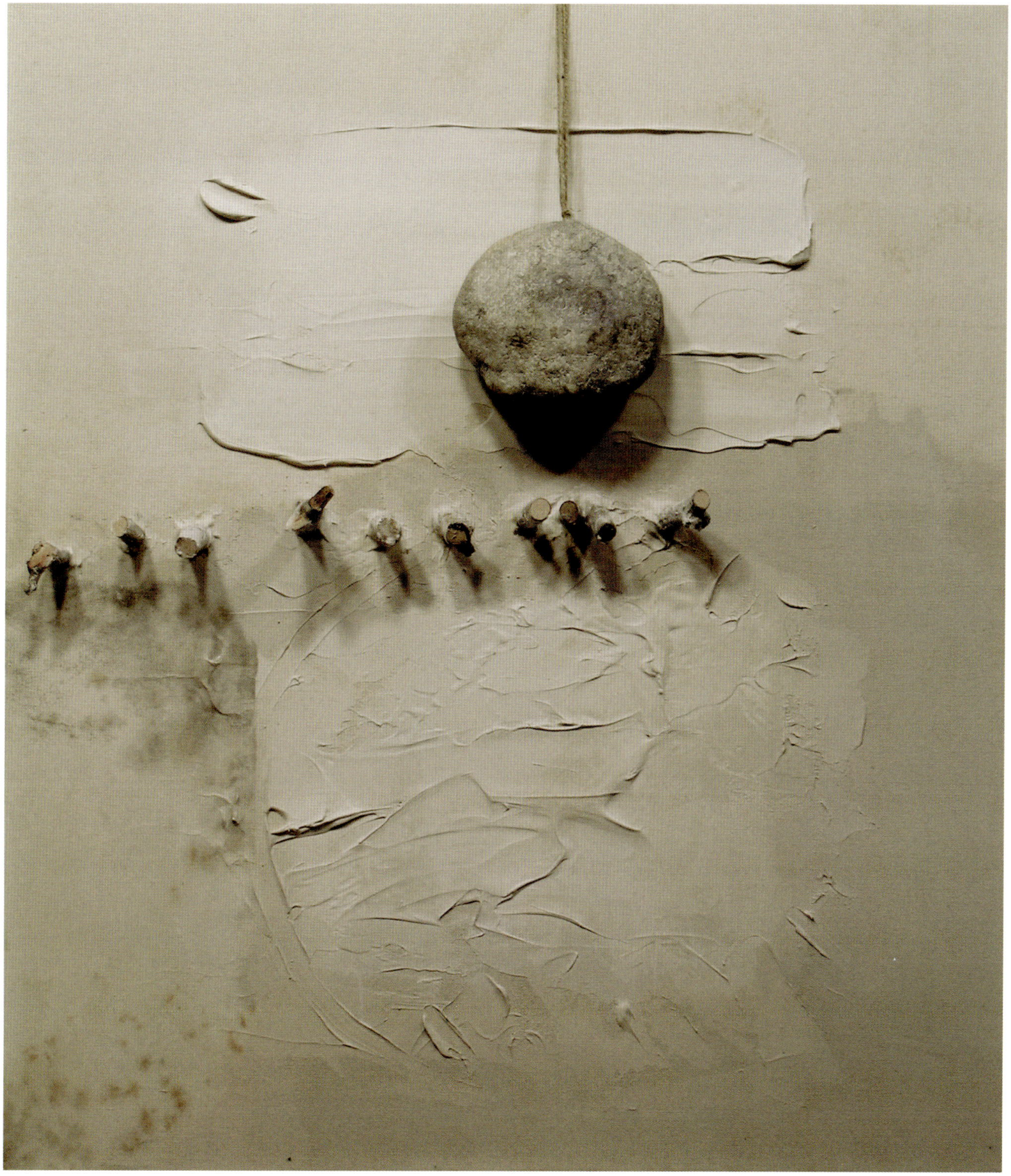

Existence Series “有”系列

Acrylic, rice paper, wood on linen with stone, papier mache
86.5 x 76cm
1988

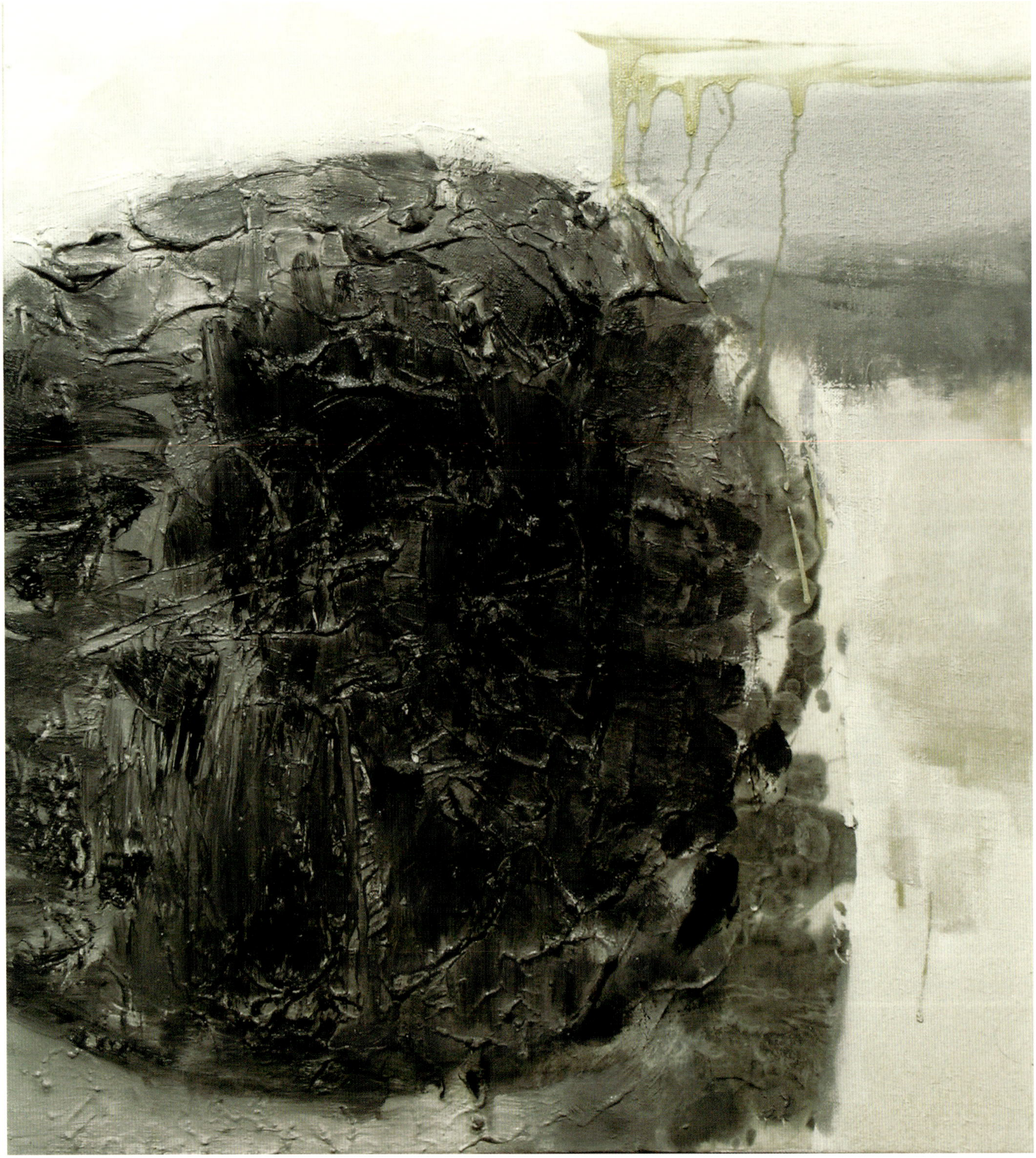

Existence Series “有” 系列
Oil paint, rice paper, sumi-ink on canvas
86.5 x 76 cm
1988

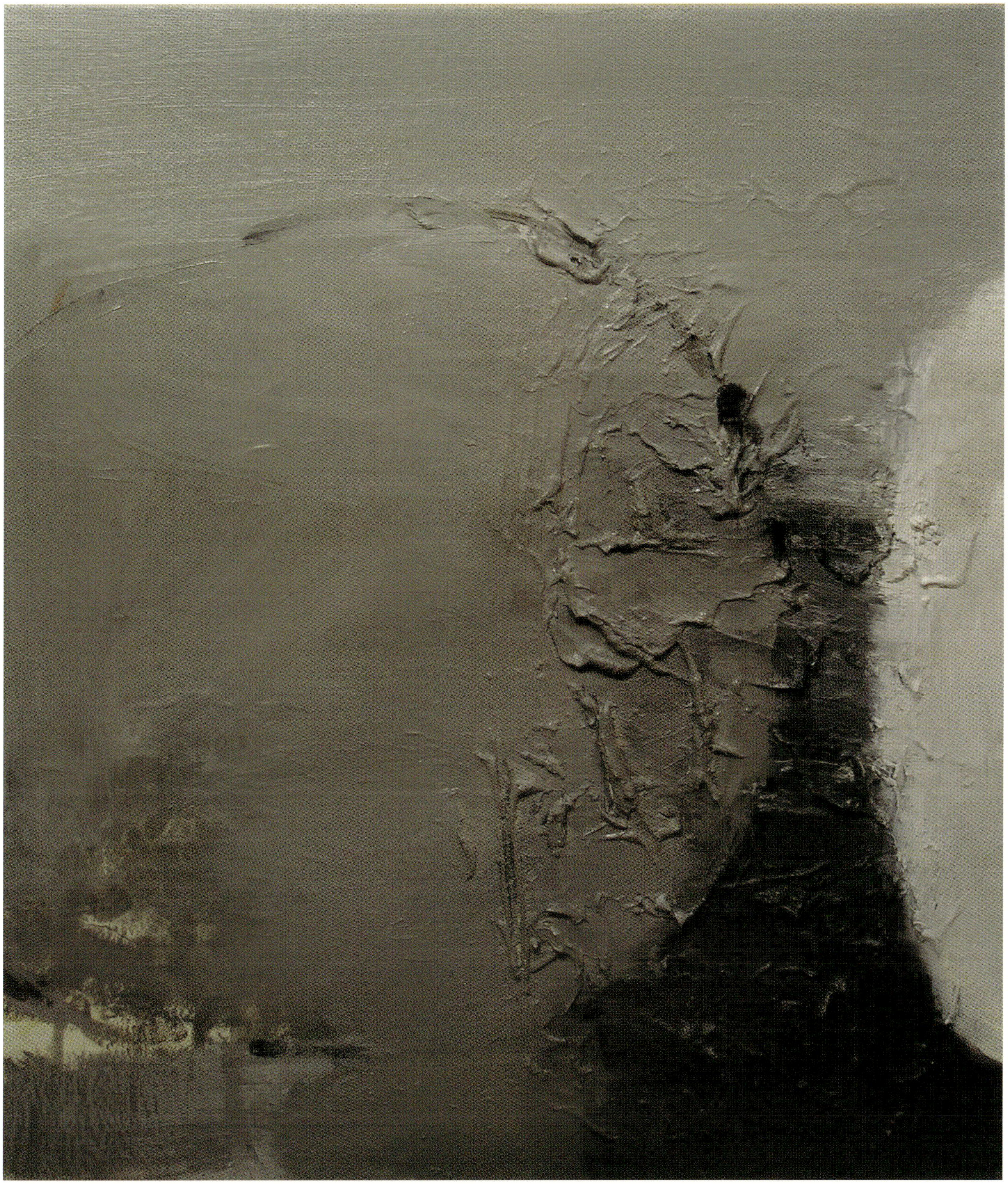

Existence Series “有”系列

Oil paint, rice paper, sumi-ink on canvas
86.5 x 76 cm
1988

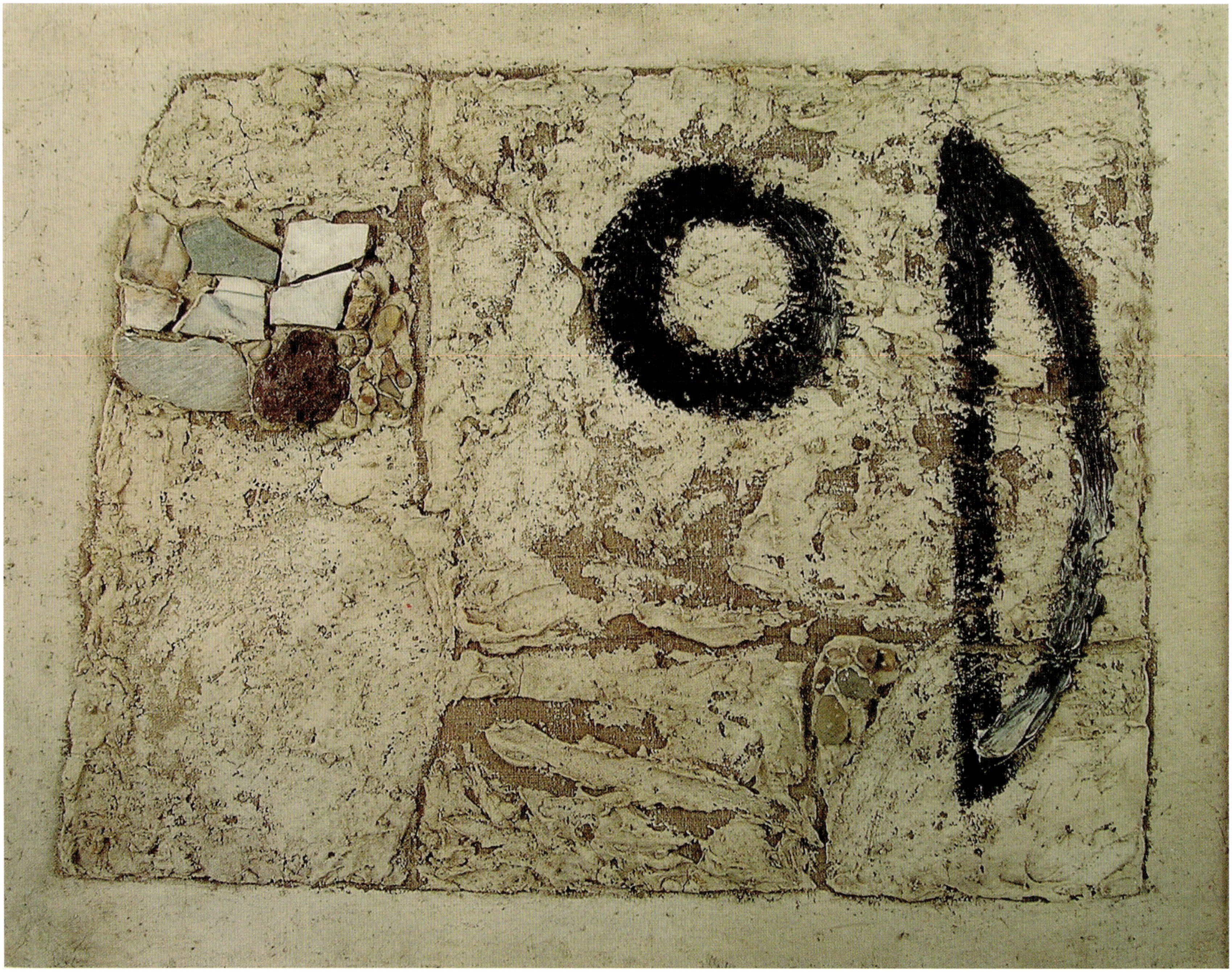

Eternal Dialog 永恆的對話

Oil paint, sand, stone on linen
67 x 92 cm
1982

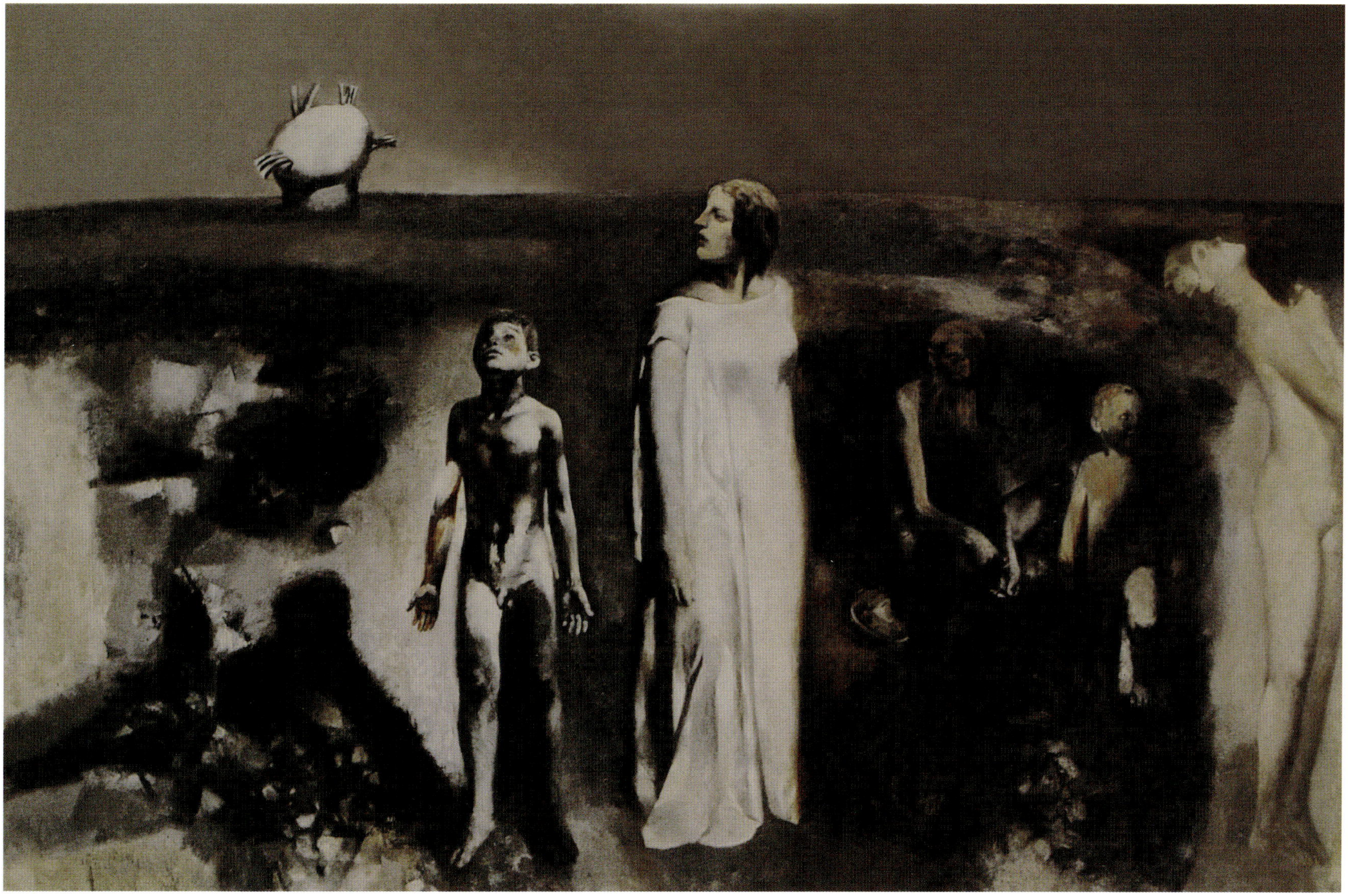

Human Beings with Their Clock #1 人類與他們的鐘

Oil paint on linen
220 x 340 cm
1986

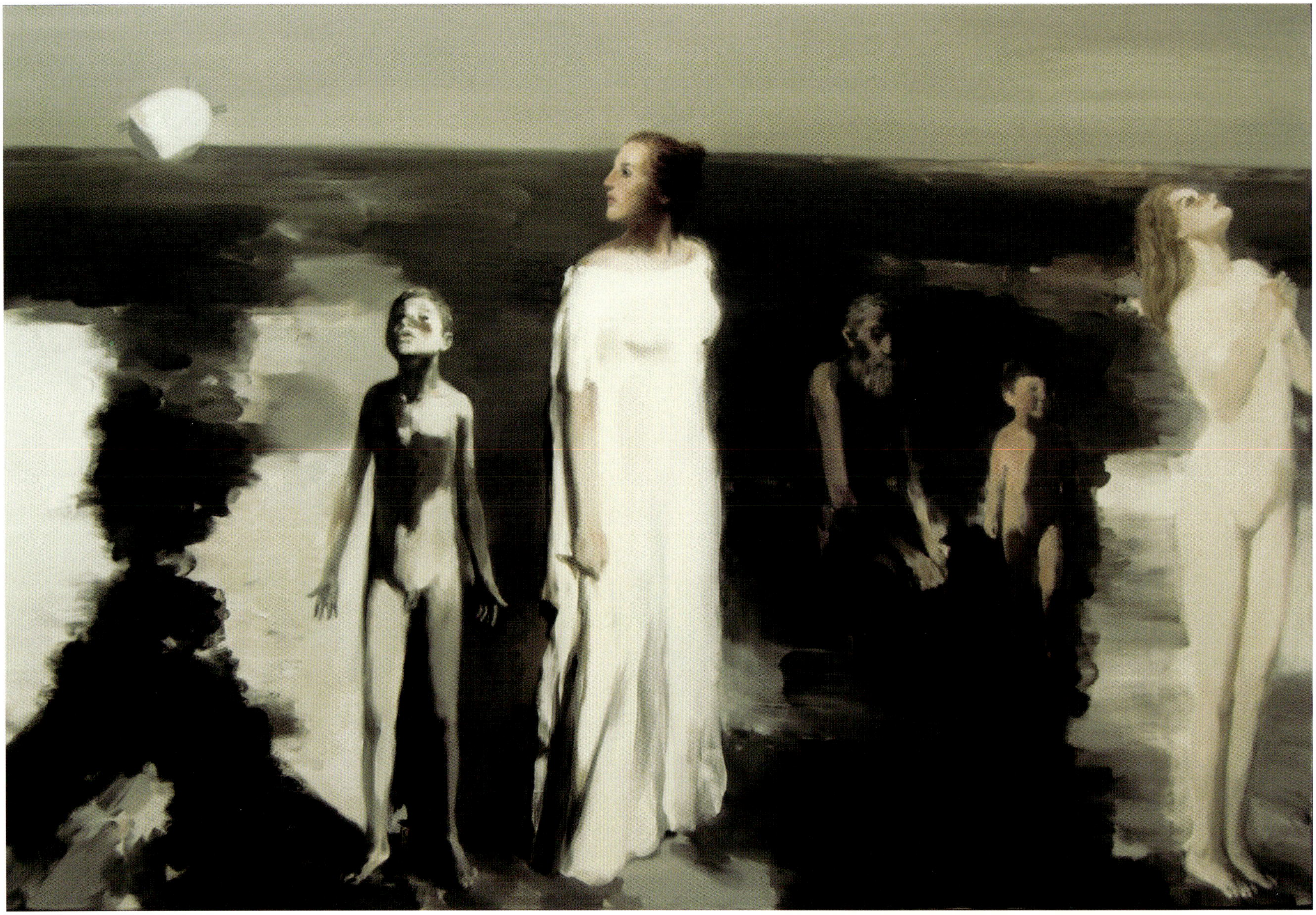

Human Beings with Their Clock #3 人類與他們的鐘
Oil paint on canvas
196 x 300 cm
2005

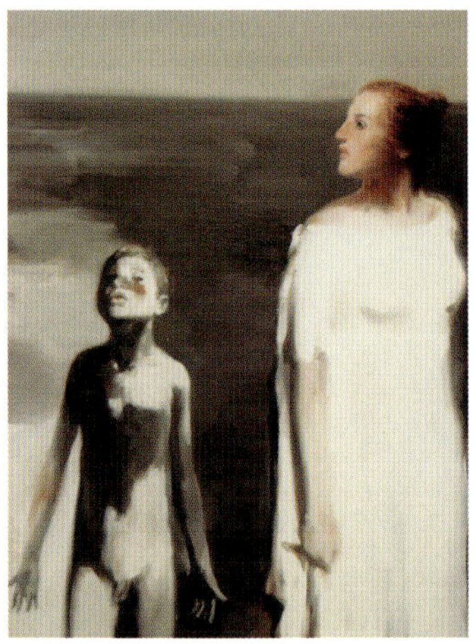

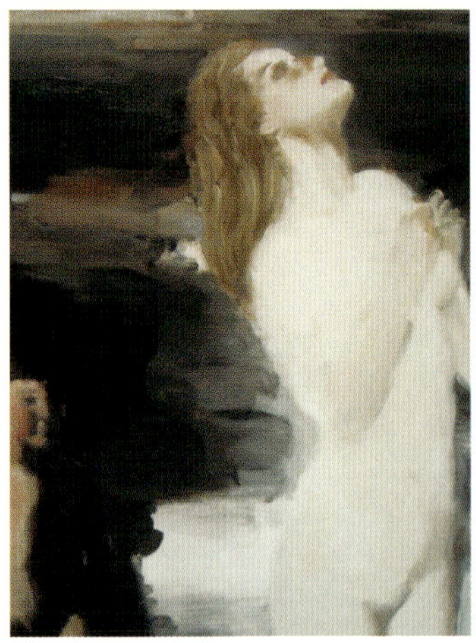

Human Beings with Their Clock #3 (detail) 人類與他們的鐘（局部）
Oil paint on canvas
196 x 300 cm
2005

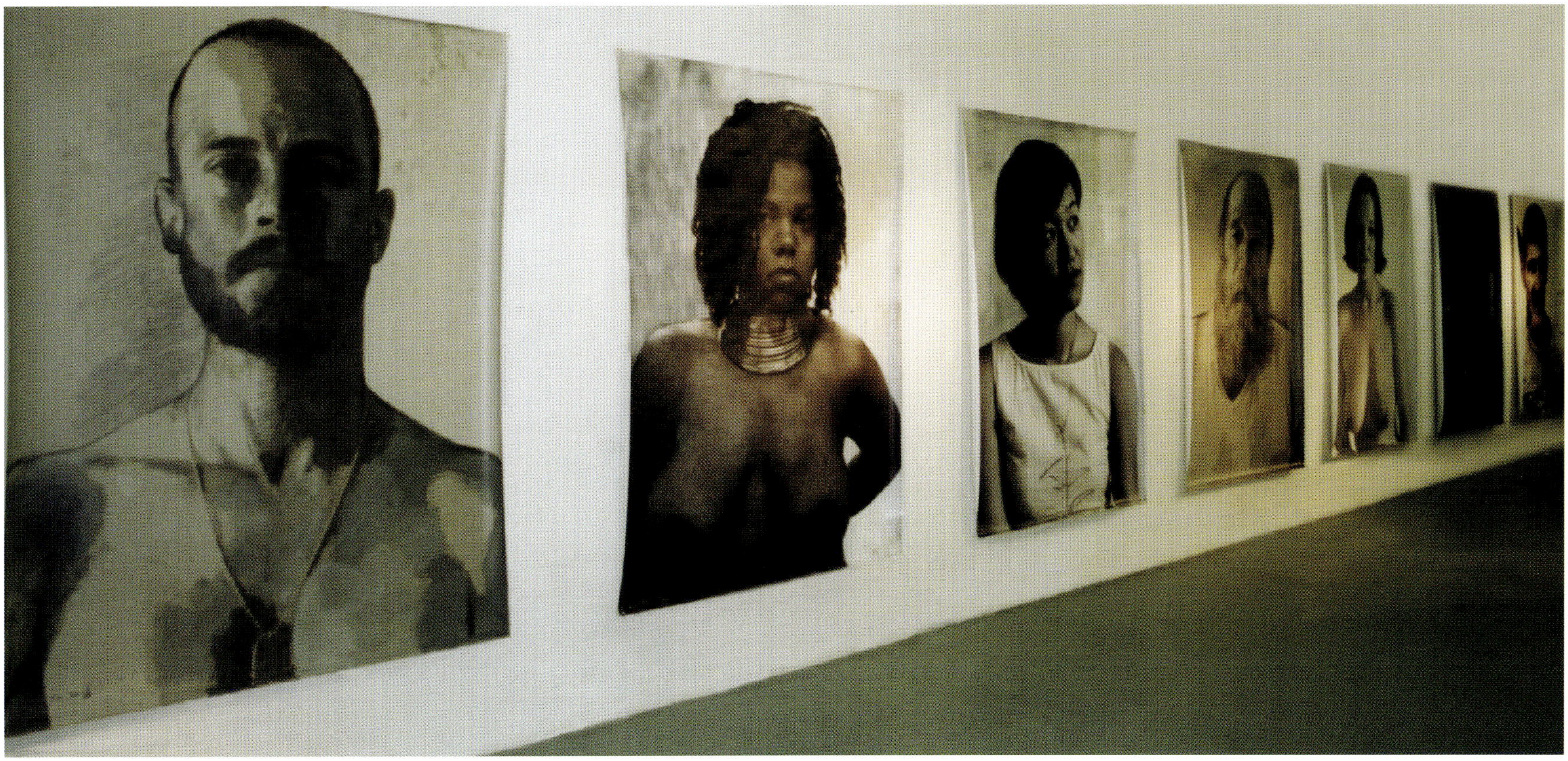

Human Chapter 人類篇 *(Installation), Oil paint, graphite, photo emulsion on canvas, time, document books, sound recordings, 203 x 150 cm (each panel), 2002*

At the Guangdong Museum of Art, Guangzhou, China; and LA Artcore Gallery, Los Angeles, California, USA.

In conclusion, it is necessary to cite a work by Zhang, entitled Human Chapter, in which the artist photographed people individually as portraits from the perspective of a frontal position. He used a special emulsion to print the photographs that would cause the images eventually to fade from view. Before the fading process took effect, Zhang would draw over the photographic portrait using oil paint and graphite. He would then re-photograph his photo/paintings every three months in order to record the fading process. This recurrent activity continued until only the painted and drawn section of the images remained. As the outset of the works, the artist asked each of his subjects to answer seven questions based on their perceptions of themselves. The responses were, in turn, recorded and played during the exhibition. Human Chapter was originally shown at the Guangdong Museum of Art in Guangzhou, China in 2002 and later shown at the LA Artcore Gallery in Los Angeles. Perhaps, the significance of this work can be estimated in terms of Zhang's phenomenological involvement with time as a process, with time as the basis of historical development, and finally with time as the human measure that we use called memory. It seems to me that Zhang Jian-Jun is trying to rehabilitate the importance of memory as an essential human attribute through a conceptual methodology that keeps history, tradition,and culture alive in the present.

為總結此文，我有必要談論張建君題為《人類篇》的作品。他在當中給個別的人從正面照相，然后再用一種特別的感光乳劑來沖洗照片，使照片影像最終無不淡化消失。張建君就趁影像尚未開始淡化以前，用油彩及石墨在照片上作畫。他每隔三個月都會對著這些照片/繪畫照相，以記錄影像的淡化過程。如此反復進行，直到畫面隻剩下素描或上色的部分為止。張建君在開始創作之前，都先請他的攝影對象各回答七道問題，涉及他們對自我的看法。他們的答復都錄了下來，並在展覽中播放。《人類篇》原先於2002年在中國廣州的廣東美術館展出，后來再到洛杉磯的LA藝術核心畫廊(LA Artcore Gallery)續展。要評價這件作品的特殊意義，也許可以聯系張建君對時間的三大層次的現象學交接。這三大層次是：時間之作為一種過程、時間之作為歷史發展的基礎，以及時間之作為人對事物的一種計量（即我們所謂“記憶”）。

在我看來，張建君其實是在嘗試重振記憶作為人類關鍵屬性的重要性。他旨在達到這一點的手段，是通過概念化的方法，讓歷史、傳統和文化在當前保持生機不絕。

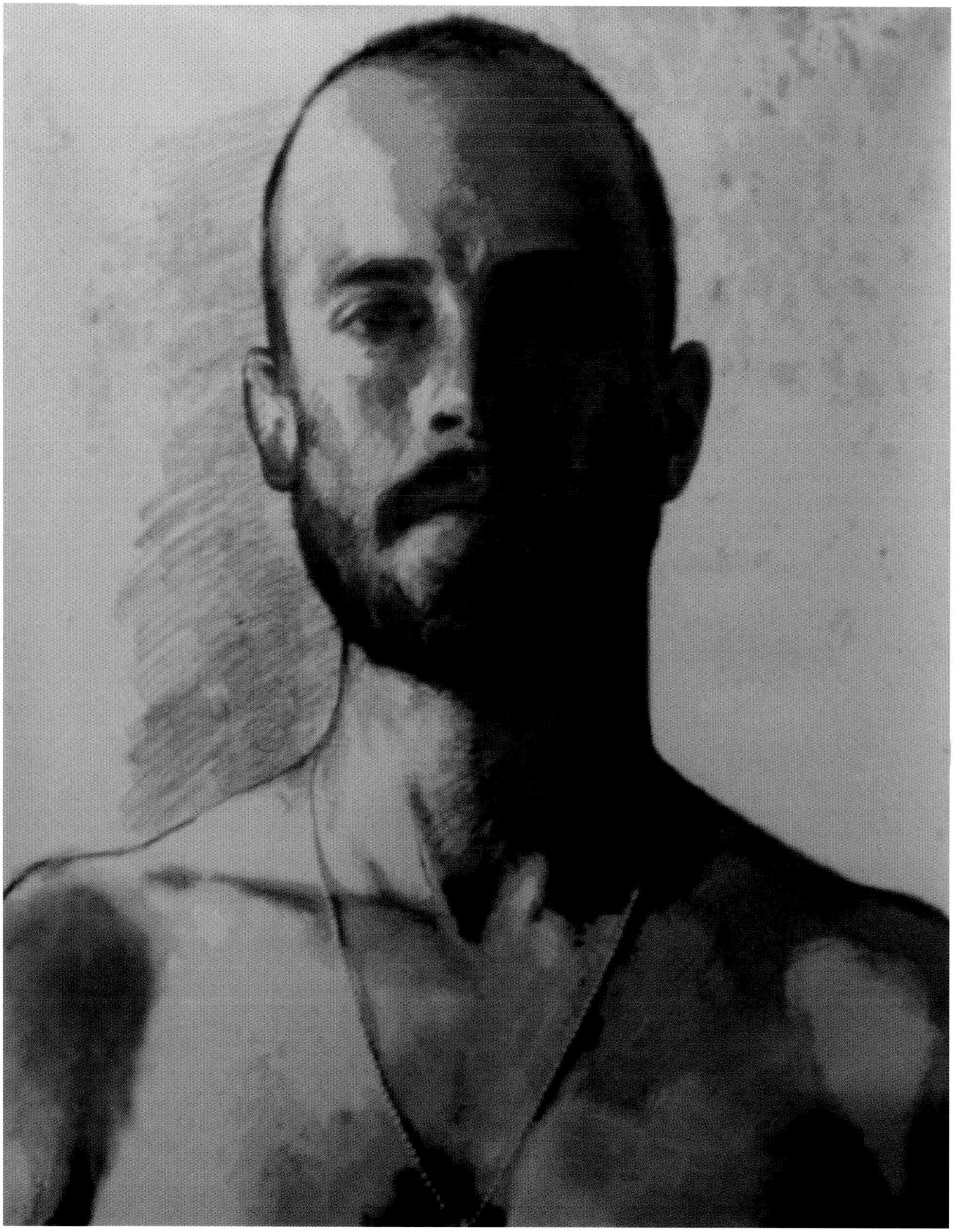

Human Chapter (Jonathan Wooster 強納森・沃斯特)

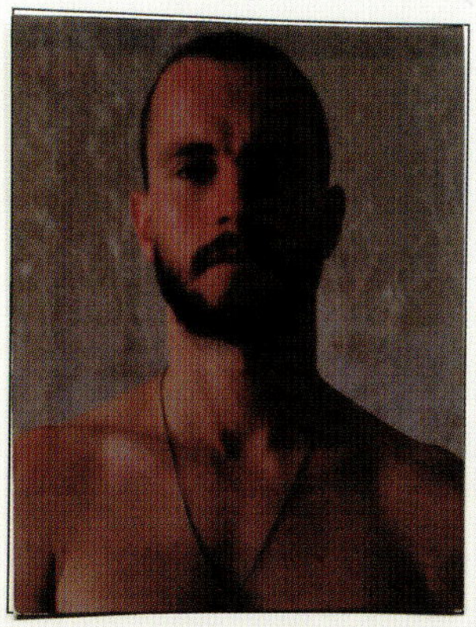

Date of Image: 04. 2002

Name: JONATHAN WOOSTER

Occupation: DANCER/PERFORMANCE ARTIST

Nationality: BRITISH

Original Ethnicity: WHITE EUROPEAN

Human Chapter

(2002)

◆ What would you like to say to people 100 years in the future?

Stop killing each other.

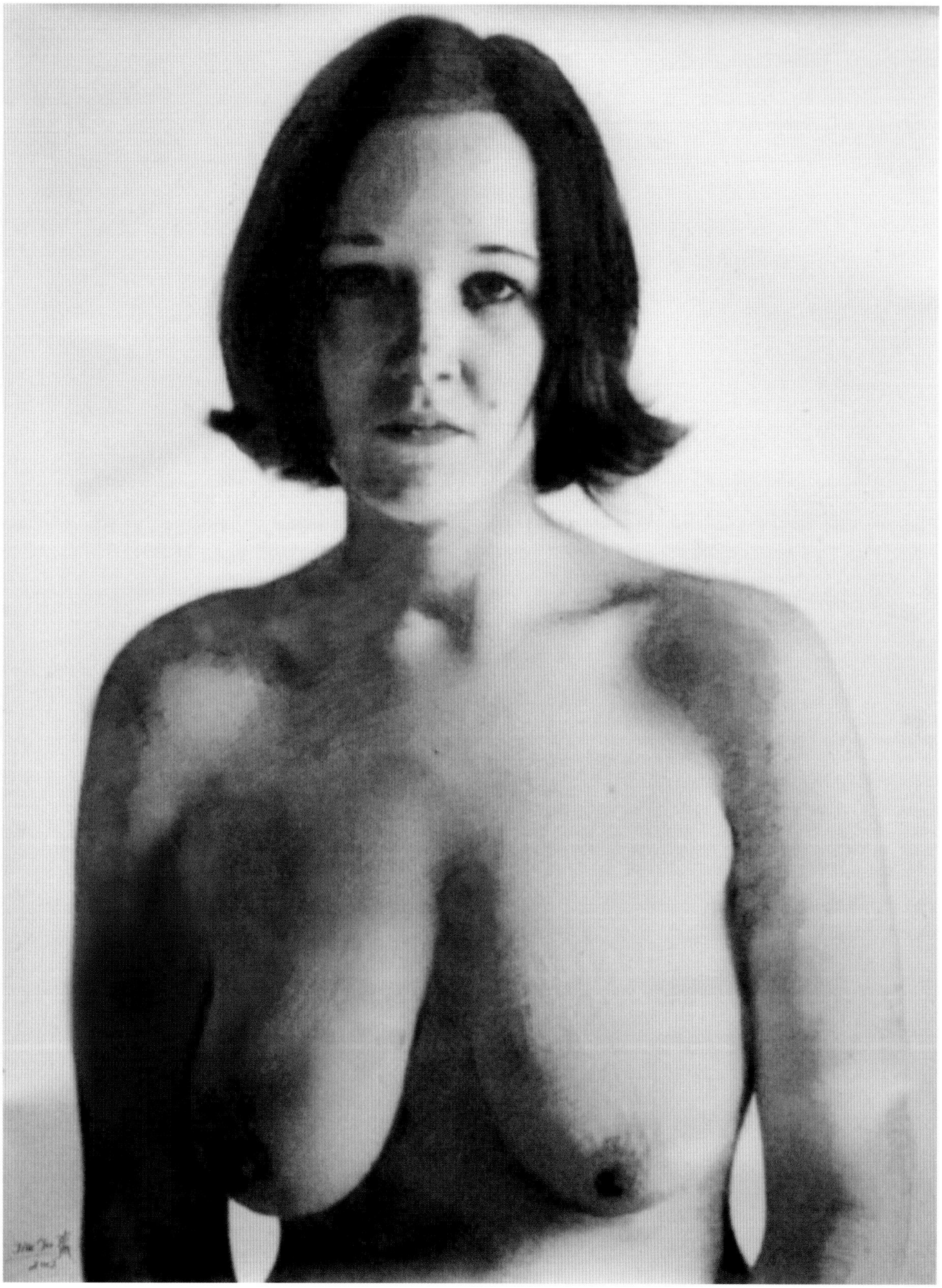

Human Chapter (Rebecca Griffin 芮貝卡・格裡芬)

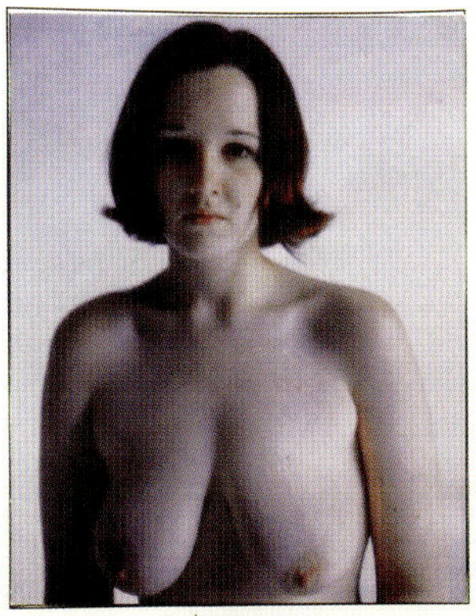

Date of Image: 5/9/02

Name: Rebecca Griffin

Occupation: Student

Nationality: American

Original Ethnicity: Irish & Scottish

Human Chapter

(2002)

◆ What would you like to say to people 100 years in the future?

Don't vote Republican. Or just don't vote at all. It doesn't really matter anyway.

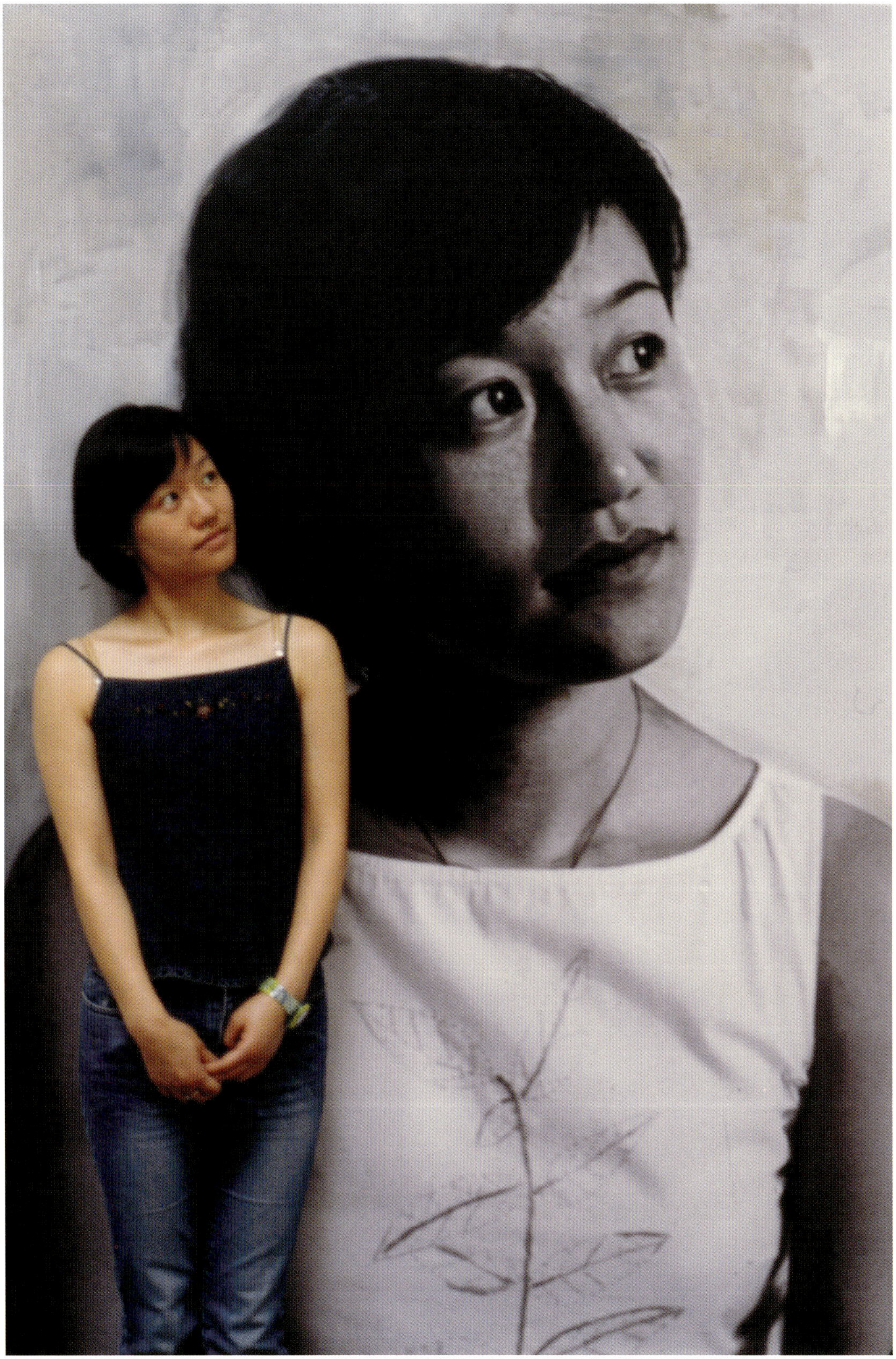

Human Chapter (Mao Ai Min 毛愛民)

Human Chapter

(2002)

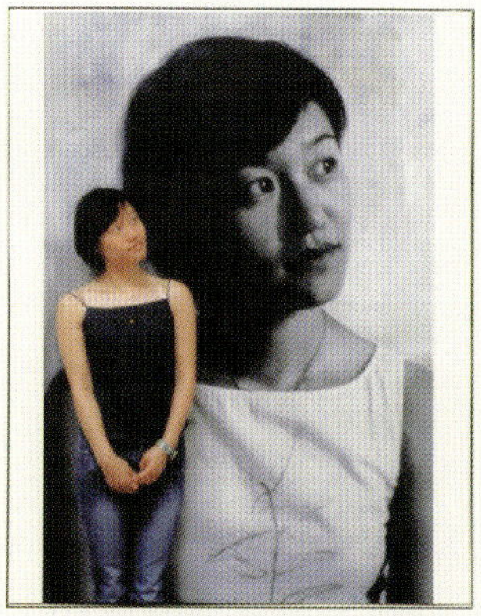

Date of Image: 2002.6.21

Name: 王晨民

Occupation: 美术馆的管理

Nationality: 中国

Original Ethnicity: 汉族

Human Chapter

(2002)

◆ What would you like to say to people 100 years in the future?

或许人类的前景并不太美好，我很希望他们能有充足的水、充足的空气、充足的食物和弹性、快乐的心情。

Afterword

Fang Zengxian

后 跋

方增先

Zhang Jian-Jun called from New York a few days ago and asked me to write an afterword for his catalogue which was to be published soon. I have known Zhang for more than twenty years. In my impression, he has always been attached to his own artistic world, dissociated from what is fashionable. Such sincerity towards art has endowed him with substantial capabilities and influence.

The fact is: Zhang had already impressed me deeply in 1985 when I became the Director of the Shanghai Art Museum. He was very young then, about twenty or thirty years old. Nevertheless, even then, he was very much an important painter amongst the young people in Shanghai who were exploring modern art.

The Shanghai Art Museum was known as the Shanghai Art Gallery prior to my arrival. Its main task was to provide an exhibition venue for the Shanghai Artists' Association. I was there to set up a professional academic institution – the newly instituted Shanghai Art Museum. In the process of doing so, I decided to put Zhang in charge of the department of academic research. I then appointed him to be Assistant Director of the Museum a year later. Shortly after, he proposed to me the idea of setting up an Experimental Gallery in the Museum. It was an unprecedented feature in the art museum network of the entire nation at that time. It provided a museum-level platform for interaction of artists with unique styles, talents and potentials. As an academic project, it truly invigorated the academic climate of the art circles in Shanghai, driving to some extent the development of contemporary art in this city in the mid- and late- 1980s. We, of course, had to bear some pressure from various sources as a result. Nevertheless, I felt that what we did represented a certain inevitable trend and direction. Moreover, it was only conducive to the development of art for people to explore different forms and styles. So I was very supportive of Zhang. The gallery for experimental artworks kept on developing for a long time thereafter, but had unfortunately slipped into oblivion after Zhang left the Museum in 1989.

Although it was highly time-consuming to head the Museum's academic researches, Zhang managed to produce a great number of works energetically in those days. I have always felt that the Museum's academic researchers need to have experiences of this sort with artistic activities, as well as the

日前張建君從紐約打電話來，要我為他即將出版的畫冊寫個跋，我和張建君相識已有20多年，在我的印象裡，他始終執著於自己的藝術世界之中，而游離在流行之外，這種對藝術的真摯為他帶來了一份厚實的實力和影響力。

其實我在1985年任上海美術館館長時，張建君便給予我很深的印象。他那時很年輕，二三十歲，但當時的他已經確確實實是上海青年一代探索現代藝術中一位重要的畫家了。

在我去美術館之前，上海美術館還隻是上海美術展覽館，主要的工作范圍是為上海美術家協會提供展覽場地等事務，我當時去就是為組建新成立的上海美術館，建立一個專業的學術機構。在組建過程中，我選擇了張建君負責學術研究部的工作，一年后又任命他為館長助理。擔任工作后不久，他就向我提出要開辟美術館的實驗展廳。這在當時全國范圍的美術館系統內也是一個前所未有的舉措，這樣，為許多有獨特藝術風格的、有才華、有潛力的藝術家提供了一個美術館層面的交流平台，而這一個學術活動項目也確實活躍了上海美術界的學術空氣，對80年代中后期的上海當代藝術的發展起到了一定的推動作用。當然，也因此有了來自各個方面的壓力，但我感覺到了這是一種趨勢和方向，而且對藝術的形式、風格進行探索，才會有利於發展，所以我是十分支持他的，這個項目之后持續地發展了很久。很可惜，實驗作品展廳這個項目在89年張建君離開美術館后就不了了之了。

擔任美術館的學術組織工作當然是耗費佔用了不少的時間，但張建君在那期間還是精力旺盛地創作了許許多多的作品。而我也一直覺得在美術館的學術研究人員需要這種藝術活動的經驗以及對美術作品的判斷能力。作為視覺藝術，除了理論以外，這種對藝術的直覺也是格外重要的。所以當時他們在學術部門的成員都相對擁有不少的創作時間。在這期間，張建君在美術館樓上那間不大的畫室中不斷創作積累了相當數量的《有》系列作品。

ability to assess artworks. Theoretical knowledge aside, it is particularly important for people dealing with visual art to have an artistic intuition. For this reason, members of the Art Research Department had, relatively, plenty of time to engage in art creation. Zhang himself kept painting during this period in the small studio upstairs in the Museum, resulting in a considerable number of works of the *Existence* series *(pages 84 - 88)*.

This series had been taking shape gradually since the early 1980s. Here, Zhang's direct use of such natural materials as stones, sand, wood and paper on the canvas interplays with brush strokes executed in oils or ink, combining natural "existence" with cultural content in his abstract visuals to form spiritual dialogues between Man and Nature.

At around this time (probably between 1985 and 1986), Zhang also painted a large, figurative albeit conceptually metaphysical oil painting entitled *Human Beings with Their Clock*. Not only did it win Zhang the First Prize in the 1st Shanghai Young Artists' Exhibition, he also came to be one of the representative artists of Shanghai at that time, having significant influence on the younger generation in particular.

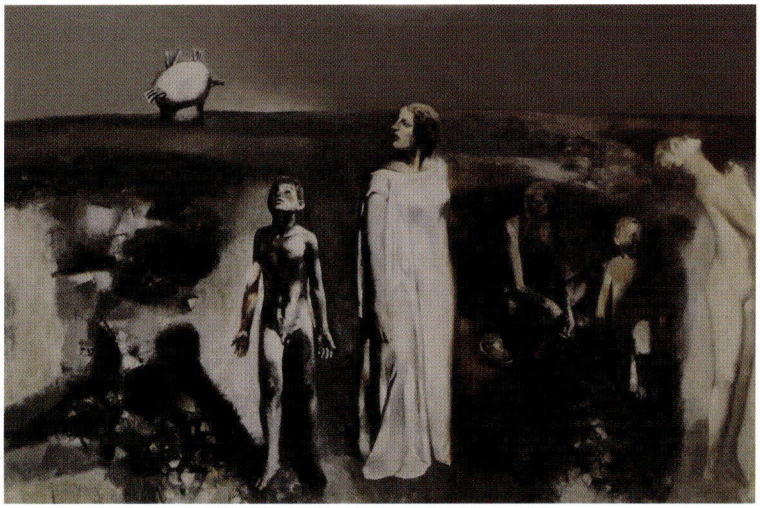

Human Beings with Their Clock #1 人類與他們的鐘, *Oil paint on linen, 220 x 340 cm, 1986*

In the summer of 1986, Zhang began to assist me in the organisation of the 1st Inaugural Exhibition of the Shanghai Art Museum. Scheduled to open in the autumn of 1986, the Exhibition might have been a little too ahead of its time in terms of the diverse styles and manner of selection of the works, such that the news media were unusually silent about it. Later, Zhang took the initiative to ask some friends from the media about it. The response was: *it was already nice of us to not criticise your Museum*... Now, after so many years, when we try to gather relevant material for the celebration of the Shanghai Art Museum's 50th Anniversary, all information regarding this Inaugural Exhibition has long been lost.

這個系列作品是從80年代初期逐漸形成的。他在畫布上直接地使用了一些自然物質，如石、沙、木、紙等和油畫或者水墨的筆觸相互作用，將自然的“存在”和文化的內涵共同組合在抽象畫面之中，形成了人和自然之間精神領域的對話。

與此同時，大概是在1985年至86年間，他也畫了一幅具有具像風格，但觀念卻相當形而上的大幅油畫《人類與他們的鐘》，這幅作品為他贏得了首屆上海市中青年藝術作品大展一等獎的榮譽，這也使他成為當時上海的代表性畫家之一，尤其在青年一代中獲得了相當的影響力。

1986年夏，張建君開始協助我組織籌備“首屆上海美術館開館展”。展覽開幕設定在1986年秋，這個展覽多樣性的作品風格以及評選作品的方式可能在當時有些超前了，所以當時的新聞媒體都一反常態地保持了沉默。張建君好像事后還去特意問了一些媒體方面的朋友，回答是沒有批評你們美術館已經很不錯了 …… 時過境遷，當我們現在為上海美術館50周年館慶尋找相關資料的時候，所有關於這個開幕展覽的信息也隨著時間而煙消雲散了。

1987年秋冬，張建君應美國洛克菲勒基金會亞洲文化協會的邀請去了紐約，在那裡研究、創作當代藝術，回國后不久，於1989年再次移居紐約。

我們的再次見面是在1994年的紐約。他還是和以前一樣精力充沛，沉浸在藝術創作的生活之中。我們去看了紐約現代美術館、大都會博物館，我們也聊了很久關於現代藝術、中國當代藝術與本土文化的關聯。

Upon the invitation of the Rockefeller Foundation's Asian Cultural Council in the USA, Zhang went to New York sometime in the autumn or winter of 1987 to engage in the research and creation of contemporary art. He went to New York again to settle down in 1989, shortly after hehad returned to China.

The next time we met was in 1994 in New York. He remained the way he was – energetic and engrossed in producing art. We went to New York's Museum of Modern Art and the Metropolitan Museum of Art. We also talked for a long time about the relationship between modern art and China's contemporary art and local culture.

Perhaps his having lived and worked in two different cultural backgrounds gives him a unique visual experience and way of thinking. It makes him seem at ease with the variegated global cultural background of today, and enables his works to find just the right artistic languages for expressing what is within him.

I am a great admirer of one of Zhang's series in which the medium of ink and wash is used to portray Time. In the works of this series, the Zen-like feel of ink and water is given new interpretations as it is re-situated in the context of contemporary art. If one argues that the sentiments flaunted in *Fog Inside* (1992, Poland) are still distinctly Oriental, then surely *To Fuse* (1994, USA) and *Footprint* (1997, Tokyo) reveal a more contemporary bent in his work. Indeed, in some of Zhang's larger installations – such as *Sumi-Ink Garden of Re-Creation* (2002, He Xiangning Art Museum (Shenzhen) and Shanghai Art Museum) – all cultural elements have been disintegrated into artistic vocabularies and situated in a cultural dialogue that spans across time and space. This kind of dialogue is apparently given full reins to an even greater extent in Zhang's new multimedia creation *Vestiges of a Process: Water* (2005, Shanghai Art Museum). Here, the artist himself becomes a listener and spectator, dissociated from the dialogue itself.

The expansive and multiplex world we live in provides artists with all kinds of possibilities to work with. It is in this spirit that Zhang Jian-Jun's artworks are flowing freely and transforming in its own wayward manner.

Note: The writer is Chairman of the Shanghai Artists' Association and Director of the Shanghai Art Museum.

可能是他在兩種不同文化背景中的生活、創作，給他帶來了一種獨特的視覺經驗、思維方式，使他在當今多樣化的世界文化背景下顯得從容而自在，也讓他作品的內心表達可以找到各種恰如其分的藝術語言。

我很欣賞他的一系列以水墨作為材料媒介來表現時間的作品。在張建君的作品中，水和墨的禪意被拿來放置於當代藝術的語境中作了新的注解。如果說《內在的霧》（1992年，波蘭）升騰的還是明顯的東方情結，那麼《融》（1994年，美國）和《足跡》（1997年，日本東京）則讓他的作品具有了更加當代的傾向。甚至在他的一些大型裝置作品，如《墨園》（2002年，深圳何香凝美術館、上海美術館）中，所有的文化元素，被分解成藝術語匯，放置於跨越時空的一場文化對話之中，而這種對話在張建君的多媒體新作《過程的瞬間：水》（2005年，上海美術館）則顯得更為地隨心所欲，他本人開始脫離了對話本身，而成為一名聽眾和觀者。

大千世界，給藝術家的創作提供了各種各樣的可能性。張建君的藝術作品也是這樣自在地流動著，率性地變化著。

注：作者為上海美術家協會主席、上海美術館館長。

CURRICULUM VITAE

1955 : Shanghai, People's Republic of China

Education

1978 : Fine Arts Department, Shanghai Drama Institute, China

Positions

1997 - Present : Adjunct Professor, Fine Arts Department, New York University

2005 : Member, Artistic Advisory Committee, Sixth Shanghai Biennale, Shanghai Art Museum, China

2000 : Participant, International Curatorial Workshop, Museum of Modern Art, New York

: Member, Artistic Advisory Committee, Third Shanghai Biennale, Shanghai Art Museum, China

1996 : Member, Artistic Advisory Committee, First Shanghai Biennale, Shanghai Art Museum, China

1987 - 1989 : Assistant Director, Shanghai Art Museum, China

1986 - 1989 : Director of the Curatorial and Art Research Department, Shanghai Art Museum, China

1978 - 1979 : Lecturer, Graduate School of Fine Arts, China National Artists Association, Shanghai Branch, China

Fellowships

1997 : The New York Foundation for the Arts, Sculpture

: The Connemara Conservancy, Dallas, Texas

1994 : The Djerassi Foundation, Resident Artist Program, California, The Gustavo Nicolich Fellowship and Permanent Collection

1987 - 1988 : Asian Cultural Council, The Rockefeller Foundation, U.S.A., (To create artwork in the United States, and to survey contemporary art.)

Grants & Honours

2002 : The Annie Wong Foundation, Hong Kong

1996 : The Pollock-Krasner Foundation, New York, U.S.A.

1995 : Art Matters Inc., New York, U.S.A.

1990 : The Pollock-Krasner Foundation, New York, U.S.A.

1986 : First Prize, The Shanghai Young Artist's Exhibition, China

: Second Prize, Shanghai Art Museum, Ministry of Culture, China

1985 : Third Prize, The Shanghai Art Exhibition, Shanghai

簡歷

1955 出生於中國・上海市

學歷

1978 畢業於上海戲劇學院美術系油畫專業

職業

1997–至今 美國紐約大學（NYU）藝術院客座教授

2006 第六屆上海雙年展學術委員會委員

2000 美國紐約現代美術館國際策展人工作小組成員

第三屆上海雙年展學術委員會委員

1996 第一屆上海雙年展學術委員會委員

1987–1989 上海美術館館長助理

1986–1989 上海美術館學術部主任

1978–1979 上海美術家協會油畫進修班任教

獎勵（簡略）

2002 梁潔華藝術基金會獎，*香港*

1997 紐約藝術基金獎（雕塑/裝置藝術），*美國紐約*

康納瑪拉藝術獎，*美國德克薩斯州*

1996 波洛克藝術基金獎，*美國紐約*

1995 藝術事態基金獎，*美國紐約*

1994 捷拉斯藝術基金獎，*美國加利福尼亞州*

尼古拉齊藝術基金獎，*美國德克薩斯州*

1990 波洛克藝術基金獎，*美國紐約*

1987—1988 洛克菲勒基金會亞洲文化協會訪問藝術家獎，*美國紐約*

1986 "首屆上海市青年藝術大展"一等獎，*中國上海*

收藏（部分）

J. P. 摩根銀行藝術館，*中國香港*

上海美術館，*中國*

廣東美術館，*中國*

Art Museum, Ministry of Culture, China

Permanent Collections
JP Morgan, Hong Kong
International Artists Museum, Lodz, Poland
Shanghai Art Museum, China
Shenzhen Art Institute, Shenzhen, China
Guangdong Museum of Art, Guangzhou, China
Dow Jones Company, New Jersey, U.S.A.
Djerassi Foundation Collection, California, U.S.A.
Frederick R. Weisman Foundation of Art, California, U.S.A.

Solo Exhibitions
2007 :"Vestiges of a Process: Shanghai", Ethan Cohen Fine Arts, New York, New York, U.S.A.
:"Zhang Jian-Jun: Vestiges of a Process", iPreciation Gallery, Singapore
2005 :"Vestiges of a Process", Asian American Art Centre, New York, New York, U.S.A.
:"Garden of Wishing Trees", Maiden Lane Exhibition Space, New York, New York, U.S.A.
2004 :"Vestiges of a Process: Chelsea Chapter", DTW Gallery, New York, New York, U.S.A.
2003 :"Mountain & River", Art Projects International Gallery, New York, New York, U.S.A.
2002 :"Sumi-Ink Garden of Recreation", He Xiangning Art Museum, Shenzhen, China
:"Vestiges of a Process: Guangzhou Chapter", Guangdong Museum of Art, Guangzhou, China
:"China Chapter", Museum of the Shenzhen Art Institute, Shenzhen, China
2001 :Art Projects International, New York, New York, U.S.A.
1997 :"Footprint", Gallerie Deux, Tokyo, Japan
1995 :Art Projects International Gallery, New York, New York, U.S.A.
1994 :"The Paradox of the Fish", Gallery Contempo, New York, New York, U.S.A.
1989 :Nerlino Gallery, New York, New York, U.S.A.
1988 :Key Gallery, Illinois, U.S.A.
:Harvard University, Massachusetts, U.S.A.
1987 :Shanghai Art Museum, China

Group Exhibitions (selected)
2007 :"Asia Europa Meditation: Asian Attitude", Posnan National Museum of Art, Posnan, Poland
2006 :"Entry Gate: Chinese Aeshetics of Heterogeneity", 1st Envisage, Museum of Contemporary Art, Shanghai, China

深圳畫院，*中國*
羅茲藝術家美術館，*波蘭*
道・瓊斯總部，*美國*
捷拉斯雕塑空間，*美國*
威斯曼基金會美術館，*美國*

個展（部分）
2007 “過程的瞬間：上海”，*一森畫廊，美國紐約*
“張建君：過程的瞬間”，*誰先覺畫，新加坡*
2005 “願望樹”，*麥登・蘭藝術中心，美國紐約*
“過程的瞬間”，*美國亞洲藝術中心，美國紐約*
年度邀請展，*亞美藝術中心，美國紐約*
2004 “過程的瞬間：Chelsea篇”，*DTW畫廊，美國紐約*
2003 “山・水”，*國際藝術計劃畫廊，美國紐約*
2002 “墨園”，*何香凝美術館，中國深圳*
“過程的瞬間”，*廣東美術館，中國廣州*
“中國篇”，*深圳畫院，中國深圳*
2001 “中國篇”，*國際藝術計劃畫廊，美國紐約*
1997 “足跡”，*DEUX畫廊，日本東京*
1995 “水・火”，*國際藝術計劃畫廊，美國紐約*
1994 “魚的困惑”，*當代畫廊，美國紐約*
1989 “自然”，*NERLINO畫廊，美國紐約*
1988 “有”，*KEY畫廊，美國伊利諾斯州*
“自然”，*哈佛大學，美國馬薩諸塞州*
1987 “自然”，*上海美術館，中國上海*

群展（部分）
2007 “亞洲・歐洲之間的靜思：亞洲的认知”，*波茲南美術館，波蘭*
“橫越大西洋”，*英國倫敦*
2006 “入境：中國美學”，*上海當代藝術館，中國上海*
“實驗水墨”，*天津現代美術館，中國天津*
“接近生活”，*布魯克林藝術館，美國紐約*

Shanghai, China
:"Crossing the Atlantic", Gallery of Goldsmiths College, London, England
:"Close to Home", BlockParty Brooklyn, New York, U.S.A.
:"New Chinese Occidentalism", Ethan Cohen Fine Arts, New York, New York, U.S.A.

2005 :"Flowing River: 30 Years of Chinese Oil Painting", National Art Museum, Beijing, China
:"100 Years of Chinese Sculpture", Shanghai Sculpture Space, Shanghai, China
:"1st International Sculpture Biennale", Xu Jia Hui Park, Shanghai, China
:"Black + White", Shanghai Art Museum, Shanghai, China
:"Regards to '85", Duolun Art Museum, Shanghai, China
:"Replacement", Cathay Gallery, Beijing, China
:"Poles Apart Poles Together: Markers V", Venice Biennale, Venice, Italy
:"Anniversary Show", Beijing Film Institute, Beijing, China

2004 :"The Fourth Shenzhen International Sumi-Ink Biennale", Shenzhen, China
:"Shanghai Abstract Survey — 50 Years", Ming Yuan Art Center, Shanghai, China
:"10/20", Lui Hai Su Art Museum, Shanghai, China
:"A Grain of Dust A Drop of Water", The 5th Gwangju Biennale, Gwangju, Korea
:"On the Edge", Ethan Cohen Fine Arts, New York, New York, U.S.A.

2003 :"10-Year Anniversary", Art Projects International Gallery, New York, New York, U.S.A.
:New York University Gallery, New York, New York, U.S.A.
:"Brushworks: New Asian Calligraphy", Andrew Bae Gallery, Chicago, Illinois, U.S.A.
:"Mountain & River", Barbara Davis Gallery, Houston, Texas, U.S.A.
:Diverseworks Art Center, Houston, Texas, U.S.A.
:"5 = 1", L.A. Artcore Gallery, Los Angeles, California, U.S.A.

2002 :"Urban Creation", The Fourth Shanghai Biennale, Shanghai Art Museum, Shanghai, China
:"Guangzhou Triennial", Guangdong Museum of Art, Guangzhou, China
:"East + West", Kunstlerhaus, Vienna, Austria
:"China Triennial", Metropolitan Museum of Guangzhou, Guangzhou, China

“新西方主義”，*一森畫廊，美國紐約*

2005 “大河上下：中國油畫30年”，*中國美術館，中國北京*
“中國百年雕塑大展”，*上海雕塑藝術中心，中國上海*
“黑+白：2005形而上”，*上海美術館，中國上海*
“向85致敬”，*上海多倫現代美術館，中國上海*
“木椿之外的公共空間”，51屆威尼斯雙年展，*意意大利威尼斯*

2004 “第五屆光州雙年展”，*韓國光州*
“第四屆深圳水墨雙年展”，*中國深圳*

2003 “筆韻：亞洲當代藝術展”，*安德魯畫廊，美國芝加哥*
“山・水”，*芭芭拉・戴維斯畫廊，美國休斯頓*
“呼吸”，*紐約大學美術館，美國紐約*
“國際藝術計劃畫廊10年展”，*國際藝術計劃畫廊，美國紐約*
“靜行中的2000年”，*DIVERSEWORKS藝術中心，美國休斯頓*
“5=1”，*L. A藝術核心畫廊，美國洛杉磯*

2002 “第四屆上海雙年展 “都市營造””，*上海美術館，中國上海*
“首屆廣州三年展”，*廣東美術館，中國廣州*
“東+西中國當代藝術展”，*奧地利現代藝術館，奧地利維也納*
“中國藝術三年展”，*廣州藝術博物院，中國廣州*
“印記 II”，*EAM畫廊，德國卡塞爾*
“水墨的變奏曲”，*前波畫廊，美國紐約*
“當代筆意”，*2000中國畫廊，美國紐約*
“制造中國”，*一森畫廊，美國紐約*

2001 “第一屆成都雙年展”，*成都現代藝術館，中國成都*
“印痕”，威尼斯雙年展，*意大利威尼斯*

	: "Markers II", EAM Gallery, Kassel, Germany
	: "Variations of Ink", Chambers Fine Art, New York, New York, U.S.A.
	: "Contemporary Brush Strokes", China 2000 Gallery, New York, New York, U.S.A.
	: "Making China", Ethan Cohen Fine Arts, New York, New York, U.S.A.
2001	: "1st Chengdu Biennial", Chengdu, China
	: "Markers", Venice Biennale, Venice, Italy
	: "Metaphysics and Reality", Shanghai Art Museum, Shanghai, China
	: "Milestones for Peace", Weill Art Gallery, New York, New York, U.S.A.
2000	: "DMZ_2000", Korean Gallery, New York, U.S.A.
	: "Construction in Process VII: This Earth is a Flower", The International Artists' Museum, Lodz, Poland
	: "Cow Parade", New York, New York, U.S.A.
	: "Milestones for Peace", Jerusalem Art Festival, Jerusalem, Israel
	: "Conceptual Ink", Ethan Cohen Fine Arts, New York, New York, U.S.A.
	: "The International Artists' Museum in New York", 83 Mercer Street Gallery, New York, New York, U.S.A.
1999	: "Wrap the World", The Kitchen, New York, New York, U.S.A.
	: "Transience: Chinese Experimental Art at the End of the Twentieth Century", Smart Museum of Art, Chicago, Illinois, U.S.A.
	: "Language", Ethan Cohen Fine Art, New York, New York, U.S.A.
1998	: Observatoire 4 Galerie, Montreal, Quebec, Canada
	: "Chinese Artists Working in New York", Purdue University Gallery, Indiana, U.S.A.
1997	: "Basic Elements", Art Beatus Gallery, Vancouver, B.C., Canada
	: "Bank: Inside the Counting Room", Lower Manhattan Cultural Council, New York, New York, U.S.A.
	: Art Projects International Gallery, New York, New York, U.S.A.
	: "Sculpture 1997", Connemara Conservancy Sculpture Park, Dallas, Texas
1996	: "Open Space", Shanghai Art Museum Biennale, China
	: Pennsylvania University Art Museum, U.S.A.
	: "Eastern Fusion: Contemporary Asian American Art in New York", Hillwood Art Museum, New York, U.S.A.

	"形而上・現實"，*上海美術館，中國上海*
2000	"DMZ_2000"，*韓國藝術中心，美國紐約*
	"建構的過程Ⅶ:地球是花朵"，*國際藝術家美術館，波蘭畢德戈西*
	"都市之牛"，紐約環境雕塑專題展，*美國紐約*
	"和平的裡程碑"，耶路撒冷藝術節，*以色列耶路撒冷*
	"墨的觀念"，*一森畫廊，美國紐約*
1999	"覆蓋世界"，*紐約現代多媒體藝術中心，美國紐約*
	"過渡:二十世紀末中國實驗藝術"，*芝加哥大學美術館，美國芝加哥*
	"語言"，*一森畫廊，美國紐約*
1998	"中國當代藝術家作品展"，*OBSERVATOIRE4畫廊，加拿大魁北克*
	"中國藝術家在紐約"，*普渡大學美術館，美國印地安納*
1997	"基本元素"，*ART BEATUS藝術畫廊，加拿大溫哥華*
	"在銀行內"，*紐約文化藝術中心，美國紐約*
	"雕塑1997"，康納瑪拉室外雕塑空間，*美國達拉斯*
1996	"首屆上海雙年展：開放的空間"，*上海美術館，中國上海*
	"東方視角"，*HILLWOOD美術館，美國紐約*
1995	"都塞多夫國際藝術節"，*都塞多夫現代藝術中心，德國都塞多夫*
	"和平　地球　復原"，廣島核爆紀念國際展，*日本廣島*
1993	"建構的過程Ⅵ"，*藝術家美術館，波蘭洛茲*
	"93NY50"，蘇格拉底雕塑公園，*美國紐約*
1992	"中國藝術家聯展"，*柏林廢墟美術館，德國柏林*
	"對話"，*藝術家美術館，波蘭洛茲*

1995 : Grosse Kunstausstelung, Dusselsorf, Germany
: "Peace, Earth, Healing", Hiroshima, Japan
1993 : "Construction in Process #4", The Artists' Museum, Lodz, Poland
: "93NY50", Socrates Sculpture Park, Long Island City, New York, U.S.A.
1992 : Ruine der Kunst, Berlin, Germany
: "Conversations", The Artists' Museum, Lodz, Poland
: "Workspace '92", Jamaica Arts Center, New York, New York, U.S.A.
: City University of New York, New York, U.S.A.
: Natural History Museum, New York, New York, U.S.A.
: Miami Art International Festival, Florida, U.S.A.
1991 : San Diego State University Gallery, California, U.S.A.
: "Annual", Asian American Art Center, New York, New York, U.S.A.
1990 : East West Contemporary Inc. Gallery, Chicago, Illinois, U.S.A.
: Exhibition Space Gallery, New York, New York, U.S.A.
1989 : Nerlino Gallery, New York, New York, U.S.A.
: Tokyo Gallery, Tokyo, Japan
: Han Art Gallery, Hong Kong
: "China/Avant Garde", China National Art Gallery, Beijing, China
: Han Art Gallery, Taipei, Taiwan
1988 : "Last Supper" (performance), Shanghai Art Museum, China
: Art West/Art East Gallery, Hamburg, Germany
: Art Waves Gallery, New York, New York, U.S.A.
: Art Museum of Nanjing, China
: "Annual" Shanghai Art Museum, China
1987 : Hong Kong Art Centre, Hong Kong
: Alisan Gallery, Hong Kong
: Pacific Asia Museum, Pasadena, California, U.S.A.
1986 : Tokyo Municipal Museum, Tokyo, Japan
: "Annual" Shanghai Art Museum, China
: 4 group exhibitions, Shanghai Art Museum, China
1985 : "Annual" Shanghai Art Museum, China
: Shanghai Drama Institute Gallery, China
1983 : Fudan University Gallery, Shanghai, China
1982 : "Annual" Shanghai Art Museum, China
1981 : "Annual" Shanghai Art Museum, China
1980 : Shanghai Art Museum, China
1979 : "Annual" Shanghai Art Museum, China

"工作空間92"，*JAMAICA藝術中心，美國紐約*
1991 "聯展"，*聖地亞哥州立大學美術館，美國加州*
"亞美藝術中心年度展"，*亞美藝術中心，美國紐約*
1990 "聯展"，*空間畫廊，美國紐約*
1989 "聯展"，*NERLINO畫廊，美國紐約*
"中國當代藝術展"，*東京畫廊，日本東京*
"墨玄"，*漢雅軒畫廊，中國香港*
"首屆中國當代藝術大展"，*中國美術館，中國北京*
1988 "最后的晚餐"，*上海美術館，中國上海*
"5畫家畫展"，*西方/東方畫廊，德國漢堡*
"上海美術館展"，*上海美術館，中國上海*
1987 "蛻變中的上海當代藝術"，*香港藝術中心，中國香港*
"藝倡畫廊"，*中國香港*
"開放"，*亞太美術館，美國加州*
1986 "第九回東京美術館聯展"，*東京美術館，日本東京*
"上海美術館展"，*上海美術館，中國上海*
"首屆上海青年藝術大展"，*上海美術館，中國上海*
1985 "上海美術館展"，*上海美術館，中國上海*
1983 "83'階段繪畫實驗展"，復旦大學，*中國上海*
1982 "上海美術館展"，*上海美術館，中國上海*
1981 "上海美術館展"，*上海美術館，中國上海*
1980 "上海美術館展"，*上海美術館，中國上海*
1979 "上海美術館展"，*上海美術館，中國上海*